Collins

C000132156

Year 8

NEW MATHS FRAMEWORKING

Matches the revised KS3 Framework

Kevin Evans, Keith Gordon, Trevor Senior, Brian Speed

Contents

Introduction

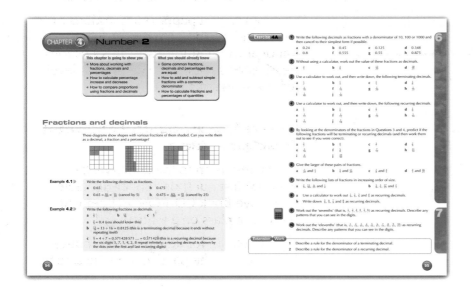

Learning objectives

See what you are going to cover and what you should already know at the start of each chapter. The purple and blue boxes set the topic in context and provide a handy checklist.

National Curriculum levels

Know what level you are working at so you can easily track your progress with the colour-coded levels at the side of the page.

Worked examples

Understand the topic before you start the exercises by reading the examples in blue boxes. These take you through how to answer a question step-by-step.

Functional Maths

Practise your Functional Maths skills to see how people use Maths in everyday life.

Look out for the Functional Maths icon on the page.

Extension activities

Stretch your thinking and investigative skills by working through the extension activities. By tackling these you are working at a higher level.

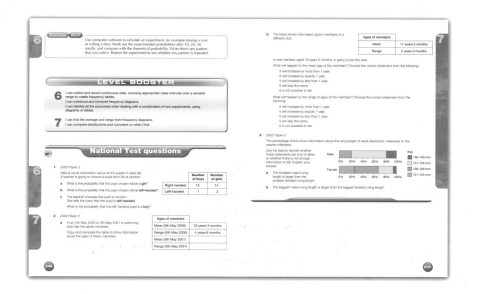

Level booster

Progress to the next level by checking the Level boosters at the end of each chapter. These clearly show you what you need to know at each level and how to improve.

National Test questions

Practise the past paper Test questions to feel confident and prepared for your KS3 National Curriculum Tests. The questions are levelled so you can check what level you are working at.

Extra interactive National Test practice

Watch and listen to the audio/visual National Test questions on the separate Interactive Book CD-ROM to help you revise as a class on a whiteboard.

 Look out for the computer mouse icon on the page and on the screen.

Functional Maths activities

Put Maths into context with these colourful pages showing real-world situations involving Maths. You are practising your Functional Maths skills by analysing data to solve problems.

Extra interactive Functional Maths questions and video clips

Extend your Functional Maths skills by taking part in the interactive questions on the separate Interactive Book CD-ROM. Your teacher can put these on the whiteboard so the class can answer the questions on the board.

See Maths in action by watching the video clips and doing the related Worksheets on the Interactive Book CD-ROM. The videos bring the Functional Maths activities to life and help you see how Maths is used in the real world.

 Look out for the computer mouse icon on the page and on the screen.

CHAPTER 1

Number and Algebra **1**

This chapter is going to show you

- How to multiply and divide negative numbers
- How to find the highest common factor and the lowest common multiple of sets of numbers
- How to find the prime factors of a number
- How to generate and describe number patterns

What you should already know

- How to add and subtract negative integers
- How to generate terms of a simple number sequence
- Recognise the square and triangle number sequences
- How to test numbers for divisibility

Multiplying and dividing negative numbers

Example 1.1 ▷ Find the missing number in: **a** $\boxed{} \times 3 = -6$ **b** $-12 \div \boxed{} = 3$

a The inverse problem is $\boxed{} = -6 \div +3$, so the missing number is -2

b The inverse problem is $\boxed{} = -12 \div +3$, so the missing number is -4

Example 1.2 ▷ Work out: **a** $-3 \times -2 + 5$ **b** $-3 \times (-2 + 5)$

a Using BODMAS, do -3×-2 first: $-3 \times -2 + 5 = +6 + 5 = +11$

b This time the bracket must be done first: $-3 \times (-2 + 5) = -3 \times +3 = -9$

Example 1.3 ▷ Work out: **a** $(-3 + 1)^2 \times -3$ **b** $(+2 - 5) \times (-2 + 5)^2$

a Using BODMAS, do the bracket first: $(-3 + 1)^2 \times -3 = (-2)^2 \times -3 = 4 \times -3 = -12$

b $(+2 - 5) \times (-2 + 5)^2 = -3 \times 3^2 = -3 \times 9 = -27$

Exercise 1A

1 Work out the following.

a $-7 + 8$ **b** $-2 - 7$ **c** $+6 - 2 + 3$ **d** $-6 - 1 + 7$ **e** $-3 + 4 - 9$

f $-3 - 7$ **g** $-4 + -6$ **h** $+7 - +6$ **i** $-3 - 7 + -8$ **j** $-5 + -4 - -7$

2 In these 'walls', subtract the right-hand from the left-hand number to find the number in the brick below.

a
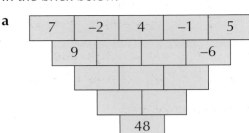

| 7 | −2 | 4 | −1 | 5 |

| 9 | | | −6 |

| | | |

| | |

| 48 |

b
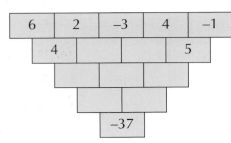

| 6 | 2 | −3 | 4 | −1 |

| 4 | | | 5 |

| | | |

| | |

| −37 |

3 Work out the answer to each of these.

a	$+5 \times -3$	**b**	-3×-4	**c**	$-7 \times +12$	**d**	-16×-3
e	$-3 \times +24$	**f**	$+16 \times -7$	**g**	$+18 \times +4$	**h**	-25×-14
i	$-12 \times -3 \times -2$	**j**	$-12 \times +4 \times -5$	**k**	$+72 \div -3$	**l**	$-24 \div -4$
m	$-64 \div +8$	**n**	$-36 \div -3$	**o**	$-328 \div +8$	**p**	$+6 \div -10$
q	$+4 \div -8$	**r**	$-35 \div -2$	**s**	$-12 \times -3 \div -24$	**t**	$-12 \times -3 \div -6$

4 The answer to the question on this blackboard is −12.

Using multiplication and/or division signs, write down at least five different calculations that give this answer.

5 Copy and complete the following multiplication grids.

a

×	−2	3	−4	5
−3	6			
6				
−2				
5				

b

×	−1	−3	4	
−2	6			
		12		
	−5			
7			−42	

c

×				−8
−2		−12		
	−15		21	
4			28	
		−30		

6 Find the missing number in each calculation. (Remember that the numbers without a + or − sign in front of them are actually positive, as we do not always show every positive sign when writing a calculation.)

a	$2 \times -3 = \boxed{}$	**b**	$-2 \times \boxed{} = -8$	**c**	$3 \times \boxed{} = -9$
d	$\boxed{} \div -5 = -15$	**e**	$-4 \times -6 = \boxed{}$	**f**	$-3 \times \boxed{} = -24$
g	$-64 \div \boxed{} = 32$	**h**	$\boxed{} \times 6 = 36$	**i**	$-2 \times 3 = \boxed{}$
j	$\boxed{} \times -6 = -48$	**k**	$-2 \times \boxed{} \times 3 = 12$	**l**	$\boxed{} \div -4 = 2$
m	$5 \times 4 \div \boxed{} = -10$	**n**	$-5 \times \boxed{} \div -2 = -10$	**o**	$\boxed{} \times -4 \div -2 = 14$

7 Work out the following.

| **a** | -2×-2 | **b** | -4×-4 | **c** | $(-3)^2$ | **d** | $(-6)^2$ |

e Explain why it is impossible to get a negative answer when you square any number.

8 Work out the following.

   a $2 \times -3 + 4$ **b** $2 \times (-3 + 4)$ **c** $-2 + 3 \times -4$ **d** $(-2 + 3) \times -4$

   e $-5 \times -4 + 6$ **f** $-5 \times (-4 + 6)$ **g** $-12 \div -6 + 2$ **h** $-12 \div (-6 + 2)$

9 Put brackets in each of these to make them true.

   a $2 \times -5 + 4 = -2$ **b** $-2 + -6 \times 3 = -24$ **c** $9 - 5 - 2 = 6$

10 Work out the answer to each of these.

   a $(-4)^2 \times +3$ **b** $3 \times (-5)^2$ **c** $12 \div (-2)^2$

   d $(-4 + 6)^2 \times -2$ **e** $7 \times (-7 + 4)^2$ **f** $(-5 - 2)^2 - (3 - 5)^2$

   g $-12 \div (-6 + 4)^2$ **h** $(-7 + 4)^2 \div (-2)^2$ **i** $-6 \times (-2 + 6)^2$

11 Calculators work in different ways. Make sure you can use the sign-change and brackets keys on your calculator.

Work out -4^2. On your calculator, you might key in   `–`   `4`   `x²`   `=` .

Now work out $(-4)^2$. Key in   `(`   `–`   `4`   `)`   `x²`   `=` .

Explain why the answers are different.

Extension **Work**

This is an algebraic magic square.

What is the 'Magic expression' that every row, column and diagonal adds up to?

Find the value in each cell when $a = 7$, $b = 9$, $c = 2$.

Find the value in each cell when $a = -1$, $b = -3$, $c = -5$.

$a + c$	$c - a - b$	$b + c$
$b + c - a$	c	$a + c - b$
$c - b$	$a + b + c$	$c - a$

HCF and LCM

Remember that:

   HCF stands for **highest common factor**

   LCM stands for **lowest common multiple**

Look at the diagrams. What do you think they are showing?

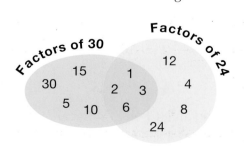

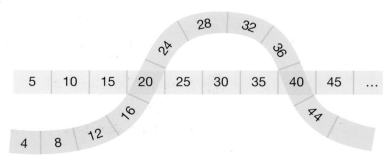

Example 1.4 ▶ Find the lowest common multiple (LCM) of the following pairs of numbers.

a 3 and 7   **b** 6 and 9

a Write out the first few multiples of each number:

3, 6, 9, 12, 15, 18, ⑳①, 24, 27, …

7, 14, ⑳①, 28, 35, …

You can see that the LCM of 3 and 7 is 21.

b Write out the multiples of each number: 6, 12, ⑱, 24, …

9, ⑱, 27, 36, …

You can see that the LCM of 6 and 9 is 18.

Example 1.5 ▶ Find the highest common factor (HCF) of the following pairs of numbers.

a 15 and 21   **b** 16 and 24

a Write out the factors of each number: 1, ③, 5, 15

1, ③, 7, 21

You can see that the HCF of 15 and 21 is 3.

b Write out the factors of each number: 1, 2, 4, ⑧, 16

1, 2, 3, 4, 6, ⑧, 12, 24

You can see that the HCF of 16 and 24 is 8.

Exercise 1B

1 Write down the first five multiples of the following numbers.

   a 4   **b** 5   **c** 8   **d** 15   **e** 20

2 Write down all the factors of the following numbers.

   a 15   **b** 20   **c** 32   **d** 35   **e** 60

3 Use your answers to Question 1 to help find the LCM of the following pairs of numbers.

   a 5 and 8   **b** 4 and 20   **c** 4 and 15   **d** 8 and 15

4 Use your answers to Question 2 to help find the HCF of the following pairs of numbers.

   a 15 and 20   **b** 15 and 60   **c** 20 and 60   **d** 20 and 32

5 Find the LCM of the following pairs.

   a 5 and 9   **b** 5 and 25   **c** 3 and 8   **d** 4 and 6

   e 8 and 12   **f** 12 and 15   **g** 9 and 21   **h** 7 and 11

6 Find the HCF of the following pairs.

   a 15 and 18   **b** 12 and 32   **c** 12 and 22   **d** 8 and 12

   e 2 and 18   **f** 8 and 18   **g** 18 and 27   **h** 7 and 11

7 a Two numbers have an LCM of 24 and an HCF of 2. What are they?

   b Two numbers have an LCM of 18 and an HCF of 3. What are they?

   c Two numbers have an LCM of 60 and an HCF of 5. What are they?

8 **a** What is the HCF and the LCM of: **i** 5, 7   **ii** 3, 4   **iii** 2, 11.

b Two numbers, x and y, have an HCF of 1. What is the LCM of x and y?

9 **a** What is the HCF and LCM of: **i** 5, 10   **ii** 3, 18   **iii** 4, 20.

b Two numbers, x and y (where y is bigger than x), have an HCF of x. What is the LCM of x and y?

10 Copy and complete the table.

x	y	Product	HCF	LCM
4	14	56	2	28
9	21			
12	21			
18	24			

Describe any relationships that you can see in the table.

Extension Work

The triangle numbers are $T_1 = 1$, $T_2 = 3$, $T_3 = 6$, $T_4 = 10$, $T_5 = 15$, $T_6 = 21$, …

The nth triangle number is Tn.

Investigate whether these statements are always true.

- The sum of two consecutive triangle numbers is always a square number, for example, $T_1 + T_2 = 1 + 3 = 4 = 2^2$

- If T is a triangle number then $9 \times T + 1$ is also a triangle number, for example, $9 \times T_1 + 1 = 9 \times 1 + 1 = 10 = T_4$

- A triangle number can never end in 2, 4, 7 or 9.

- If T is a triangle number then $8 \times T + 1$ is always a square number, for example, $8 \times T_1 + 1 = 8 \times 1 + 1 = 9 = 3^2$

- If you keep on working out the sum of digits of any triangle number until a single digit is obtained the answer is always 1, 3, 6 or 9.

- The sum of n consecutive cubes starting from 1 is equal to the square of the nth triangle number, for example, $T_4^2 = 10^2 = 100 = 1^3 + 2^3 + 3^3 + 4^3$

Powers and roots

Look at these cubes. Is cube B twice as big, four times as big or eight times as big as cube A? How many times bigger is cube C than cube A?

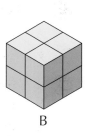
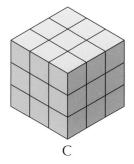

A   B   C

Example 1.6 ▷

Use a calculator to work out: **a** 4^3 **b** 5.5^2 **c** $(-3)^4$

a $4^3 = 4 \times 4 \times 4 = 64$

b $5.5^2 = 5.5 \times 5.5 = 30.25$ (most calculators have a button for squaring, usually marked x^2)

c $(-3)^4 = -3 \times -3 \times -3 \times -3 = +9 \times +9 = 81$

Example 1.7 ▷

Use a calculator to work out: **a** $\sqrt{12.25}$ **b** $\sqrt{33\,124}$

a   Depending on your calculator, sometimes you type the square root before the number, and sometimes the number comes first. Make sure you can use your calculator. The answer is 3.5.

b   The answer is 182.

Exercise 1C

1 The diagrams at the beginning of this section show cubes made from smaller 1 cm cubes. Copy and complete this table.

Length of side	1 cm	2 cm	3 cm	4 cm	5 cm	6 cm	7 cm	8 cm	9 cm	10 cm
Area of face	1 cm²	4 cm²	9 cm²							
Volume of cube	1 cm³	8 cm³	27 cm³							

2 Use the table in Question 1 to work out the following.

    a $\sqrt{4}$ **b** $\sqrt{64}$ **c** $\sqrt{81}$ **d** $\sqrt{100}$ **e** $\sqrt{25}$

    f $\sqrt[3]{27}$ **g** $\sqrt[3]{125}$ **h** $\sqrt[3]{1000}$ **i** $\sqrt[3]{512}$ **j** $\sqrt[3]{729}$

3 Find two values of x that make the following equations true.

    a $x^2 = 36$ **b** $x^2 = 121$ **c** $x^2 = 144$ **d** $x^2 = 2.25$

    e $x^2 = 196$ **f** $x^2 = 5.76$ **g** $x^2 = 2.56$ **h** $x^2 = 3600$

4 Use a calculator to find the value of the following.

    a 13^2 **b** 13^3 **c** 15^2 **d** 15^3 **e** 21^2 **f** 21^3

    g 1.4^2 **h** 1.8^3 **i** 2.3^3 **j** 4.5^2 **k** 12^3 **l** 1.5^3

5 Use a calculator to find the value of the following.

    a 2^4 **b** 3^5 **c** 3^4 **d** 2^5 **e** $(-4)^4$ **f** 5^4

    g 7^4 **h** 8^3 **i** $(-2)^7$ **j** 2^9 **k** 2^{10} **l** 3^{10}

6 Without using a calculator, write down the values of the following. (*Hint:* Use the table in Question 1 and some of the answers from Question 5 to help you.)

    a 20^2 **b** 30^3 **c** 50^3 **d** 20^5 **e** 70^2 **f** 200^3

7 $10^2 = 100$, $10^3 = 1000$: Copy and complete the following table.

Number	100	1000	10 000	100 000	1 000 000	10 000 000
Power of 10	10^2	10^3				

8 Work out: **a** 1^2 **b** 1^3 **c** 1^4 **d** 1^5 **e** 1^6

f Write down the value of 1^{223}

9 Work out: **a** $(-1)^2$ **b** $(-1)^3$ **c** $(-1)^4$ **d** $(-1)^5$ **e** $(-1)^6$

f Write down the value of: **i** $(-1)^{223}$ **ii** $(-1)^{224}$

10 You can see from the table in Question 1 that 64 is a square number (8^2) and a cube number (4^3).

a One other cube number (apart from 1) in the table is also a square number. Which is it?

b Which is the next cube number that is also a square number?

(*Hint*: Look at the pattern of such cube numbers so far, i.e. 1^3, 4^3, ...)

Extension **Work**

If you have a basic calculator with only [+] [×] [÷] [−] keys, how can you find a square root?

For example, find $\sqrt{7}$ to two decimal places.

You know that the answer is between 2 and 3 ($\sqrt{4} = 2$ and $\sqrt{9} = 3$).

Try $2.5^2 = 6.25$. This is too low.
Try $2.6^2 = 6.76$. This is too low.
Try $2.7^2 = 7.29$. This is too high.
Try $2.65^2 = 7.0225$. This is very close but a bit high.
Try $2.64^2 = 6.9696$. This is very close but too low.

The answer is $\sqrt{7} = 2.65$ to two decimal places.

Using only the [×] key, find the following square roots to two decimal places.

1 $\sqrt{20}$ **2** $\sqrt{15}$ **3** $\sqrt{120}$ **4** $\sqrt{70}$

A computer spreadsheet can be used for this activity.

Prime factors

What are the **prime factors** of 120 and 210?

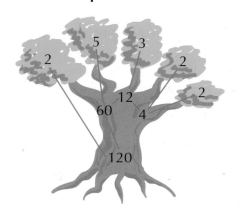

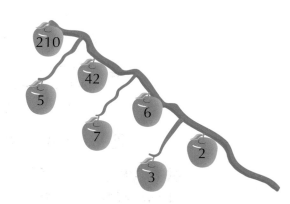

Example 1.8 ▶ Write 18 as the product of its prime factors.

Using a prime factor tree, split 18 into 3×6 and 6 into 3×2.

The prime factors of 18 are 2, 3, 3.

So, $18 = 2 \times 3 \times 3 = 2 \times 3^2$

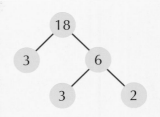

Example 1.9 ▶ Write 24 as the product of its prime factors.

Using the division method:

```
2 | 24
2 | 12
2 |  6
3 |  3
       1
```

The prime factors of 24 are 2, 2, 2, 3.

So, $24 = 2 \times 2 \times 2 \times 3 = 2^3 \times 3$

Example 1.10 ▶ Use prime factors to find the highest common factor (HCF) and lowest common multiple (LCM) of 24 and 54.

$24 = 2 \times 2 \times 2 \times 3$, $54 = 2 \times 3 \times 3 \times 3$

You can see that 2×3 is common to both lists of prime factors.

Put these in the centre, overlapping, part of the diagram.

Put the other prime factors in the outside of the diagram.

The product of the centre numbers, $2 \times 3 = 6$, is the HCF.

The product of all the numbers, $2 \times 2 \times 2 \times 3 \times 3 \times 3 = 216$, is the LCM.

Exercise 1D

1 These are the products of the prime factors of some numbers. What are the numbers?

   a $2 \times 2 \times 3$ **b** $2 \times 3 \times 3 \times 5$ **c** $2 \times 2 \times 3^2$ **d** $2 \times 3^3 \times 5$ **e** $2 \times 3 \times 5^2$

2 Using a prime factor tree, work out the prime factors of the following.

   a 8   **b** 10   **c** 16   **d** 20   **e** 28

   f 34   **g** 35   **h** 52   **i** 60   **j** 180

3 Using the division method, work out the prime factors of the following.

   a 42   **b** 75   **c** 140   **d** 250   **e** 480

4 Using the diagrams below, work out the HCF and LCM of the following pairs.

a

30 and 72

b

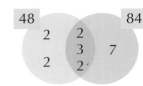

50 and 90

c

48 and 84

8

5 The prime factors of 120 are 2, 2, 2, 3, 5. The prime factors of 150 are 2, 3, 5, 5.

Put these numbers into a diagram like those in Question 4.

Use the diagram to work out the HCF and LCM of 120 and 150.

6 The prime factors of 210 are 2, 3, 5, 7. The prime factors of 90 are 2, 3, 3, 5.

Put these numbers into a diagram like those in Question 4.

Use the diagram to work out the HCF and LCM of 210 and 90.

7 The prime factors of 240 are 2, 2, 2, 2, 3, 5. The prime factors of 900 are 2, 2, 3, 3, 5, 5.

Put these numbers into a diagram like those in Question 4.

Use the diagram to work out the HCF and LCM of 240 and 900.

8 Use prime factors to work out the HCF and LCM of the following pairs.
   a 200 and 175   **b** 56 and 360   **c** 42 and 105

9 Find the LCM of the following pairs.
   a 56 and 70   **b** 28 and 38   **c** 18 and 32

Extension Work

1 Show that 60 has 12 factors.
Find three more numbers less than 100 that also have 12 factors.

2 Show that 36 has nine factors.
There are seven other numbers greater than 1 and less than 100 with an odd number of factors.
Find them all. What sort of numbers are they?

3 There are 69 three-digit multiples of 13. The first is 104 and the last is 988.
Five of these have a digit sum equal to 13.
For example, 715 is a multiple of 13 and 7 + 1 + 5 = 13.
Find the other four.

You may find a computer spreadsheet useful for this activity.

Sequences 1

Example 1.11

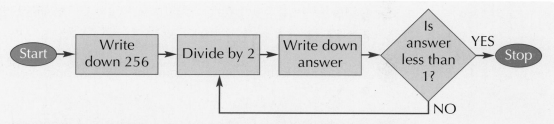

Follow the above **flow diagram** through to the end and write down the numbers generated.

These are 256, 128, 64, 32, 16, 8, 4, 2, 1, 0.5.

Example 1.12 ▷ For each of the following sequences: **i** describe how it is being generated. **ii** find the next two terms.

a 2, 6, 10, 14, 18, 22, …   **b** 1, 3, 27, 81, 243, …
i The sequence is going up by 4   **i** Each term is multiplied by 3
ii The next two terms are 26, 30   **ii** The next two terms are 729, 2187

Exercise 1E

1 Follow these instructions to generate sequences.

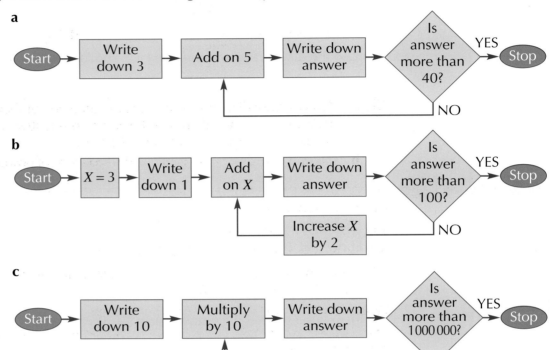

a

Start → Write down 3 → Add on 5 → Write down answer → Is answer more than 40? — YES → Stop / NO (loops back to Add on 5)

b

Start → X = 3 → Write down 1 → Add on X → Write down answer → Is answer more than 100? — YES → Stop / NO → Increase X by 2 (loops back to Add on X)

c

Start → Write down 10 → Multiply by 10 → Write down answer → Is answer more than 1000 000? — YES → Stop / NO (loops back to Multiply by 10)

2 What is the name of the sequence of numbers generated by the flow diagram in Question 1b?

3 Describe in words the sequence of numbers generated by the flow diagram in Question 1c.

4 Describe how the sequences below are generated.

a 1, 4, 7, 10, 13, 16, …   **b** 1, 4, 16, 64, 256, 1024, …
c 1, 4, 8, 13, 19, 26, …   **d** 1, 4, 9, 16, 25, 36, …

5 Write down four sequences beginning 1, 5, …, and explain how each of them is generated.

6 Describe how each of the following sequences is generated and write down the next two terms.

a 40, 41, 43, 46, 50, 55, …   **b** 90, 89, 87, 84, 80, 75, …
c 1, 3, 7, 13, 21, 31, …   **d** 2, 6, 12, 20, 30, 42, …

5

7 You are given a start number and a multiplier. Write down at least the first six terms of the sequences (for example, start 2 and multiplier 3 gives 2, 6, 18, 54, 162, 486, …).

a start 1, multiplier 3   **b** start 2, multiplier 2   **c** start 1, multiplier −1

d start 1, multiplier 0.5   **e** start 2, multiplier 0.4   **f** start 1, multiplier 0.3

8 The following patterns of dots generate sequences of numbers.

  i Draw the next two patterns of dots.

  ii Write down the next four numbers in the sequence.

a    **b**

c   **d**

9 a Draw a flow diagram to generate the triangle numbers 1, 3, 6, 10, 15, 21, …. (*Hint:* Look at the differences between consecutive terms and compare with those in the sequence from Question 1b.)

  b Draw a flow diagram to generate the sequence of powers of 2 (2, 4, 8, 16, 32, 64, …).

Extension | Work

Fibonacci numbers

You will need a calculator.

A Fibonacci sequence is: 1, 1, 2, 3, 5, 8, 13, 21, …

It is formed by writing down 1, 1 and then adding together the previous two terms, that is 5 = 3 + 2, 8 = 5 + 3, etc.

Write down the next five terms of the sequence.

Now divide each term by the previous term, that is 1 ÷ 1 = 1, 2 ÷ 1 = 2, 3 ÷ 2 = 1.5, 5 ÷ 3 = …

You should notice something happening.

You may find a computer spreadsheet useful for this activity.
If you have access to a library or the Internet, find out about the Italian mathematician after whom the sequence is named.

Sequences 2

Paving slabs 1 metre square are used to put borders around square ponds. For example:

1 × 1 m² pond
8 slabs

2 × 2 m² pond
12 slabs

3 × 3 m² pond
16 slabs

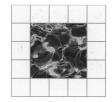

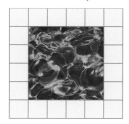

4 × 4 m² pond
20 slabs

How many slabs would fit around a 5 × 5 m² pond? What about a 100 × 100 m² pond?

Example 1.13 ▷ Generate sequences using the rules given.

  a First term 5, increase each term by a constant difference of 6.

  b First term 32, multiply each term by $-\frac{1}{2}$.

  c First term 3, subtract 1 then multiply by 2.

  a The sequence is 5, 5 + 6 = 11, 11 + 6 = 17, …, which gives 5, 11, 17, 23, 29, 35, …

  b The sequence is 32, 32 × $-\frac{1}{2}$ = –16, –16 × $-\frac{1}{2}$ = 8, etc., which gives 32, –16, 8, –4, 2, –1, $\frac{1}{2}$, $-\frac{1}{4}$, …

  c The sequence is 3, (3 – 1) × 2 = 4, (4 – 1) × 2 = 6, (6 – 1) × 2 = 10, etc., which gives 3, 4, 6, 10, 18, 34, 66, …

We can describe sequences by giving a rule for any term. This is called the general or *n*th term and is an algebraic expression.

Example 1.14 ▷ The *n*th term of the sequence 9, 13, 17, 21, 25, … is given by the expression 4*n* + 5.

  a Show this is true for the first three terms.

  b Use the rule to find the 50th term of the sequence.

  a Let *n* = 1, 4 × 1 + 5 = 4 + 5 = 9

   Let *n* = 2, 4 × 2 + 5 = 8 + 5 = 13

   Let *n* = 3, 4 × 3 + 5 = 12 + 5 = 17

  b Let *n* = 50, 4 × 50 + 5 = 200 + 5 = 205

   so the 50th term is 205.

We can describe a sequence by finding the *n*th term. This is the **generalisation** that will allow us to find any specific term.

Example 1.15 ▷ Look at the sequence with the following pattern.

(term)

Pattern number	1	2	3
Number of matchsticks	7	12	17

  a Find the generalisation (*n*th term) of the pattern.

  b Find the 50th term in the sequence.

  a The terms go up by 5 so the *n*th term is based on 5*n*.

   The first term is 7.

   For the first term *n* = 1

   So 5 × 1 + 2 = 7, giving

     nth term = 5n + 2

  b 50th term = 5 × 50 + 2 = 252

Example 1.16 ▷ Find the *n*th term of the sequence 3, 10, 17, 24, 31, …

The sequence goes up by 7 each time, so the *n*th term is based on 7*n*.

The first term is 3, and 3 − 7 = −4, so the *n*th term is 7*n* − 4.

Exercise 1F

1 For the following arithmetic sequences, write down the first term *a* and the constant difference *d*.

   a 4, 9, 14, 19, 24, 29, …   **b** 1, 3, 5, 7, 9, 11, …

   c 3, 9, 15, 21, 27, 33, …   **d** 5, 3, 1, −1, −3, −5, …

2 Given the first term *a* and the constant difference *d*, write down the first six terms of each of these sequences.

   a *a* = 1, *d* = 7   **b** *a* = 3, *d* = 2   **c** *a* = 5, *d* = 4

   d *a* = 0.5, *d* = 1.5   **e** *a* = 4, *d* = −3   **f** *a* = 2, *d* = −0.5

3 The following flow diagram can be used to generate sequences.

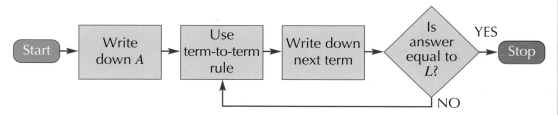

For example, if *A* = 8, the term-to-term rule is 'halve' and *L* = 0.25, the sequence is:

    8, 4, 2, 1, 0.5, 0.25

Write down the sequences generated by:

	A	Term-to-term rule	*L*
a	1 000 000	Divide by 10	1
b	1	Add 3, 5, 7, 9, 11, etc.	225
c	1	Double	1024
d	10	Subtract 5	−25
e	3	Add 2	23
f	1	Multiply by −2	1024
g	48	Halve	0.75
h	1	Double and add 1	63
i	2	Times by 3 and subtract 1	365
j	0	Add 1, 2, 3, 4, 5, 6, etc.	55

4 The *n*th term of sequences are given by the rules below. Use this to write down the first five terms of each sequence.

    a $2n - 1$ **b** $2n + 3$ **c** $2n + 2$ **d** $2n + 1$

    e   What is the constant difference in each of the sequences in **a**–**d**?

5 The *n*th term of sequences are given by the rules below. Use this to write down the first five terms of each sequence.

    a $3n + 1$ **b** $3n + 2$ **c** $3n - 2$ **d** $3n - 1$

    e   What is the constant difference in each of the sequences in **a**–**d**?

6 The *n*th term of sequences are given by the rules below. Use this to write down the first five terms of each sequence.

    a $5n - 1$ **b** $5n + 2$ **c** $5n - 4$ **d** $5n + 3$

    e   What is the constant difference in each of the sequences in **a**–**d**?

7 For each of the sequences whose *n*th term is given below, find:

    i   the first three terms.   **ii**   the 100th term.

    a $n + 1$ **b** $3n - 1$ **c** $2n - 3$

    d $5n - 2$ **e** $4n - 3$ **f** $9n + 1$

    g $\frac{1}{2}n + 1$ **h** $6n + 1$ **i** $1\frac{1}{2}n - \frac{1}{2}$

8 For each of the patterns below, find:

    i   the *n*th term for the number of matchsticks.

    ii   the number of matchsticks in the 50th term.

a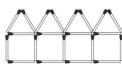

b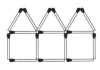

c

d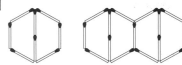

9 Find the *n*th term of each of these sequences.

    a   4, 10, 16, 22, 28, …   **b**   9, 12, 15, 18, 21, …

    c   9, 15, 21, 27, 33, …   **d**   2, 5, 8, 11, 14, …

    e   2, 9, 16, 23, 30, …   **f**   8, 10, 12, 14, 16, …

    g   10, 14, 18, 22, 26, …   **h**   3, 11, 19, 27, 35, …

    i   9, 19, 29, 39, 49, …   **j**   4, 13, 22, 31, 40, …

10 Write down a first term *A* and a term-to-term rule that you can use in the flow diagram in Question 3 so that:

    a   each term of the sequence is even.

    b   each term of the sequence is odd.

    c   the sequence is the 5 times table.

    d   the sequence is the triangle numbers.

    e   the numbers in the sequence all end in 1.

    f   the sequence has alternating odd and even terms.

    g   the sequence has alternating positive and negative terms.

Extension · Work

For each of the sequences whose *n*th term is given below, find:

i   the first three terms.   **ii**   the 99th term.

a $2(n + 1)^2$ **b** $(n - 1)(n + 1)$ **c** $\frac{1}{2}(n + 1)(n + 2)$

Solving problems

An investigation

At the start of the last section you were asked to say how many slabs would be needed to go round a square pond.

1 × 1 pond
8 slabs

2 × 2 pond
12 slabs

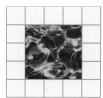
3 × 3 pond
16 slabs

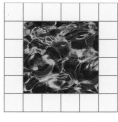
4 × 4 pond
20 slabs

To solve this problem you need to:

    Step 1: break the problem into simple parts.

    Step 2: set up a **table** of results.

    Step 3: **predict** and **test** a **rule**.

    Step 4: use your rule to answer the question.

Step 1

This is already done with the diagrams given.

Step 2

Pond side	Number of slabs
1	8
2	12
3	16
4	20

Step 3

Use the table to spot how the sequence is growing.

In this case, it is increasing in 4s.

So a 5 × 5 pond will need 24 slabs (see right).

We can also say that the number of slabs S is 4 times the pond side (P) plus 4, which we can write as:

$$S = 4P + 4$$

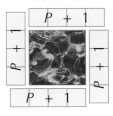

There are many other ways to write this rule, and many ways of showing that it is true.

For example:

$4P + 4$ $2(P + 2) + 2P$ $4(P + 1)$

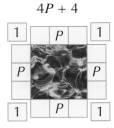 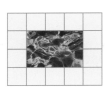 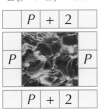

Step 4

We can now use any rule to say that for a 100 × 100 pond, 4 × 100 + 4 = 404 slabs will be needed.

Exercise 1G

Do the following investigations. Make sure you follow the steps above and explain what you are doing clearly. In each investigation you are given some hints.

1 Write a rule to show how many square slabs it takes to make a border around rectangular ponds.

First side	Second side	Slabs
1	2	10
1	3	12
2	3	14

2 The final score in a football match was 5–4. How many different half-time scores could there have been?

For a match that ended 0–0, there is only one possible half-time result (0–0).

For a match that ended 1–2, there are six possible half-time scores (0–0, 0–1, 0–2, 1–0, 1–1, 1–2).

Take some other low-scoring matches, such as 1–1, 2–1, 2–0, etc., and work out the half-time scores for these.

Set up a table like the one in Question 1.

3 There are 13 stairs in most houses. How many different ways are there of going up the stairs in a combination of one step or two steps at a time?

Take one stair. There is only one way of going up it (1).

Take two stairs. There are two ways of going up (1+1, 2).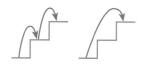

Before you think this is going to be easy, look at five stairs. There are eight ways of going up them (1+1+1+1+1, 1+1+1+2, 1+2+1+1, 1+1+2+1, 1+2+2, 2+1+2, 2+2+1, 2+1+1+1).

Work out the number of ways for three stairs and four stairs. Draw up a table and see if you can spot the rule!

LEVEL BOOSTER

4
I can write down the multiples of any whole number.
I can work out the factors of numbers under 100.

5
I can add and subtract negative numbers.
I can write down and recognise the sequence of square numbers.
I know the squares of all numbers up to 15^2 and the corresponding square roots.
I can use a calculator to work out powers of numbers.
I can find any term in a sequence given the first term and the term-to-term rule.
I know that the square roots of positive numbers can have two values, one positive and one negative.

6
I can multiply and divide negative numbers.
I can find the lowest common multiple (LCM) for pairs of numbers.
I can find the highest common factor (HCF) for pairs of numbers.
I can write a number as the product of its prime factors.
I can find any term in a sequence given the algebraic rule for the nth term.
I can find the nth term of a sequence in the form $an + b$.
I can investigate a mathematical problem.

7
I can work out the LCM and HCF of two numbers using prime factors.
I can devise flow diagrams to generate sequences.

1 *2000 Paper 1*

    a   Two numbers multiply together to make −15. They add together to make 2.
        What are the two numbers?

    b   Two numbers multiply together to make −15, but add together to make −2.
        What are the two numbers?

    c   The square of 5 is 25. The square of another number is also 25.
        What is that other number?

2 *2007 Paper 2*

Look at the information.

$$x = 4 \qquad y = 13$$

Copy and complete the rules below to show **different** ways to get y using x.

The first one is done for you.

To get y, **multiply** x by 2 and **add** 5
This can be written as $y = 2x + 5$

To get y, **multiply** x by ___ and **add** ___
This can be written as $y = $ _____

To get y, **multiply** x by ___ and **subtract** ___
This can be written as $y = $ _____

To get y, **divide** x by ___ and **add** ___
This can be written as $y = $ _____

3 *2006 Paper 1*

    a   Put these values in order of size with the **smallest first**:

        5^2 3^2 3^3 2^4

    b   Look at this information:

        5^5 is 3125

    What is 5^7?

4 *2006 Paper 2*

Look at these pairs of number sequences.

The second sequence is formed from the first sequence by adding a number or multiplying by a number.

Work out the missing nth terms.

    a   5,   9,   13,   17,   … nth term is $4n + 1$
        6,   10,   14,   18,   … nth term is …

b   12,   18,   24,   30,   ... nth term is $6n + 6$
    6,   9,   12,   15,   ... nth term is ...

c   2,   7,   12,   17,   ... nth term is $5n - 3$
    4,   14,   24,   34,   ... nth term is ...

5   *2007 Paper 1*

    a   Copy the following and **draw lines** to match each nth term rule to its number sequence.

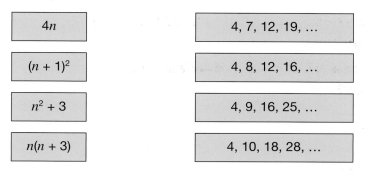

    b   Write the **first four** terms of the number sequence using the nth term rule below:

6   *2007 Paper 1*

    Here is the rule to find the **geometric mean** of two numbers.

> **Multiply** the two numbers together,
> then find the **square root** of the result.

    Example: geometric mean of 4 and 9 $= \sqrt{4 \times 9}$
                                    $= \sqrt{36}$
                                      $= 6$

    a   For the two numbers **10** and x, the geometric mean is **30**.

        What is the value of x?

    b   Reena says:

           'For the two numbers **–2** and **8**, it is **impossible** to find the geometric mean.'

        Is Reena correct?

        Explain your answer.

FM Blackpool Tower

Blackpool Tower is a tourist attraction in Blackpool, Lancashire, England. It opened to the public on 14 May 1894. Inspired by the Eiffel Tower in Paris, it rises to 518 ft 9 inches.

The foundation stone was laid on 29 September 1891. The total cost for the design and construction of the Tower and buildings was about £290 000. Five million bricks, 2500 tonnes of steel and 93 tonnes of cast steel were used to construct the Tower. The Tower buildings occupy a total of 6040 sq yards.

When the Tower opened, 3000 customers took the first rides to the top. Tourists paid 6 old pence for admission, a further 6 old pence for a ride in the lifts to the top, and a further 6 old pence for the circus.

Inside the Tower there is a circus, an aquarium, a ballroom, restaurants, a children's play area and amusements.

In 1998 a 'Walk of Faith' glass floor panel was opened at the top of the Tower. Made up of two sheets of laminated glass, it weighs half a tonne and is two inches thick. Visitors can stand on the glass panel and look straight down 380 ft to the promenade.

Use the information to help you answer these questions.

1 In what year did the Tower celebrate its centenary (100th birthday)?

2 How many years and months did it take to build the Tower?

3 The Tower is painted continuously. It takes seven years to paint the Tower completely. How many times has it been painted since it opened?

4 The aquarium in the Tower opened 20 years earlier than the Tower. What year did the aquarium celebrate its 100th birthday?

5 The largest tank in the aquarium holds 32 000 litres of water. There are approximately 4.5 litres to a gallon. How many gallons of water does the tank hold?

6 The water in the tropical fish tanks is kept at 75 °F. This rule is used to convert from degrees Fahrenheit to degrees Centigrade.

°F → Subtract 32 → Divide by 9 → Multiply by 5 → °C

Use this rule to convert 75°F to °C.

7 The circus in the base of the Tower first opened to the public on 14 May 1894. Admission fee was 6 old pence. Before Britain introduced decimal currency in 1971 there were 240 old pence in a pound.

  a What fraction, in its simplest form, is 6 old pence out of 240 old pence?

  b What is the equivalent value of 6 old pence in new pence?

8 Over 650 000 people visit the Tower every year. The Tower is open every day except Christmas day. Approximately how many people visit the Tower each day on average?

9 **a** In January 2008, it cost €12 to visit the Eiffel Tower and £9.50 to visit Blackpool Tower. The exchange rate in January 2008 was £1 = €1.35. Which Tower was cheapest to visit and by how much (answer in pounds and pence)?

  b The Eiffel Tower is 325 m high. Blackpool Tower is 519 ft high. 1 m ≈ 3.3 ft. How many times taller is the Eiffel Tower than the Blackpool Tower?

  c The Eiffel Tower gets 6.7 million visitors a year. How many times more popular is it with tourists than the Blackpool Tower?

  d The Eiffel Tower celebrated its centenary in 1989. How many years before the Blackpool Tower did it open?

10 Animals have not appeared in the Tower Circus performances since 1990.

For how many years did animals appear in the circus?

11 The top of the Tower is 518 ft and 9 inches above the base. There are 12 inches in a foot and 2.54 cm in an inch. Calculate the height of the Tower in metres.

12 The 'Walk of Faith' can withstand the weight of five baby elephants. One baby elephant weighs on average 240 kg. One adult human weighs on average 86 kg. How many adults should be allowed on the 'Walk of Faith' at any one time (if they could fit)?

13 The Tower and buildings cost approximately £290 000 to construct. Today it is estimated that the cost would be £230 million. By how many times has the cost of building gone up since the Tower was built?

14 The Tower lift makes about 75 trips up and down each day. Each ascent and descent is approximately 350 ft. There are 5280 ft in a mile. In a year (assume 360 days) approximately how many miles does the lift travel?

15 The Ballroom floor measures 36.58 m by 36.58 m. It comprises 30 602 separate blocks of mahogany, oak and walnut.

Assuming that every block is equal in area, what is the area, in square centimetres, of each block?

Give your answer to the nearest square centimetre.

16 When it is lit up, the tower has 10 000 light bulbs using an average of 15 watts per hour each. The cost of electricity is 12p per kilowatt hour (1000 watts per hour). Calculate the approximate yearly electricity bill for the lights assuming they are lit for 12 hours per day.

17 The circus ring when flooded can hold up to 190 000 litres of water to a depth of 140 cm. (1 litre = 1000 cm^3)

a How many cubic centimetres is 190 000 litres?

b Assuming that the circus ring is circular the formula for working out the radius if you know the volume, V, and the depth, d, is

$$r = \sqrt{\frac{V}{\pi \times d}}$$

Work out the radius of the circus ring.
Give your answer in metres.

18 An approximate formula for how far you can see, D kilometres, when you are m metres above the ground is

$$D = \sqrt{13m}$$

The coast of the Isle of Man is 42 km from Blackpool. Can you see it from the observation deck of the tower which is 120 m above the ground?

Show your working clearly.

This chapter is going to show you

- How to identify alternate and corresponding angles
- How to calculate the interior and exterior angles of polygons
- How to use proof in geometry
- How to classify quadrilaterals using their geometric properties
- How to draw constructions using a ruler and compasses

What you should already know

- How to use angles in parallel lines
- The sum of the interior angles of a triangle and a quadrilateral
- The names for different sided polygons
- The symmetrical properties of quadrilaterals
- How to construct triangles from given information
- How to solve algebraic equations

Alternate and corresponding angles

Look at the picture of the railway. Can you work out why the angles between the arms of the signals and the post are both the same?

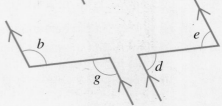

Example 2.1 ▷ Look at the diagram.

a Name pairs of angles that are alternate angles.

b Name pairs of angles that are corresponding angles.

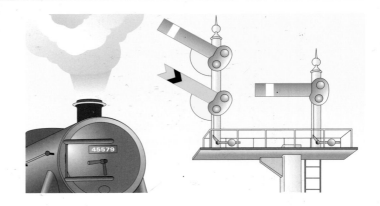

a The alternate angles are *b* and *g*, and *d* and *e*.

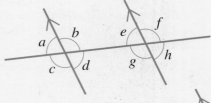

b The corresponding angles are *a* and *e*, *b* and *f*, *c* and *g*, and *d* and *h*.

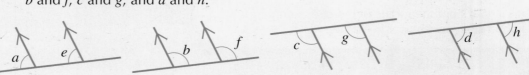

Exercise 2A

1 Copy and complete the sentences below.

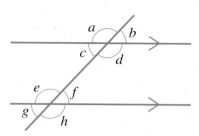

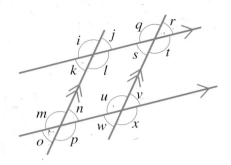

a *a* and … are corresponding angles.
b *b* and … are corresponding angles.
c *c* and … are corresponding angles.
d *d* and … are corresponding angles.
e *e* and … are alternate angles.
f *f* and … are alternate angles.
g *k* and … are corresponding angles.
h *u* and … are corresponding angles.
i *l* and … are corresponding angles.
j *r* and … are corresponding angles.
k *n* and … are alternate angles.
l *s* and … are alternate angles.

2 Work out the measurement of the lettered angles in these diagrams.

a

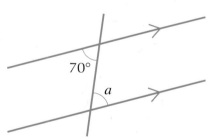

b

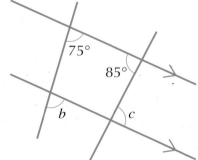

c

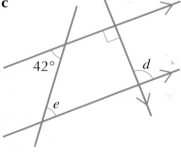

d

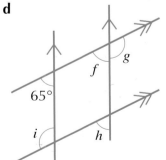

e

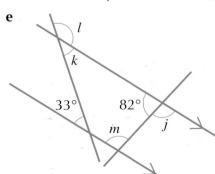

f

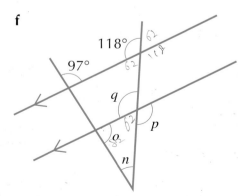

3 Calculate x in each of these diagrams. You may need to set up and solve an equation.

a
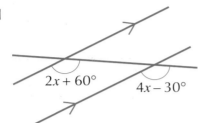
$40° + x$
$120°$

b
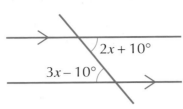
$2x + 10°$
$3x - 10°$

c
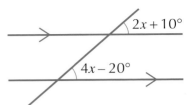
$2x + 10°$
$4x - 20°$

d
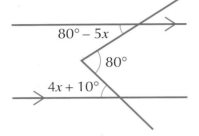
$2x + 60°$ $4x - 30°$

e
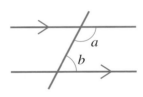
$80° - 5x$
$80°$
$4x + 10°$

Extension   Work

1   Interior angles in parallel lines

a and b are called interior angles:

$$a + b = 180°$$

a
b

Calculate x in each of the following diagrams. You may need to set up and solve an equation.

a

$52°$
x

b
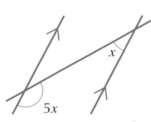
x
$5x$

c
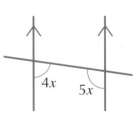
$4x$ $5x$

d
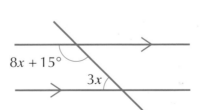
$8x + 15°$
$3x$

e
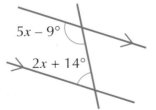
$5x - 9°$
$2x + 14°$

2 Drawing parallel lines using a ruler and a set-square

To draw a line parallel to the line AB to pass through the point C.

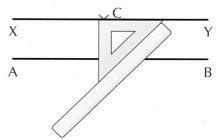

Place the ruler and the set square on the line as shown:

Slide the set-square along the ruler until it touches C. Draw the line XY to pass through C. Then XY is parallel to AB.

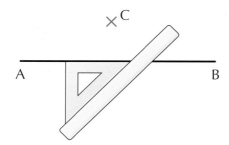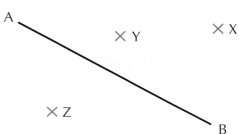

Now draw a line AB and points X, Y and Z as shown. Draw lines parallel to AB which pass through the three points.

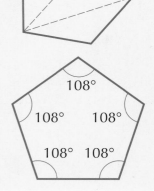

Interior and exterior angles of polygons

Interior angles

The angles inside a **polygon** are known as **interior angles**.

For a triangle, the sum of the interior angles is 180°:

$$a + b + c = 180°$$

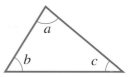

Example 2.2 ▷

Find the sum of the interior angles of a pentagon.

The diagram shows how a pentagon can be split into three triangles from one of its vertices. The sum of the interior angles for each triangle is 180°.

So the sum of the interior angles of a pentagon

$$= 3 \times 180° = 540°$$

From this, we can deduce that each interior angle of a regular pentagon is:

$$540° \div 5 = 108°$$

Remember: A regular polygon has equal sides and equal angles.

Exterior angles

If we extend a side of a polygon, the angle formed outside the polygon is known as an **exterior angle**.

In the diagram, *a* is an exterior angle of the quadrilateral.

At any vertex of a polygon, the interior angle plus the exterior angle = 180° (angles on a straight line).

In the diagram, *a* + *b* = 180°.

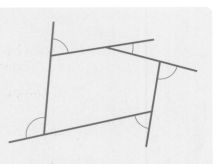

This is shown for the quadrilateral, but remember it is true for *any* polygon.

Example 2.3 ▶

On the diagram, all the sides of the pentagon have been extended to show all the exterior angles.

If you imagine standing on a vertex and turning through all the exterior angles on the pentagon, you will have turned through 360°.

This is true for all polygons. The sum of the exterior angles for any polygon is 360°.

For a regular pentagon, each exterior angle is
360° ÷ 5 = 72°

Exercise 2B

1 a Find the sum of the interior angles of: **i** a hexagon. **ii** an octagon by splitting each polygon into triangles.

b Copy and complete the table below. The pentagon has been done for you. You should not draw the polygons.

Name of polygon	Number of sides for the polygon	Number of triangles inside the polygon	Sum of interior angles for the polygon
Triangle			
Quadrilateral			
Pentagon	5	3	540°
Hexagon			
Heptagon			
Octagon			
n-sided polygon			

2 Calculate the measurement of the lettered angle in each of the following polygons.

a

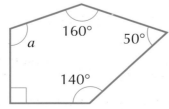

b

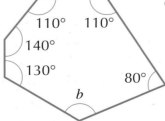

c

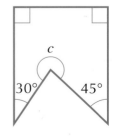

3 Calculate the size of the interior angle for each of the following.

a A regular hexagon **b** A regular octagon **c** A regular decagon

4 Calculate the size of the lettered angle in each of the following polygons.

a

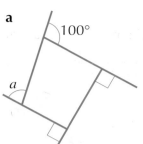

b

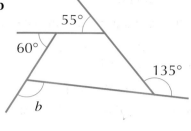

c

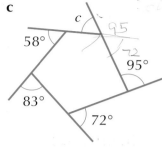

5 Copy and complete the table below for regular polygons. The regular pentagon has been done for you.

Regular polygon	Number of sides	Sum of exterior angles	Size of each exterior angle
Equilateral triangle			
Square			
Regular pentagon	5	360°	72°
Regular hexagon			
Regular octagon			
Regular decagon			
Regular *n*-sided polygon			

6 A regular dodecagon is a polygon with 12 equal angles.
- **a** Calculate the sum of the interior angles.
- **b** Work out the size of each interior angle.
- **c** Work out the size of each exterior angle.

Extension **Work**

1 Calculate the value of *x* in each of the following polygons:

a

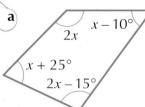

b

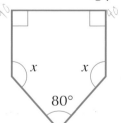

c

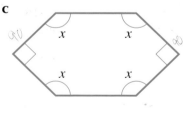

2 The size of each interior angle in a regular polygon is 162°. How many sides does the polygon have?

3 The size of each exterior angle in a regular polygon is 20°. How many sides does the polygon have?

4 If you start at any vertex of a polygon, then follow each side around and back to your starting position, then you will have made a complete turn of 360°.

Use computer software such as Logo to demostrate this, and to explain why 360° is the sum of the exterior angles of any polygon.

Geometric proof

The following two examples show you how to **prove** geometric statements. **Proofs** start from basic geometric facts about parallel lines and polygons which are known to be true. Algebra is used to combine the basic facts into more complex statements which must be true as well.

Example 2.4 ▷ *The sum of the angles of a triangle is 180°.*

To prove $a + b + c = 180°$:

Draw a line parallel to one side of the triangle. Let x and y be the other two angles formed on the line with a. Then $x = b$ (alternate angles), $y = c$ (alternate angles) and $a + x + y = 180°$ (angles on a line).

So $a + b + c = 180°$

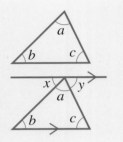

Example 2.5 ▷ *The exterior angle of a triangle is equal to the sum of the two interior opposite angles.*

x is an exterior angle of the triangle. To prove $a + b = x$:

Let the other interior angle of the triangle be c. Then $a + b + c = 180°$ (angles in a triangle) and $x + c = 180°$ (angles on a straight line).

So $a + b = x$

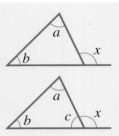

Exercise 2C

1 Write a proof to show that $a + b = 90°$ in the right-angled triangle.

2 Write a proof to show that the sum of the interior angles of a quadrilateral is 360°. (*Hint:* Divide the quadrilateral into two triangles.)

3 Write a proof to show that $x + y = 180°$.

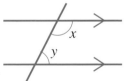

4 Prove that the opposite angles of a parallelogram are equal. (*Hint:* Draw a diagonal on the parallelogram and use alternate angles.)

Extension Work

1 Prove that the sum of the exterior angles of a triangle is 360° (see diagram).

2 Prove that the sum of the interior angles of a pentagon is 540°.

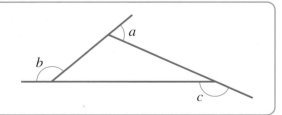

The geometric properties of quadrilaterals

Read carefully and learn all the properties of the **quadrilaterals** below.

Square
- Four equal sides
- Four right angles
- Opposite sides parallel
- Diagonals bisect each other at right angles
- Four lines of symmetry
- Rotational symmetry of order four

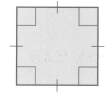

Rectangle
- Two pairs of equal sides
- Four right angles
- Opposite sides parallel
- Diagonals bisect each other
- Two lines of symmetry
- Rotational symmetry of order two

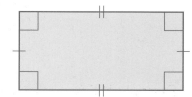

Parallelogram
- Two pairs of equal sides
- Two pairs of equal angles
- Opposite sides parallel
- Diagonals bisect each other
- No lines of symmetry
- Rotational symmetry of order two

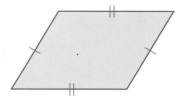

Rhombus
- Four equal sides
- Two pairs of equal angles
- Opposite sides parallel
- Diagonals bisect each other at right angles
- Two lines of symmetry
- Rotational symmetry of order two

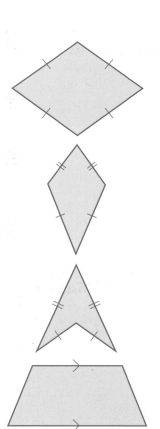

Kite
- Two pairs of adjacent sides of equal length
- One pair of equal angles
- Diagonals intersect at right angles
- One line of symmetry

Arrowhead or delta
- Two pairs of adjacent sides of equal length
- One pair of equal angles
- Diagonals intersect at right angles outside the shape
- One line of symmetry

Trapezium
- One pair of parallel sides
- Some trapeziums have one line of symmetry

Exercise 2D

1 Copy the table below and put each of these quadrilaterals in the correct column: square, rectangle, parallelogram, rhombus, kite, arrowhead, trapezium.

No lines of symmetry	One line of symmetry	Two lines of symmetry	Four lines of symmetry

2 Copy the table below and put each of these quadrilaterals in the correct column: square, rectangle, parallelogram, rhombus, kite, arrowhead, trapezium.

Rotational symmetry of order one	Rotational symmetry of order two	Rotational symmetry of order four

3 A quadrilateral has four right angles and rotational symmetry of order two. What type of quadrilateral is it?

4 A quadrilateral has rotational symmetry of order two and no lines of symmetry. What type of quadrilateral is it?

5 Rachel says:

> A quadrilateral with four equal sides must be a square.

Is she right or wrong? Explain your answer.

6 Robert says:

> A quadrilateral with rotational symmetry of order two must be a rectangle.

Is he right or wrong? Explain your answer.

7 Sharon knows that a square is a special kind of rectangle (a rectangle with four equal sides). Write down the names of other quadrilaterals that could also be given to a square.

8 The three-by-two rectangle shown is to be cut into squares along its grid lines:

This can be done in two different ways:

Three squares   and   Six squares

Use squared paper to show the number of ways different sizes of rectangle can be cut into squares.

1 The tree classification diagram below shows how to sort a set of triangles.

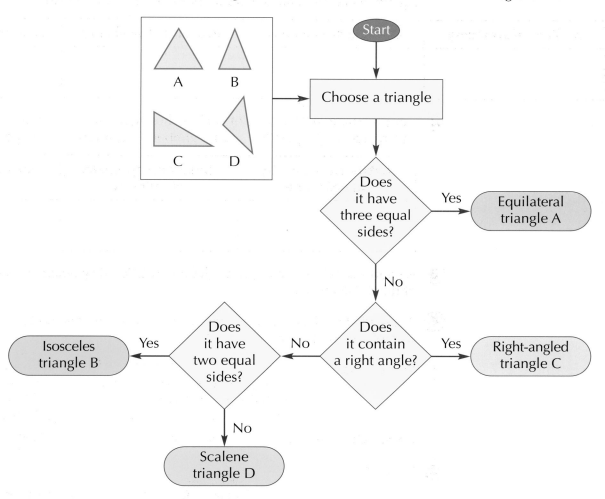

Draw a tree classification diagram to sort a given set of quadrilaterals. Make a poster to show your diagram and display it in your classroom.

2 The instructions below are to draw the parallelogram shown.

REPEAT TWICE:

    [FORWARD 10
    TURN RIGHT 120°
    FORWARD 6
    TURN RIGHT 60°]

Write similar instructions to draw different quadrilaterals. Choose your own measurements for each one.

If you have access to a computer, you may be able to draw the shapes by using programs such as Logo.

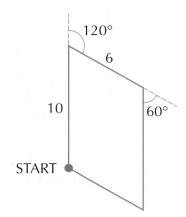

Constructions

The following examples are four important geometric **constructions**. You have already met the first two in Year 7. Carefully work through them yourself. They are useful because they give exact measurements and are therefore used by architects and in design and technology. You will need a sharp pencil, a **straight edge** (or ruler), **compasses** and a protractor. Draw the initial diagram as large as you like. Leave all your construction lines on the diagrams.

Example 2.6 ▶

To construct the mid-point and the perpendicular bisector of the line AB:

- Draw a line segment AB of any length.
- Set compasses to any radius greater than half the length of AB.
- Draw two arcs with the centre at A, one above and one below AB.
- With compasses set at the same radius, draw two arcs with the centre at B, to intersect the first two arcs at C and D.
- Join C and D to intersect AB at X. X is the **mid-point** of the line AB.
- The line CD is the **perpendicular bisector** of the line AB.

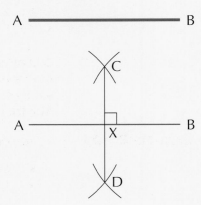

Example 2.7 ▶

To construct the bisector of the angle ABC:

- Draw an angle (∠) ABC of any size.
- Set compasses to any radius. With the centre at B, draw an arc to intersect BC at X and AB at Y.
- With compasses set to any radius, draw two arcs with the centres at X and Y, to intersect at Z.
- Join BZ.
- BZ is the **bisector** of the angle ABC.
- Then ∠ABZ = ∠CBZ.

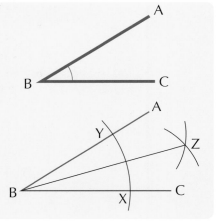

Example 2.8 ▶

To construct the perpendicular from a point P to a line segment AB:

- Set compasses to any suitable radius. Draw arcs from P to intersect AB at X and Y.
- With compasses set at the same radius, draw arcs with the centres at X and Y to intersect at Z below AB.
- Join PZ.
- PZ is perpendicular to AB.

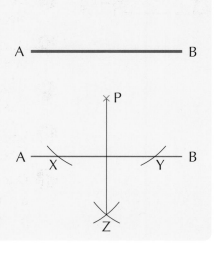

Example 2.9 ▶

To construct the perpendicular from a point Q on a line segment XY:

- Set compasses to a radius that is less than half the length of XY. With the centre at Q, draw two arcs on either side of Q to intersect XY at A and B.
- Set compasses to a radius that is greater than half the length of XY and, with the centres at A and B, draw arcs above and below XY to intersect at C and D.
- Join CD.
- CD is the perpendicular from the point Q.

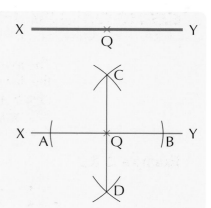

You already know how to construct a triangle given two sides and the included angle (abbreviated SAS) or two angles and the included side (ASA) or three sides (SSS). The example below shows you how to construct a triangle given a right angle, the hypotenuse (the longest side) and another side (RHS).

Example 2.10 ▶

To construct the right-angled triangle ABC:

- Draw line BC 4 cm long.
- Use the method in Example 2.9 to construct the perpendicular from B. (You will need to extend the line BC.)
- Set compasses to a radius of 5 cm. With centre at C, draw an arc to intersect the perpendicular from B.
- The intersection of the arc and the perpendicular is A.

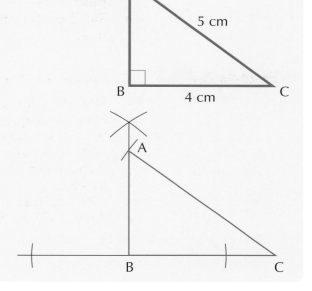

1. Draw a line AB 10 cm in length. Using compasses, construct the perpendicular bisector of the line.

2. Draw a line CD of any length. Using compasses, construct the perpendicular bisector of the line.

3. Using a protractor, draw an angle of 80°. Using compasses, construct the angle bisector of this angle. Measure the two angles formed to check that they are both 40°.

4. Using a protractor, draw an angle of 140°. Using compasses, construct the angle bisector of this angle. Measure the two angles formed to check that they are both 70°.

5. Draw a line XY that is 8 cm in length.
   a Construct the perpendicular bisector of XY.
   b By measuring the length of the perpendicular bisector, draw a rhombus with diagonals of length 8 cm and 5 cm.

6 Draw a circle of radius 6 cm and centre O. Draw a line AB of any length across the circle, as in the diagram (AB is called a chord). Construct the perpendicular from O to the line AB. Extend the perpendicular to make a diameter of the circle.

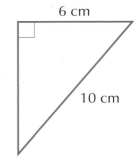

7 Construct each of the following right-angled triangles. Remember to label all the sides.

a

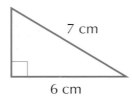

7 cm

6 cm

b

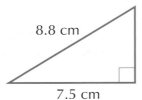

8.8 cm

7.5 cm

c

6 cm

10 cm

8 A 10 m ladder leans against a wall with its foot on the ground 3 m from the wall.
  a Use a scale of 1 cm to 1 m to construct an accurate scale drawing.
  b Find how far up the wall the ladder actually reaches.
  c Find the angle the ladder makes with the ground.

Extension Work

1 *To construct an angle of 60°:*

Draw a line AB of any length. Set your compasses to a radius of about 4 cm. With centre at A, draw a large arc to intersect the line at X. Using the same radius and, with the centre at X, draw an arc to intersect the first arc at Y. Join A and Y. Then ∠YAX is 60°.

Explain how you could use this construction to construct angles of 30° and 15°.

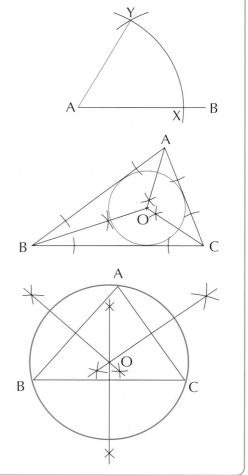

2 *To construct the inscribed circle of a triangle:*

Draw a triangle ABC with sides of any length. Construct the angle bisectors for each of the three angles. The three angle bisectors will meet at a point O in the centre of the triangle. Using O as the centre, draw a circle to touch the three sides of the triangle.

The circle is known as the inscribed circle of the triangle.

3 *To construct the circumscribed circle of a triangle:*

Draw a triangle ABC with sides of any length. Construct the perpendicular bisector for each of the three sides. The three perpendicular bisectors will meet at a point O. Using O as the centre, draw a circle to touch the three vertices of the triangle.

The circle is known as the circumcircle of the triangle, and O is known as the circumcentre.

5
I know the symmetrical properties of quadrilaterals.
I can construct triangles from given information.

6
I can use alternate and corresponding angles in parallel lines.
I can use the interior and exterior angle properties of polygons.
I can use proof in geometry.
I can solve problems using the geometrical properties of quadrilaterals.
I can draw constructions using a ruler and compasses.

National Test questions

1 *2005 Paper 1*

This shape has been made from two congruent **isosceles** triangles.

What is the size of angle p?

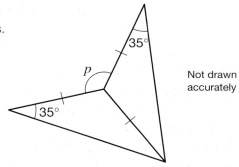

Not drawn
accurately

2 *2002 Paper 2*

The diagram shows a rectangle.

Work out the size of angle a. You must show
your working.

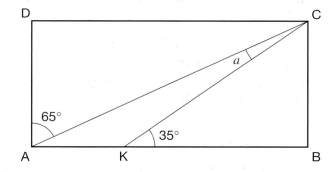

3 *2001 Paper 1*

Look at the triangle drawn on the straight
line PQ.

a Write x in terms of y.

b Now write x in terms of t and w.

c Use your answers to **a** and **b** to show
that $y = t + w$.

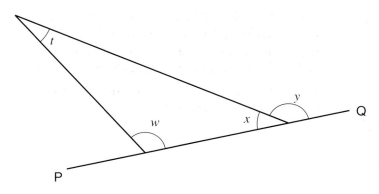

4 *2002 Paper 1*

Draw two points 5 cm apart and label them C and D as below.

.C   .D

Use a straight edge and compasses to draw all points that are the *same distance* from C as from D.

Leave in your construction lines.

5 *2003 Paper 2*

This pattern has rotation symmetry of order 6

a What is the size of angle *w*?

Show your working.

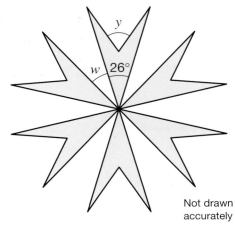

Not drawn accurately

b Each quadrilateral in the pattern is made from two congruent **isosceles** triangles.

What is the size of angle *y*?

Show your working.

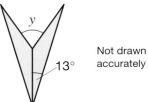

Not drawn accurately

This chapter is going to show you

- How to work out probabilities in different situations
- How to use experimental probability to make predictions
- How to compare experimental and theoretical probability

What you should already know

- Some basic ideas about chance and probability
- How to collect data from a simple experiment
- How to record data in a table or chart
- How to use fractions and decimals

Probability

Look at the pictures. Which one is most likely to happen where you live today?

Many processes are said to be **random**. This means that the result is not **predictable**. So we cannot say for certain that a particular **event** will happen. However, we can use **probability** to decide how likely it is that different events will happen.

You may remember that the probability of an event is given by:

$$p(\text{event}) = \frac{\text{number of outcomes in the event}}{\text{total number of possible outcomes}}$$

Example 3.1 ▶ What is the probability of rolling a dice and obtaining a prime number?

There are 6 possible outcomes: 1, 2, 3, 4, 5 or 6 and 2, 3 and 5 are prime numbers, so there are 3 possible prime numbers to roll.

So, $p(\text{prime}) = \frac{3}{6} = \frac{1}{2}$

Example 3.2 ▶ A dice is rolled 60 times and a 6 turns up 5 times. Is the dice biased?

$p(6) = \frac{1}{6}$ so we would expect to see $60 \times \frac{1}{6} = 10$ sixes

So, there are half the number of expected sixes, suggesting that the dice is biased.

6

1 Bag A contains 10 red marbles, 5 blue marbles and 5 green marbles. Bag B contains 8 red marbles, 2 blue marbles and no green marbles. A girl wants to pick a marble at random from a bag. Which bag should she choose to have the better chance of:

Bag A 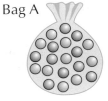 Bag B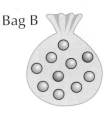

a a red marble? **b** a blue marble? **c** a green marble?

Explain your answers.

2 I roll a dice 30 times. How many times should I expect to see:

a the number 5? **b** an even number? **c** a number less than 5?

3 A pack of cards is shuffled and one drawn at random. This happens 60 times. How many times would you expect to see:

a a red card? **b** a club?

c an Ace? **d** either a Queen or a King?

4 If I toss a fair coin 100 times, how many heads should I expect to see?

5 a Write down the four different results after flipping a 2p coin and a 10p coin.

b If you flipped the two coins 100 times, how many times would you expect to see:

i two heads? **ii** two tails? **iii** a head and a tail?

6 In Mr Speed's class there are 16 boys and 12 girls. He always chooses at random a pupil to give out the books. He takes this class 72 times in the year and every pupil is always there.

How many times would you expect that the person giving out the books is:

a a boy? **b** a girl?

7 A coin is flipped 60 times. It lands on heads 36 times.

Do you think that the coin is biased? Explain your answer.

8 The probability of winning a major prize on a national lottery is 0.000 000 2.

Ben had a go on this lottery twice a week and every week for 60 years.

a How many times could he expect to win this lottery?

b How long should he live, going on this lottery twice a week, in order to expect having won once?

9 The probability of winning a small prize on a national lottery is 0.0095.

Fiya had a go on this lottery twice a week, every week.

How many times could she expect to win a small prize on this lottery in a year?

Extension Work

Carry out a survey by asking many people in your class to give you five different numbers between 1 and 20.

Record the results and write a brief report to say whether you think that each number has the same chance of being chosen.

Probability scales

Probabilities can be written as either fractions or decimals. They always take values from 0 to 1 inclusive. The **probability** of an **event** can be shown on the probability scale:

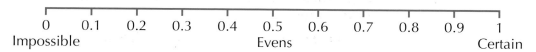

```
   0    0.1   0.2   0.3   0.4   0.5   0.6   0.7   0.8   0.9    1
Impossible                      Evens                      Certain
```

For example, before we go outside, we might think about rain. There are only two possible events: raining, and not raining. The probabilities of all the possible events must add up to 1. So if the probability of it raining is p, then the probability of it not raining is $1 - p$.

The weather is very complex. We could look out of the window and guess that the probability of it raining is 0.2. A weather service will collect lots of data, and might forecast the probability as 0.3.

In simpler situations, we can give the probabilities exactly. For example, the event of drawing a diamond from a pack of playing cards consists of 13 of the 52 possible **outcomes**. So the probability of drawing a diamond is $\frac{13}{52} = \frac{1}{4} = 0.25$. The probability of not drawing a diamond is $1 - 0.25 = 0.75$ (or $\frac{39}{52} = 0.75$).

Example 3.3 ▸

The probability that a woman washes her car on Sunday is 0.7. What is the probability that she does not wash her car on Sunday?

These two events are opposites of each other, so the probabilities add up to 1. The probability that she does not wash her car is $1 - 0.7 = 0.3$.

Example 3.4 ▸

A girl plays a game of tennis. The probability that she wins is $\frac{2}{3}$. What is the probability that she loses?

The probability of not winning (losing) is $1 - \frac{2}{3} = \frac{1}{3}$.

Example 3.5 ▸

Here are the probabilities of different events happening. What are the probabilities of these events not happening?

a 0.4 **b** 0.8 **c** 0.75 **d** 0.16 **e** $\frac{1}{4}$ **f** $\frac{3}{5}$ **g** $\frac{3}{8}$

The probabilities of the events not happening are:

a $1 - 0.4 = 0.6$ **b** $1 - 0.8 = 0.2$ **c** $1 - 0.75 = 0.25$

d $1 - 0.16 = 0.84$ **e** $1 - \frac{1}{4} = \frac{3}{4}$ **f** $1 - \frac{3}{5} = \frac{2}{5}$ **g** $1 - \frac{3}{8} = \frac{5}{8}$

Example 3.6 ▷

A number of discs marked 1, 2, 3 and 4 are placed in a bag. The probabilities of randomly drawing out discs marked with a particular number are given as:

$$p(1) = 0.2 \qquad p(2) = 0.3 \qquad p(3) = 0.25$$

What is the probability of drawing a disc marked: **a**   1, 2 or 3   **b**   4

a   The probability of drawing a disc marked 1, 2 or 3 is
0.2 + 0.3 + 0.25 = 0.75

b   The probability of drawing a disc marked 4 is
1 − 0.75 = 0.25

Exercise 3B

1   Here is a probability scale:

The probabilities of events A, B, C and D happening are shown on the scale. Copy the scale and mark on it the probabilities of A, B, C and D not happening.

2   Copy and complete the table.

Event	Probability of event occurring (p)	Probability of event not occurring ($1 - p$)
A	$\frac{1}{4}$	
B	$\frac{1}{3}$	
C	$\frac{3}{4}$	
D	$\frac{9}{10}$	
E	$\frac{2}{15}$	
F	$\frac{7}{8}$	
G	$\frac{7}{9}$	

3   A card is chosen at random from a pack of 52 playing cards. Calculate the probability that it is:

a   not an ace.   **b**   not a diamond.

c   not a picture card.   **d**   not the six of hearts.

4   In a city taxi fleet there are 25 black cabs, 8 yellow cabs and 7 blue cabs.

Mr Adams does not like riding in a yellow taxi cab.

a   What is the probability that the first cab to come along for Mr Adams is not yellow?

b   Mr Adams travels by taxi approximately 100 times a year. How many of these times would you expect him to travel in a taxi that is:

i   not yellow?   **ii**   blue?   **iii**   not black?

5 A bag contains 32 counters that are either black or white. The probability that a counter is black is $\frac{1}{4}$.

How many white counters are in the bag? Explain how you worked it out.

6 A bag contains many counters that are red, blue, green or yellow. The probabilities of randomly drawing out a counter of a particular colour are given as:

p(red)   = 0.4
p(blue) = 0.15
p(green) = 0.3

Calculate the probability that a counter drawn out is:

a   red or blue.

b   red, blue or green.

c   yellow.

7 In a game there are three types of prize: jackpot, runners-up and consolation. The probability of winning the jackpot is $\frac{1}{100}$, the probability of a runners-up prize is $\frac{1}{10}$, and the probability of a consolation prize is $\frac{1}{2}$.

a   Calculate the probability of winning a prize.

b   Calculate the probability of not winning a prize.

c   Which event is more likely to happen: winning a prize or not winning a prize?

d   After many games the jackpot had been won three times. How many games would you expect to have been played?

Extension   Work

Design a spreadsheet to convert the probabilities of events happening into the probabilities that they do not happen.

Mutually exclusive events

You have a dice and are trying to throw numbers less than 4, but you are also looking for even numbers. Which number is common to both events?

When two events overlap like this, we say that the events are **not mutually exclusive**. This means they can both happen at once.

When you repeatedly throw a dice like this, you are conducting an **experiment**. Each throw is called a **trial**.

Example 3.7

The woman shown is choosing fruit. Here is a list of events:

Event A: She chooses strawberries.
Event B: She chooses red fruit.
Event C: She chooses green apples.
Event D: She chooses red apples.
Event E: She chooses oranges.
Event F: She chooses bananas.
Event G: She chooses fruit with thick skins that need peeling.

She chooses one item only. State whether each of the following pairs of events is mutually exclusive or not.

a A and B   **b** A and E   **c** B and C   **d** B and D   **e** E and F   **f** E and G

a   Strawberries are red fruit, so the events are not mutually exclusive.

b   Strawberries are not oranges, so the events are mutually exclusive.

c   Green apples are not red fruit, so the events are mutually exclusive.

d   Red apples are red fruit, so the events are not mutually exclusive.

e   Oranges are not bananas, so the events are mutually exclusive.

f   Oranges are fruits with thick skins that need peeling, so the events are not mutually exclusive.

Exercise 3C

1 A number square contains the numbers from 1 to 100. A number is chosen from the number square. Here is a list of events:

Event A: The number chosen is greater than 50.

Event B: The number chosen is less than 10.

Event C: The number chosen is a square number (1, 4, 9, 16, …).

Event D: The number chosen is a multiple of 5 (5, 10, 15, 20, …).

Event E: The number chosen has at least one 6 in it.

Event F: The number chosen is a factor of 100 (1, 2, 4, 5, 10, …).

Event G: The number chosen is a triangle number (1, 3, 6, 10, …).

1	2	3	4	5	6	7	8	9	10
11	12	13	14	15	16	17	18	19	20
21	22	23	24	25	26	27	28	29	30
31	32	33	34	35	36	37	38	39	40
41	42	43	44	45	46	47	48	49	50
51	52	53	54	55	56	57	58	59	60
61	62	63	64	65	66	67	68	69	70
71	72	73	74	75	76	77	78	79	80
81	82	83	84	85	86	87	88	89	90
91	92	93	94	95	96	97	98	99	100

State whether each of the following pairs of events is mutually exclusive or not.

a A and B **b** A and C **c** B and C **d** C and D
e B and F **f** C and F **g** C and G **h** D and E
i D and G **j** E and F **k** E and G **l** F and G

2 A till contains lots of 1p, 2p, 5p, 10p, 20p, 50p, £1 and £2 coins.

A woman is given two coins in her change. List all the different amounts of money that she could have received in her change.

3 Look back at Example 3.7. On one particular day the woman decides to buy two types of fruit from bananas, apples, oranges or strawberries. List all the possible combinations that she could choose.

4 Two fair spinners are spun.

a Complete the table to show the different pairs of scores.

Spinner 1	Spinner 2	Total score
+2	0	2
+2	−1	1

b What is the most likely score?

What is the probability of:

c a score of 2? **d** a positive score? **e** a negative score?

5 A sampling bottle contains 40 different coloured beads. (A sampling bottle is a plastic bottle in which only one bead can be seen at a time.)

a After 20 trials a boy has seen 12 black beads and 8 white beads. Does this mean that there are only black and white beads in the bottle? Explain your answer.

b The boy is told that there are 20 black beads, 15 white beads and 5 red beads in the bottle. State which of the following events are mutually exclusive.

  i Seeing a black bead and seeing a white bead
  ii Seeing a black bead and seeing a bead that is not white
  iii Seeing a black bead and seeing a bead that is not black
  iv Seeing any colour bead and seeing a red bead

Extension Work

Imagine a horse race between two horses (called A and B). They could finish the race in two different ways, AB or BA.

Now look at a three-horse race. How many ways can they finish the race?

Extend this problem to four horses, and so on. Put your results into a table. See if you can work out a pattern to predict how many different ways a 10-horse race could finish.

When you have finished this, you can explore what the factorial ! button does on a calculator (you may be able to relate this to the horse problem).

Calculating probabilities

Look at the spinners. Which one is more likely to land on red?

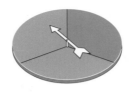 

Remember:

$$p(\text{event}) = \frac{\text{number of outcomes in the event}}{\text{total number of possible outcomes}}$$

Landing on red is an event. The sectors on the spinners are the possible outcomes.

Sometimes you will look at more than one event happening at the same time. Diagrams called **sample spaces** will help you do this. A sample space contains all the possible outcomes of the combined experiment. Look at the sample space for a **coin** and a **dice**:

	1	2	3	4	5	6
Head	H, 1	H, 2	H, 3	H, 4	H, 5	H, 6
Tail	T, 1	T, 2	T, 3	T, 4	T, 5	T, 6

You can now work out the probability of throwing both a head and a 6.

Example 3.8 ▶

An ice-cream man sells 10 different flavours of ice cream. A girl picks a tub at random (without looking). What is the probability that the girl picks her favourite flavour?

She has only one favourite, so the probability that she picks that one out of 10 flavours is $\frac{1}{10}$.

Example 3.9 ▶

Toni has been shopping and is carrying two bags. The first bag contains tins of beans and spaghetti. The second bag contains white and brown bread. One item is picked from each bag. List all the combinations that could be chosen.

The combinations are:
Beans and white bread
Spaghetti and white bread
Beans and brown bread
Spaghetti and brown bread

Exercise 3D

1. A set of cards is numbered from 1 to 200. One card is picked at random. Give the probability that it:

   a   is even.
   b   has a 7 on it.
   c   has a 3 on it.
   d   is a prime number.
   e   is a multiple of 6.
   f   is a square number.
   g   is less than 110.
   h   is a factor of 180.

2. Two pupils are chosen from a class with an equal number of boys and girls.

   a   Write down the four possible boy/girl combinations that could be chosen.
   b   Jo says that the probability of choosing two boys is $\frac{1}{3}$. Explain why he is wrong.

3 A bag contains apples, bananas and pears. Two fruits are chosen at random. List the possible outcomes.

4 Jacket potatoes are sold either plain, with cheese or with beans. Clyde and Delroy each buy a jacket potato.

a Copy and complete the table:

Clyde	Delroy
plain	plain
plain	cheese

b Give the probability of:
i Clyde choosing plain.
ii Delroy choosing plain.
iii Both choosing plain.
iv Clyde choosing plain and Delroy choosing beans.
v Clyde choosing beans and Delroy choosing cheese.
vi Both choosing the same.
vii Both not choosing plain.
viii Both choosing different.

5 Two dice are rolled and the scores are added together. Copy and complete the sample space of scores.

	1	2	3	4	5	6
1	2	3				
2	3					

a What is the most likely total?

b Give the probability that the total is:
i 4   **ii** 5   **iii** 1
iv 12   **v** less than 7
vi less than or equal to 7   **vii** greater than or equal to 10
viii even   **ix** 6 or 8

Extension Work

Make up your own question using two different spinners as follows. Draw the spinners and put different numbers on each section. Now make a sample space diagram and write three of your own questions followed by the answers.

Experimental probability

Will the train be late again today?

Look at the picture. How could you **estimate** the probability that a train will be late?

The train arriving late is an event. You could keep a record of the number of times that the train arrives late and not late over a period of 10 days. You could then use the results of these trials to estimate the probability that the train will be late in future. This is the **experimental probability** of the event:

$$\text{Experimental probability} = \frac{\text{number of trials in which event occurred}}{\text{total number of trials carried out}}$$

The arrival of a train is a very complex process. For simpler processes (such as throwing a pair of dice) you can first calculate the **theoretical probability** of an event (such as throwing 7). You have already met this:

$$\text{Theoretical probability} = \frac{\text{number of outcomes in the event}}{\text{total number of possible outcomes}}$$

So you can make **predictions**: you know what to **expect** when you carry out the experiment. You can then compare the experimental probability of an event with the theoretical probability.

Example 3.10 ▶

An electrician wants to estimate the probability that a new light bulb lasts less than 1 month. He fits 20 new bulbs, and 3 of them fail within 1 month.

a What is his estimate of the probability that a new light bulb will fail within 1 month?

b The manufacturer of the bulbs claims that 1 in 10 of all bulbs produced fail within 1 month. Do you think the electrician will agree with him?

a 3 out of 20 bulbs fail, so his experimental probability is $\frac{3}{20}$.

b 1 in 10 or $\frac{2}{20}$ is less than 3 in 20 or $\frac{3}{20}$, so the electrician will not agree with the manufacturer.

Example 3.11 ▶

A dentist keeps a record of the number of fillings she gives her patients over 2 weeks. Here are her results:

Number of fillings	None	1	More than 1
Number of patients	80	54	16

Estimate the probability that a patient did not need a filling (there are 150 records altogether).

The experimental probability is $\frac{80}{150} = \frac{8}{15}$.

Example 3.12 ▷ A company manufactures items for computers. The number of faulty items is recorded as shown below.

Number of items produced	Number of faulty items	Experimental probability
100	8	0.08
200	20	
500	45	
1000	82	

a Copy and complete the table.

b Which is the best estimate of the probability of an item being faulty? Explain your answer.

a

Number of items produced	Number of faulty items	Experimental probability
100	8	0.08
200	20	0.1
500	45	0.09
1000	82	0.082

b The last result (0.082), as the experiment is based on more results.

Example 3.13 ▷ Two dice are thrown by three players. Each player has a rule which gains them a point whenever it is satisfied. The rules are:

Rule 1: a total of 7

Rule 2: a total of more than 8

Rule 3: a double

a Calculate the theoretical probability of obtaining a point using each rule.

b Test these predictions for a game of just 12 throws, and examine the results.

a

First dice

		1	2	3	4	5	6
	1	2	3	4	5	6	7
	2	3	4	5	6	7	8
Second dice	**3**	4	5	6	7	8	9
	4	5	6	7	8	9	10
	5	6	7	8	9	10	11
	6	7	8	9	10	11	12

The theoretical probabilities are:

for rule 1: $\frac{6}{36} = \frac{1}{6} = 0.16$

for rule 2: $\frac{10}{36} = \frac{5}{18} = 0.27$

for rule 3: $\frac{6}{36} = \frac{1}{6} = 0.16$

Therefore you would expect rules 1 and 3 to give the same number of points, and rule 2 to give more points than rules 1 and 3.

Example 3.13 ▷

continued

b Here are some experimental results from 12 throws:

Rule 1	Rule 2	Rule 3
2	4	3

The experimental probabilities are:

for rule 1: $\frac{2}{12} = \frac{1}{6} = 0.16$

for rule 2: $\frac{4}{12} = \frac{1}{3} = 0.3$

for rule 3: $\frac{3}{12} = \frac{1}{4} = 0.25$

The experimental probabilities are not all the same as the theoretical probabilities. Rules 2 and 3 gave a different number of points from those expected. The most likely reason is that there were not enough trials. A less likely reason is that the dice were biased.

Exercise 3E

1 A boy decides to carry out an experiment to estimate the probability of a drawing pin landing with the pin pointing up. He drops 50 drawing pins and records the result. He then repeats the experiment several times. Here are his results:

Number of drawing pins	Number pointing up
50	32
100	72
150	106
200	139

a From the results, would you say that there is a greater chance of a drawing pin landing point up or point down? Explain your answer.

b Which result is the most reliable, and why?

c From these data, how could the boy estimate the probability of a drawing pin landing point up?

d How could he improve the experiment?

e If you spilt a box of 500 drawing pins on the floor, how many would you expect to land point up?

2 a Draw a table showing all the possible combinations when you roll two dice, one blue and one red.

b You roll two dice in a typical game of Monopoly about 100 times. Use your table to predict how many times you would expect to roll:

i a double 6. **ii** a double.

iii a total of 7. **iv** a total more than 8.

3 Two dice are thrown by three players. Each player has a rule which gains them a point whenever it is satisfied. The rules are as follows.

Rule 1: the product is odd

Rule 2: the sum is even

Rule 3: the difference is 1

a Calculate the theoretical probability of obtaining a point using each rule.

b Test the predictions with a game of 30 throws, and examine the results.

4 Some pupils rolled three fair dice.
They recorded how many times the numbers on
the dice were the same.

Name	Number of throws	Results		
		All different	**Two the same**	**All the same**
Ali	50	33	15	2
Mark	150	86	61	3
Kate	30	15	14	1
Rashid	100	53	43	4

a Who is the pupil whose data are most likely to give the best estimate of the
probability of getting each result? Explain your answer.

b This table shows the pupils' results altogether.

Number of throws	Results		
	All different	**Two the same**	**All the same**
330	187	133	10

Use these data to estimate the probability of throwing numbers that are all
different.

c The theoretical probability of each result is shown below.

	All different	**Two the same**	**All the same**
Probability	$\frac{17}{30}$	0.41	0.03

Use these probabilities to calculate, for 330 throws, how many times you would
theoretically expect to get each result.

d Explain why the pupils' results are not the same as the theoretical results.

e Ria says to her daughter, 'If you roll three dice 100 times, you will get the same
three numbers 18 times'.

Explain why she is wrong to say this.

Extension **Work**

Decide on an experiment of your own. You should choose a process that has a few
clearly different outcomes, and that you can observe lots of times. Write a report of how
you would carry out the experiment and how you would record your results.

6

6 I can identify all the outcomes from two events.

I can use tables to show the outcomes.

I understand what is meant by mutually exclusive.

I can use the fact that the total of mutually exclusive events in a situation is 1.

7 I know how to identify bias in an experiment.

I know how to compare outcomes of experiments.

National Test questions

1 *2000 Paper 1*

There are some cubes in a bag. The cubes are either red (R) or black (B). The teacher says:

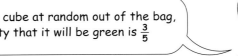

If you take a cube at random out of the bag, the probability that it will be red is $\frac{1}{5}$

a What is the probability that the cube will be black?

b A pupil takes one cube out of the bag. It is red.

What is the smallest number of black cubes there could be in the bag?

c Then the pupil takes another cube out of the bag. It is also red.

From this new information, what is the smallest number of black cubes there could be in the bag?

d A different bag has blue (B), green (G) and yellow (Y) cubes in it. There is at least one of each of the three colours.

The teacher says:

If you take a cube at random out of the bag, the probability that it will be green is $\frac{3}{5}$

There are 20 cubes in the bag.

What is the greatest number of yellow cubes there could be in the bag? Show your working.

2 *2005 Paper 2*

A spinner has the numbers 1 to 4 on it.

The probability of spinning a number 4 is 0.1.

The probability of spinning a number 1 is 0.6.

The probability of spinning a number 2 is the same as the probability of spinning a number 3.

Calculate the probability of spinning a **number 3**.

3 *2007 Paper 1*

A teacher has some coins in his pocket.

He is going to take one of the coins at random.

He says:

> There are **more than four** coins in my pocket.
>
> The total value of the coins is **25p**.
>
> The probability that I will take a **1p** coin is $\frac{1}{4}$.

List **all the coins** that must be in his pocket.

4 *2007 Paper 2*

A computer is going to choose a letter at random from an English book.

The table shows the probabilities of the computer choosing each vowel.

Vowel	A	E	I	O	U
Probability	0.08	0.13	0.07	0.08	0.03

What is the probability that it will **not** choose a vowel?

5 *2007 Paper 2*

The table shows the number of boys and girls in two different classes.

A teacher is going to choose a pupil at random from each of these classes.

In which class is she **more likely** to choose a boy?

You **must** show your working.

	Class 9A	Class 9B
Boys	13	12
Girls	15	14

Fun in the fairground

The fair has come to town.

Hoopla

You can buy five hoops for £1.25.

You win a prize by throwing a hoop over that prize, but it must also go over the base that the prize is standing on!

Ben spent some time watching people have a go at this stall and started to count how many goes they had and how many times someone won.

The table below shows his results.

Prize	Number of throws	Number of wins
Watch	320	1
£10 note	240	4
£1 coin	80	2

Hook a duck

This is a game where plastic ducks float around a central stall. They all have numbers stuck to their underside which cannot be seen until hooked up on a stick and presented to the stall holder.

In the game, if the number under the duck is a:

- 1 – you win a lollipop
- 2 – you win a yo-yo
- 5 – you win a cuddly toy

Each time a duck is hooked, it is replaced in the water.

Cindy, the stall holder, set up the stall one week with:

- 45 plastic ducks
- Only one of which had the number 5 underneath
- Nine had the number 2 underneath
- All the rest had a number 1 underneath

Cindy charged 40p for one stick, to hook up just one duck.

Use the information on Hoopla to answer these questions.

1 From the results shown, what is the probability of someone aiming for and winning a:

  a £1 coin?

  b £10 note?

  c watch?

2 What would you say is the chance of someone winning a prize with:

  a one hoop?

  b five hoops?

3 After watching this, Ben decided to try for a £10 note.

He bought 25 hoops and all his throws were aimed at the £10 note.

  a How much did this cost him?

  b What is his probability of winning a £10 note?

4 On a Saturday afternoon, the stall would expect about 500 people to buy a set of hoops.

Assume that the throws would have been aimed at the various prizes in the same proportion as Ben observed.

  a How many of each prize would the stall expect to have to give away?

  b How much income would be generated from the 500 people?

  c If the watches cost £18, how much profit would the stall expect to make on a Saturday afternoon?

5 How many sets of five hoops would someone have to use to give themselves a good chance of expecting to win:

  a £1 coin?

  b £10 note?

  c watch?

6 What is the probability of winning anything other than a lollipop?

7 Tom wanted his sister, Julie, to win a yo-yo.
  a How many ducks should Julie hook to expect to have picked up at least one with a number 2 underneath?
  b How much will it cost Tom to pay for the number of ducks hooked to expect Julie to win a yo-yo?

8 Before lunch on Sunday, Cindy took £100 from the stall.
  a How many ducks had been hooked that morning?
  b How many cuddly toys would you expect Cindy to have given away that morning?
  c How many yo-yos would you expect Cindy to have given away that morning?

9 Cindy bought in the cuddly toys for £4 each and the yo-yos for 50p each. She gets the lollipops in a jar of 100 for £4.
  Cindy expects to take £250 on a Friday night.
  a How many ducks will she expect to be hooked that night?
  b How many lollipops will she expect to give away that evening?
  c How many yo-yos will she expect to give away that evening?
  d How many cuddly toys will she expect to give away that evening?
  e What will be the value of all the prizes she expects to give away that night?

10 In the first week Cindy expects to have 1500 ducks hooked.
  Cindy expects to take £250 on a Friday night.
  a How many of each prize would Cindy expect to give away?
  b What profit would Cindy expect to make in that first week?

This chapter is going to show you	What you should already know
• More about working with fractions, decimals and percentages • How to calculate percentage increase and decrease • How to compare proportions using fractions and decimals	• Some common fractions, decimals and percentages that are equal • How to add and subtract simple fractions with a common denominator • How to calculate fractions and percentages of quantities

Fractions and decimals

These diagrams show shapes with various fractions of them shaded. Can you write them as a decimal, a fraction and a percentage?

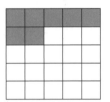 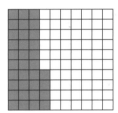 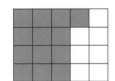

Example 4.1 ▶ Write the following decimals as fractions.

    a   0.65   **b**   0.475

    a $0.65 = \frac{65}{100} = \frac{13}{20}$ (cancel by 5)   **b** $0.475 = \frac{475}{1000} = \frac{19}{40}$ (cancel by 25)

Example 4.2 ▶ Write the following fractions as decimals.

    a $\frac{2}{5}$ **b** $\frac{13}{16}$ **c** $\frac{4}{7}$

    a $\frac{2}{5} = 0.4$ (you should know this)

    b $\frac{13}{16} = 13 \div 16 = 0.8125$ (this is a terminating decimal because it ends without repeating itself)

    c $\frac{4}{7} = 4 \div 7 = 0.571428\,571 \ldots = 0.\dot{5}7142\dot{8}$ (this is a recurring decimal because the six digits 5, 7, 1, 4, 2, 8 repeat infinitely; a recurring decimal is shown by the dots over the first and last recurring digits)

Exercise 4A

1. Write the following decimals as fractions with a denominator of 10, 100 or 1000 and then cancel to their simplest form if possible.

   a 0.24 **b** 0.45 **c** 0.125 **d** 0.348

   e 0.8 **f** 0.555 **g** 0.55 **h** 0.875

2. Without using a calculator, work out the value of these fractions as decimals.

   a $\frac{3}{5}$ **b** $\frac{3}{8}$ **c** $\frac{13}{20}$ **d** $\frac{18}{25}$

3. Use a calculator to work out, and then write down, the following terminating decimals.

   a $\frac{1}{2}$ **b** $\frac{1}{4}$ **c** $\frac{1}{5}$ **d** $\frac{1}{8}$

   e $\frac{1}{10}$ **f** $\frac{1}{16}$ **g** $\frac{1}{20}$ **h** $\frac{1}{25}$

   i $\frac{1}{40}$ **j** $\frac{1}{50}$

4. Use a calculator to work out, and then write down, the following recurring decimals.

   a $\frac{1}{3}$ **b** $\frac{1}{6}$ **c** $\frac{1}{7}$ **d** $\frac{1}{9}$

   e $\frac{1}{11}$ **f** $\frac{1}{12}$ **g** $\frac{1}{13}$ **h** $\frac{1}{14}$

   i $\frac{1}{15}$ **j** $\frac{1}{18}$

5. By looking at the denominators of the fractions in Questions 3 and 4, predict if the following fractions will be terminating or recurring decimals (and then work them out to see if you were correct).

   a $\frac{2}{3}$ **b** $\frac{4}{5}$ **c** $\frac{3}{7}$ **d** $\frac{2}{9}$

   e $\frac{3}{16}$ **f** $\frac{5}{8}$ **g** $\frac{7}{12}$ **h** $\frac{11}{14}$

   i $\frac{4}{15}$ **j** $\frac{39}{50}$

6. Give the larger of these pairs of fractions.

   a $\frac{7}{20}$ and $\frac{1}{3}$ **b** $\frac{5}{9}$ and $\frac{11}{20}$ **c** $\frac{7}{8}$ and $\frac{4}{5}$ **d** $\frac{2}{3}$ and $\frac{16}{25}$

7. Write the following lists of fractions in increasing order of size.

   a $\frac{2}{9}$, $\frac{13}{50}$, $\frac{6}{25}$ and $\frac{1}{4}$ **b** $\frac{5}{8}$, $\frac{3}{5}$, $\frac{17}{25}$ and $\frac{2}{3}$

8. **a** Use a calculator to work out $\frac{1}{9}$, $\frac{2}{9}$, $\frac{3}{9}$ and $\frac{4}{9}$ as recurring decimals.

   b Write down $\frac{5}{9}$, $\frac{6}{9}$, $\frac{7}{9}$ and $\frac{8}{9}$ as recurring decimals.

9. Work out the 'sevenths' (that is, $\frac{1}{7}$, $\frac{2}{7}$, $\frac{3}{7}$, $\frac{4}{7}$, $\frac{5}{7}$, $\frac{6}{7}$) as recurring decimals. Describe any patterns that you can see in the digits.

10. Work out the 'elevenths' (that is, $\frac{1}{11}$, $\frac{2}{11}$, $\frac{3}{11}$, $\frac{4}{11}$, $\frac{5}{11}$, $\frac{6}{11}$, $\frac{7}{11}$, $\frac{8}{11}$, $\frac{9}{11}$, $\frac{10}{11}$) as recurring decimals. Describe any patterns that you can see in the digits.

Extension Work

1 Describe a rule for the denominator of a terminating decimal.

2 Describe a rule for the denominator of a recurring decimal.

Adding and subtracting fractions

All of the grids below contain 100 squares. Some of the squares have been shaded in. The fraction shaded is shown below the square in its lowest terms. Use the diagrams to work out $1 - (\frac{1}{5} + \frac{7}{20} + \frac{11}{25} + \frac{1}{25})$.

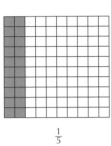

$\frac{1}{5}$

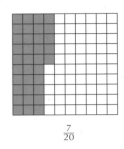

$\frac{7}{20}$

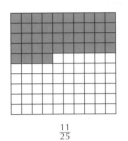

$\frac{11}{25}$

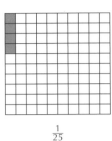

$\frac{1}{25}$

Example 4.3 ▷

Work out:

a $\frac{2}{5} + \frac{1}{4}$ b $\frac{2}{3} + \frac{2}{7}$ c $\frac{1}{3} + \frac{5}{6} + \frac{3}{4}$

a   The common denominator is 20, as this is the lowest common multiple of 4 and 5, hence $\frac{2}{5} + \frac{1}{4} = \frac{8}{20} + \frac{5}{20} = \frac{13}{20}$

b   The common denominator is 21, hence $\frac{2}{3} + \frac{2}{7} = \frac{14}{21} + \frac{6}{21} = \frac{20}{21}$

c   The common denominator is 12, hence $\frac{1}{3} + \frac{5}{6} + \frac{3}{4} = \frac{4}{12} + \frac{10}{12} + \frac{9}{12} = \frac{23}{12} = 1\frac{11}{12}$

    Note that the last answer is a top-heavy fraction, and so should be written as a mixed number.

Example 4.4 ▷

Work out:

a $\frac{2}{3} - \frac{1}{4}$ b $\frac{5}{6} - \frac{4}{9}$

a   The common denominator is 12, so $\frac{2}{3} - \frac{1}{4} = \frac{8}{12} - \frac{3}{12} = \frac{5}{12}$

b   The common denominator is 18, so $\frac{5}{6} - \frac{4}{9} = \frac{15}{18} - \frac{8}{18} = \frac{7}{18}$

Exercise 4B

1 Find the lowest common multiple of the following pairs of numbers.

   a   3, 4   b   5, 6   c   3, 5   d   2, 3

   e   4, 5   f   2, 4   g   6, 9   h   4, 6

2 Convert the following fractions to equivalent fractions with a common denominator. Then work out the answer to the addition or subtraction. Cancel down or write as a mixed number if appropriate.

   a $\frac{2}{3} + \frac{1}{4}$ b $\frac{2}{5} + \frac{1}{6}$ c $2\frac{1}{3} + \frac{2}{5}$ d $2\frac{1}{3} + 1\frac{1}{2}$

   e $4\frac{1}{5} + 1\frac{3}{4}$ f $1\frac{1}{2} + 1\frac{5}{6}$ g $3\frac{5}{6} + 1\frac{1}{9}$ h $1\frac{1}{6} + 2\frac{7}{8}$

   i $\frac{1}{3} - \frac{1}{4}$ j $\frac{2}{5} - \frac{1}{6}$ k $2\frac{2}{5} - 1\frac{1}{3}$ l $3\frac{1}{2} - 1\frac{1}{3}$

   m $3\frac{2}{5} - 1\frac{3}{4}$ n $3\frac{1}{2} - 1\frac{5}{6}$ o $3\frac{5}{6} - 1\frac{1}{9}$ p $2\frac{5}{6} - 1\frac{7}{8}$

3 Work out the following fraction additions and subtractions.

a $\frac{3}{4} + \frac{9}{14}$ **b** $\frac{2}{9} + \frac{4}{21}$ **c** $\frac{1}{12} + \frac{2}{21}$ **d** $\frac{7}{18} + \frac{11}{24}$

e $\frac{5}{56} - \frac{3}{70}$ **f** $\frac{11}{28} - \frac{9}{38}$ **g** $\frac{17}{18} - \frac{15}{32}$ **h** $\frac{19}{25} - \frac{11}{15}$

i $1\frac{11}{18} + 1\frac{7}{24}$ **j** $3\frac{1}{21} - 1\frac{6}{35}$

4 Convert the following fractions to equivalent fractions with a common denominator. Then work out the answers. Cancel down or write as mixed numbers if appropriate.

a $1\frac{1}{3} - \frac{7}{8}$ **b** $2\frac{2}{3} + \frac{4}{7}$ **c** $1\frac{2}{3} + 2\frac{1}{4}$ **d** $3\frac{2}{3} - 1\frac{1}{5}$

5 Copy the diagram shown. Shade in the following fractions without overlapping: $\frac{1}{12}, \frac{5}{24}, \frac{1}{8}, \frac{1}{4}$ and $\frac{1}{6}$. Write down the answer, in its simplest form, to $1 - (\frac{1}{12} + \frac{5}{24} + \frac{1}{8} + \frac{1}{4} + \frac{1}{6})$.

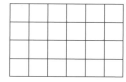

6 A rectangle measures $3\frac{5}{9}$ cm by $7\frac{5}{6}$ cm. Calculate its perimeter.

7 A knife is $13\frac{2}{3}$ cm long in total. The handle is $6\frac{3}{4}$ cm. How long is the blade?

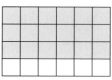

$13\frac{2}{3}$ cm

$6\frac{3}{4}$ cm

Extension Work

The ancient Egyptians only used unit fractions, that is fractions with a numerator of 1. So they would write $\frac{5}{8}$ as $\frac{1}{2} + \frac{1}{8}$.

1 Write the following as the sum of two unit fractions.

     a $\frac{3}{8}$ **b** $\frac{3}{4}$ **c** $\frac{7}{12}$ **d** $\frac{2}{3}$

2 Write the following as the sum of three unit fractions.

     a $\frac{7}{8}$ **b** $\frac{5}{6}$ **c** $\frac{5}{8}$ **d** $\frac{23}{24}$

Multiplying and dividing fractions

You can use grids to work out fractions of quantities.

This grid shows that $\frac{3}{4}$ of 24 is equal to 18:

This grid shows that $\frac{2}{3}$ of 24 is equal to 16:

Example 4.5 ▷ Use this grid to work out $\frac{3}{10}$ of 30.

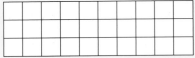

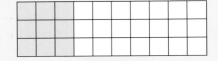

$\frac{3}{10}$ of 30 = 9

Example 4.6 ▷ Work out:

a $\frac{3}{4}$ of £28   **b** $5 \times \frac{2}{3}$ **c** $\frac{2}{3} \div 6$

a $\frac{1}{4}$ of £28 = £7, so $\frac{3}{4}$ of £28 = 3 × £7 = £21

b $5 \times \frac{2}{3} = \frac{5 \times 2}{3} = \frac{10}{3} = 3\frac{1}{3}$

c $\frac{2}{3} \div 6 = \frac{2}{3 \times 6} = \frac{2}{18} = \frac{1}{9}$

Exercise 4C

1 Use any method to work out each of these.

a $\frac{1}{8}$ of 32   **b** $\frac{3}{8}$ of 32   **c** $\frac{1}{4}$ of 32   **d** $\frac{3}{4}$ of 32

e $\frac{1}{5}$ of 25   **f** $\frac{3}{5}$ of 25   **g** $\frac{2}{3}$ of 45   **h** $\frac{5}{6}$ of 120

2 Work out the following.

a $\frac{5}{8}$ of £32   **b** $\frac{3}{16}$ of 64 kg   **c** $\frac{2}{3}$ of £45   **d** $\frac{5}{6}$ of 240 cm

e $\frac{6}{7}$ of 28 cm   **f** $\frac{9}{10}$ of 40 grams   **g** $\frac{3}{8}$ of £72   **h** $\frac{3}{4}$ of 48 km

3 Work out the following. Cancel down or write as mixed numbers if appropriate.

a $5 \times \frac{3}{4}$ **b** $7 \times \frac{4}{5}$ **c** $9 \times \frac{2}{3}$ **d** $4 \times \frac{7}{8}$

e $8 \times \frac{9}{10}$ **f** $6 \times \frac{3}{7}$ **g** $9 \times \frac{5}{6}$ **h** $10 \times \frac{3}{4}$

4 Work out the following.

a $\frac{3}{4} \div 5$ **b** $\frac{4}{5} \div 8$ **c** $\frac{2}{3} \div 6$ **d** $\frac{5}{9} \div 7$

e $\frac{2}{7} \div 5$ **f** $\frac{8}{9} \div 2$ **g** $\frac{3}{5} \div 7$ **h** $\frac{7}{8} \div 6$

5 Copy and complete the following sentence.

Multiplying by a fraction between 0 and 1 makes the answer …

6 Copy and complete the following sentence.

Dividing a fraction between 0 and 1 by a whole number makes the answer …

Extension **Work**

Put these in order of size smallest to biggest.

a $24 \times \frac{5}{8}$ $36 \times \frac{1}{4}$ $35 \times \frac{2}{7}$

b $\frac{3}{8} \div 4$ $\frac{1}{4} \div 3$ $\frac{2}{7} \div 5$

Percentages

Example 4.7 ▶   Without using a calculator, find:

a   18 as a percentage of 25.   **b**   39 as a percentage of 300.

a   Write as a fraction $\frac{18}{25}$. Multiply the top and bottom by 4, which gives $\frac{72}{100}$. So 18 is 72% of 25.

b   Write as a fraction $\frac{39}{300}$. Cancel the top and bottom by 3, which gives $\frac{13}{100}$. So 39 is 13% of 300.

Example 4.8 ▶   **a**   What percentage of 80 is 38?   **b**   What percentage of 64 is 14?

a   Write as a fraction $\frac{38}{80}$. Divide through to give the decimal 0.475. Then multiply by 100 to give $47\frac{1}{2}$%. Or, simply multiply $\frac{38}{80}$ by 100.

b   Write as a fraction $\frac{14}{64}$. Divide through to give the decimal 0.218 75. Then multiply by 100 giving 22% (rounded off from 21.875). Or, simply multiply $\frac{14}{64}$ by 100.

Example 4.9 ▶   Ashram scored 39 out of 50 in a Physics test, 56 out of 70 in a Chemistry test and 69 out of 90 in a Biology test. In which science did he do best?

Convert each mark to a percentage:

Physics   = 78%
Chemistry = 80%
Biology   = 77% (rounded off)

So Chemistry was the best mark.

Exercise 4D

1   Without using a calculator, express the following as percentages.

a	32 out of 50	**b**	17 out of 20	**c**	24 out of 40	**d**	16 out of 25
e	122 out of 200	**f**	93 out of 300	**g**	640 out of 1000	**h**	18 out of 25

2   In each of the following, use a calculator to express the first number as a percentage of the second (round off to the nearest percent if necessary).

a	33, 60	**b**	18, 80	**c**	25, 75	**d**	26, 65
e	56, 120	**f**	84, 150	**g**	62, 350	**h**	48, 129

3 In the National Curriculum test, Trevor scored 39 out of 60 in Maths, 42 out of 70 in English and 54 out of 80 in Science. Convert all these scores to a percentage. In which test did Trevor do best?

4 In a Maths exam worth 80 marks, 11 marks are allocated to Number, 34 marks are allocated to Algebra, 23 marks are allocated to Geometry and 12 marks are allocated to Statistics. Work out the percentage allocated to each topic (round the answers off to the nearest percent) and add these up. Why is the total more than 100%?

5 A table costs a carpenter £120 to make. He sells it for £192.

   a How much profit did he make?

   b What percentage of the cost price was the profit?

6 A dealer buys a painting for £5500. He sells it at a loss for £5000.

   a How much did he lose?

   b What percentage of the original price was the loss?

7 Mr Wilson pays £60 a month to cover his electricity, gas and oil bills. Electricity costs £24, gas costs £21 and the rest is for oil. What percentage of the total does each fuel cost?

8 My phone bill last month was £45. Of this, £13 went on Internet calls, £24 went on long-distance calls and the rest went on local calls. What percentage of the bill was for each of these types of call?

9 Last week the Smith family had a bill of £110.57 at the supermarket. Of this, £65.68 was spent on food, £35.88 on drinks and £9.01 on cleaning products. Work out what percentage of the total bill was for food, drinks and cleaning products (round off the answers to the nearest percent). Add the three percentages up. Why do they not total 100%?

10 Fred drove from Barnsley to Portsmouth. The total distance was 245 miles. Of this, 32 miles was on B roads, 145 miles on A roads and 68 miles on motorways. What percentage of the journey was on each type of road?

Extension Work

1 Write down 20% of 100.

2 Write down 20% of 120.

3 If £100 is increased by 20%, how much do you have?

4 If £120 is decreased by 20%, how much do you have?

5 Draw a poster to explain why a 20% increase followed by a 20% decrease does not return you to the value you started with.

Percentage increase and decrease

SPORTY SHOES
$\frac{1}{3}$ off all trainers

SHOES-FOR-YOU
30% off all trainers

Which shop gives the better value?

Example 4.10 ▷

a A shop has a sale and reduces its original prices by 15%. How much is the sale price of:

   i a microwave originally costing £95?   **ii** a washer originally costing £225?

   i 15% of 95 is (10% + 5%) of 95 = 9.5 + 4.75 = 14.25. So the microwave costs £95 – £14.25 = £80.75.

   ii 15% of 225 is 22.5 + 11.25 = 33.75. So the washer costs £225 – £33.75 = £191.25.

b A company gives all its workers a 3.2% pay rise. What is the new wage of:

   i Joan, who at present earns £260 per week?

   ii Jack, who at present earns £8.40 per hour?

   i 3.2% of 260 is 3.2 ÷ 100 × 260 = £8.32
     So Joan gets £260 + £8.32 = £268.32 per week

   ii 3.2% of 8.40 is 3.2 ÷ 100 × 8.40 = £0.2688 = 27p
     So Jack gets £8.40 + 27p = £8.67 per hour

Exercise 4E

Do not use a calculator for the first three questions.

1 Work out the final amount when:

  a £72 is increased by 10%   **b** £36 is decreased by 10%
  c £1.40 is increased by 20%   **d** £99 is decreased by 20%
  e £175 is increased by 15%   **f** £220 is decreased by 15%
  g £440 is increased by 25%   **h** £422 is decreased by 25%
  i £9.60 is increased by 35%   **j** £6.40 is decreased by 15%

2 A bat colony has 40 bats. Over the breeding season the colony increases by 30%.

  a How many bats are there in the colony after the breeding season?

  b The colony increases by 30% again the next year. How many bats are there after the second year?

3 In a wood there are 20 000 midges. During the evening bats eat 45% of the midges.

  a How many midges were left after the bats had finished eating for the evening?

  b Assuming that the midges do not increase in number during the following day and the bats eat 45% of the remaining midges, how many are there after the second night?

You may use a calculator for the rest of this exercise.

4 a In a sale all prices are reduced by 3.5%. Give the new price of items costing:

    i £19.40   **ii** £36   **iii** £42.60   **iv** £94.60?

b An electrical company increases its prices by 12.2%. Calculate the new price of items costing:

    i £550   **ii** £630   **iii** £885   **iv** £199?

5 A Petri dish contains 2400 bacteria. These increase overnight by 23%.

a How many extra bacteria are there?

b How many bacteria are there the next morning?

6 A rabbit colony has 230 rabbits. As a result of a disease, 47% die.

a How many rabbits die from the disease?

b How many rabbits are left after the disease?

c What percentage of the rabbits remain?

7 Work out the final price in euros when:

a €65 is increased by 12%   **b** €65 is decreased by 14%

c €126 is increased by 22%   **d** €530 is decreased by 28%

e €95 is increased by 132%   **f** €32 is decreased by 31%

g €207 is increased by 155%   **h** €421 is decreased by 18%

i €6.82 is increased by 236%   **j** €5.40 is decreased by 28%

8 a In a sale all prices are reduced by $12\frac{1}{2}$%. Give the new price of items that previously cost:

    i £23.50   **ii** £66   **iii** £56.80   **iv** £124

b An electrical company increases its prices by $17\frac{1}{2}$% so that they include value-added tax (VAT). Give the price with VAT of items that previously cost:

    i £250   **ii** £180   **iii** £284   **iv** £199

Extension Work

The government charges you VAT at $17\frac{1}{2}$% on most things you buy. Although this seems like an awkward percentage to work out, there is an easy way to do it without a calculator! We already know that it is easy to find 10%, which can be used to find 5% (divide the 10% value by 2), which can in turn be used to find $2\frac{1}{2}$% (divide the 5% value by 2). Then 10% + 5% + $2\frac{1}{2}$% = $17\frac{1}{2}$%.

Find the VAT on an item that costs £24 before VAT is added.

10% of £24 = £2.40, 5% of £24 is £1.20, and $2\frac{1}{2}$% of £24 is £0.60.

So $17\frac{1}{2}$% of £24 = £2.40 + £1.20 + £0.60 = £4.20.

Work out the VAT on items that cost:

  1 £34   **2** £44   **3** £56   **4** £75   **5** £120   **6** £190

Real-life problems

Percentages occur in everyday life in many situations. You have already met percentage increase and decrease. Percentages are also used when buying goods on credit, working out profit and/or loss and paying tax.

Example 4.11 　A car that costs £5995 can be bought on credit by paying a 25% deposit and then 24 monthly payments of £199.

　　a　How much will the car cost on credit?

　　b　What is the extra cost as a percentage of the usual price?

　　a　The deposit is 25% of £5995 = £1498.75. The payments are 24 × £199 = £4776. Therefore, the total paid = £1498.75 + £4776 = £6274.75.

　　b　The extra cost = £6274.75 – £5995 = £279.75. This as a percentage of £5995 is (279.75 ÷ 5995) × 100 = 4.7%.

Example 4.12 　A jeweller makes a brooch for £250 and sells it for £450. What is the percentage profit?

The profit is: £450 – £250 = £200

As a percentage of £250, this is $\frac{200}{250} \times 100$
= 200 ÷ 250 × 100 = 80%.

Example 4.13 　Jeremy earns £18 000. His tax allowance is £3800. He pays tax on the rest at 22%. How much tax does he pay?

Taxable income = £18 000 – £3800 = £14 200

The tax paid is 22% of £14 200
= $\frac{22}{100} \times £14\,200$ = 22 ÷ 100 × 14 200 = £3124

Exercise 4F

 1 A mountain bike that normally costs £479.99 can be bought using three different plans:

Plan	Deposit	Number of payments	Each payment
A	20%	24	£22
B	50%	12	£20
C	10%	36	£18

　　a　Work out how much the bike costs using each plan.
　　b　Work out the percentage of the original price that each plan costs.

2 A shop buys a radio for £55 and sells it for £66. Work out the percentage profit made by the shop.

3 A CD costs £10.99. The shop paid £8.50 for it. What is the percentage profit?

4 A car that costs £6995 can be bought by paying a 15% deposit, followed by 23 monthly payments of £189 and a final payment of £1900.

 (a) How much will the car cost using the credit scheme?

 (b) What percentage of the original cost is the extra cost on the credit scheme?

 5 Work out the tax paid by the following people:

Person	Income	Tax allowance	Tax rate
Ada	£25000	£4700	22%
Bert	£32000	£5300	25%
Carmine	£10000	£3850	15%
Derek	£12000	£4000	22%
Ethel	£45000	£7000	40%

6 A shop sells a toaster for £19.99 in a sale. It cost the shop £25. What is the percentage loss?

 7 **a** What is £10 decreased by 10%?

 b Decrease your answer to **a** by 10%.

 c What is £10 decreased by 20%?

 d A shirt in a clothes shop is reduced from its original price by 20% because it has a button missing. The shop is offering a further 15% off all marked prices in a sale. John the shop assistant says:

I don't need to work out the two reductions one after the other, I can just take 35% off the original price.

 Is John correct? Explain your answer.

8 An insurance policy for a motorbike is £335. It can be paid for by a 25% deposit and then five payments of £55.25.

 (a) How much does the policy cost using the scheme?

 (b) What percentage of the original cost of the policy is the extra cost?

9 Mrs Smith has an annual income of £28000. Her tax allowance is £4500. She pays tax at 22%.

 (a) How much tax does she pay?

 (b) It is discovered that her tax allowance should have been £6000. How much tax does she get back?

10 A TV costs £450. The shop has an offer '40% deposit and then 12 equal payments, one each month for a year'.

    a How much is the deposit?   **b** How much is each payment?

 11 Which of these schemes to buy a three-piece suite priced at £999 is cheaper?

    Scheme A: no deposit followed by 24 payments of £56

    Scheme B: 25% deposit followed by 24 payments of £32

Give a reason why someone might prefer Scheme A.

LEVEL BOOSTER

5
I can work out lowest common multiples.
I can calculate a fraction of a quantity.
I can calculate percentages of a quantity.
I can multiply a fraction by a whole number (integer).

6
I can change fractions to decimals.
I can add and subtract fractions with different denominators.
I can calculate one quantity as a percentage of another.
I can use percentages to solve real-life problems.

7
I understand the effects of multiplying and dividing by numbers between 0 and 1.
I can use a multiplier to solve percentage problems.
I can use percentage change to solve more complex problems.

National Test questions

1 *2004 Paper 2*

In 2001 the average yearly wage was **£21 842**.

On average, people spent **£1644** on their family holiday.

What percentage of the average yearly wage is that?

Show your working.

2 *2006 Paper 2*

Kate asked people if they read a daily newspaper.
Then she wrote this table to show her results.

No	80 people = 40%
Yes	126 people = 60%

The values in the table **cannot** all be correct.

a The error could be in the number of people.

Copy and complete each table to show what the correct numbers could be.

No	80 people = 40%
Yes	... people = 60%

No	... people = 40%
Yes	126 people = 60%

b The error could be in the percentages.

Copy and complete the table with the correct percentages.

No	80 people = ... %
Yes	126 people = ... %

3 *2007 Paper 2*

One day, each driver entering a car park paid **exactly £1.50**.

Here is what was put into the machine that day.

Number of £1 coins   **136**
Number of 50p coins   **208**

On that day what percentage of drivers paid with **three 50p coins?**

CAR PARK

Pay exactly £1.50 to enter

Machine accepts only £1 coins
and 50p coins

4 *2006 Paper 1*

In a quiz game two people each answer **100 questions.**
They score one point for each correct answer.

The quiz game has not yet finished.
Each person has answered **90 questions.**
The table shows the results so far.

Can person B win the quiz game?

Explain your answer.

Person A	Person B
60% of the first 90 questions correct	50% of the first 90 questions correct

5 *2005 Paper 2*

A newspaper printed this information about the world's population.

On average, **how many times** as wealthy as one of the other 94 people would one of these 6 people be?

If the world was a village of 100 people,
6 people would have **59%** of the total wealth.
The other 94 people would have the rest.

a   One calculation below gives the answer to the question:

What is 70 increased by 9%?

Write down the correct one.

   70 × 0.9   70 × 1.9   70 × 0.09   70 × 1.09

b   For each of the other calculations in **a**, write a question about percentages that it represents.

c   Write down the decimal number missing from the following statement:

To decrease by 14%, multiply by …

Going on holiday

1 This table shows the outgoing flights from Leeds to Tenerife.

Flight	Mon	Tue	Wed	Thu	Fri	Sat	Sun	Departs	Arrives
LS223		✈			✈	✈		13:55	18:30
LS225					✈			07:45	12:30

This table shows the return flights from Tenerife to Leeds.

Flight	Mon	Tue	Wed	Thu	Fri	Sat	Sun	Departs	Arrives
LS224		✈			✈	✈		19:15	23:50
LS226					✈			13:30	18:05

Mr and Mrs Brown and their two children are planning a week's holiday to Tenerife.

Mr Brown goes on the Internet to find the times of the planes from Leeds to Tenerife.

a On which days can they fly out to Tenerife?

b The family decides to fly out on Friday morning and return on the latest flight on the following Friday. What are the flight numbers for the two flights?

c How long are these two flights?

d When Mr Brown books the flights, he is informed that he needs to check in at Leeds airport at least $2\frac{1}{2}$ hours before the departure time of the flight. What is the latest time the family can arrive at the airport?

e The return ticket costs £289 for an adult and £210 for a child. What is the total cost of the tickets for the family?

f Each member of the family also has to pay a fuel supplement tax at £6.08, a baggage allowance at £5.99 and £3 to book a seat. Find the total cost for the family.

2 Mr Brown decides to take some euros (€) for the holiday. The exchange rate at the bank is £1 = €1.24.

a Mr Brown changes £450 at the bank. How many euros will he receive? Give your answer to the nearest five euros.

b Mr Brown also has 120 dollars ($) from a previous holiday to change into euros at the bank. The exchange rate at the bank is $1 = £0.52. How many euros will he receive? Give your answer to the nearest five euros.

c Mr Brown returns from the holiday with €80. How much is this in pounds? Give your answer to the nearest pence.

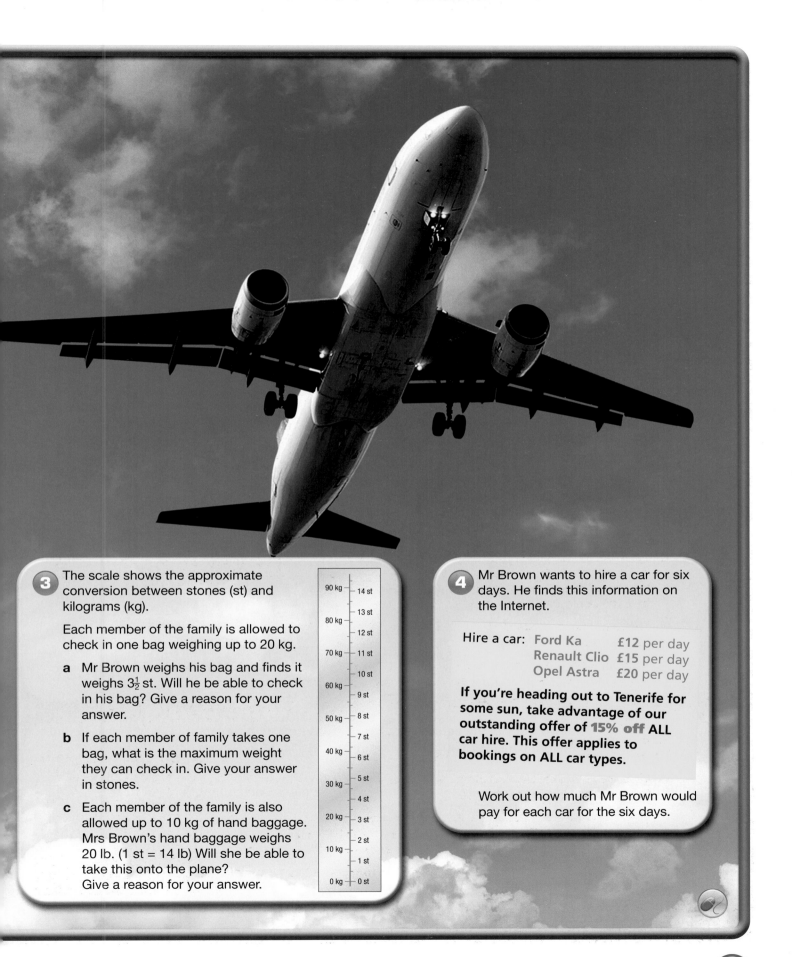

3 The scale shows the approximate conversion between stones (st) and kilograms (kg).

Each member of the family is allowed to check in one bag weighing up to 20 kg.

a Mr Brown weighs his bag and finds it weighs $3\frac{1}{2}$ st. Will he be able to check in his bag? Give a reason for your answer.

b If each member of family takes one bag, what is the maximum weight they can check in. Give your answer in stones.

c Each member of the family is also allowed up to 10 kg of hand baggage. Mrs Brown's hand baggage weighs 20 lb. (1 st = 14 lb) Will she be able to take this onto the plane?
Give a reason for your answer.

Scale:
90 kg — 14 st
— 13 st
80 kg — 12 st
70 kg — 11 st
— 10 st
60 kg — 9 st
50 kg — 8 st
— 7 st
40 kg — 6 st
— 5 st
30 kg — 4 st
20 kg — 3 st
— 2 st
10 kg — 1 st
0 kg — 0 st

4 Mr Brown wants to hire a car for six days. He finds this information on the Internet.

Hire a car:
Ford Ka	£12 per day
Renault Clio	£15 per day
Opel Astra	£20 per day

If you're heading out to Tenerife for some sun, take advantage of our outstanding offer of 15% off ALL car hire. This offer applies to bookings on ALL car types.

Work out how much Mr Brown would pay for each car for the six days.

CHAPTER 5 Algebra 2

This chapter is going to show you

- How to simplify expressions in algebra
- How to expand brackets
- How to factorise expressions
- How to use index notation with algebra

What you should already know

- How to substitute into algebraic expressions
- How to add, subtract and multiply with negative numbers

Algebraic shorthand

In algebra, to make expressions simpler, and to avoid confusion with the variable x, the multiplication sign $\times$ is usually left out. In the simpler expressions, the numbers go in front of the variables. So:

$$3 \times m = 3m \qquad a \times b = ab \qquad w \times 7 = 7w \qquad d \times 4c = 4cd \qquad n \times (d + t) = n(d + t)$$

The **division** sign $\div$ cannot be just left out. Instead, it is usually replaced by a short rule in the style of a fraction (and later on, by a forward slash). So:

$$3 \div m = \frac{3}{m} \qquad w \div 7 = \frac{w}{7} \qquad a \div b = \frac{a}{b} \qquad d \div 4c = \frac{d}{4c} \qquad n \div (d + t) = \frac{n}{d + t}$$

Division often leads to **cancelling**. You can show cancelling if you wish. Remember that $a \times 1 = a$, and $a \div 1 = \frac{a}{1} = a$. So:

$$\frac{4n}{4} = \frac{\overset{1}{\cancel{4}}n}{\underset{1}{\cancel{4}}} = n \qquad \frac{6m}{m} = \frac{6\overset{1}{\cancel{m}}}{\underset{1}{\cancel{m}}} = 6 \qquad \frac{4p}{6} = \frac{\overset{2}{\cancel{4}}p}{\underset{3}{\cancel{6}}} = \frac{2p}{3} \qquad \frac{5pq}{10p} = \frac{\overset{1}{\cancel{5}}\overset{1}{\cancel{p}}q}{\underset{2}{\cancel{10}}\underset{1}{\cancel{p}}} = \frac{q}{2}$$

$$\frac{n(d + t)}{3n} = \frac{\overset{1}{\cancel{n}}(d + t)}{3\underset{1}{\cancel{n}}} = \frac{d + t}{3}$$

The two sides of the **equals** sign (=) are always equal, although they may look different. Therefore whatever you do to one side, you must do the same to the other side.

Example 5.1 ▶

Which of the following expressions are equal to each other? Write correct mathematical statements for those that equal each other.

$$a + b \qquad b - a \qquad ab \qquad \frac{b}{a}$$
$$ba \qquad \frac{a}{b} \qquad b + a \qquad a - b$$

We can pick out $a + b$ as being equal to $b + a$ ($a + b = b + a$) and ab as being equal to ba ($ab = ba$). None of the others are the same.

Example 5.2 ▶

Solve the equation $3x + 2 = 23$.

Subtract the same value, 2, from both sides to keep the sides equal:
$$3x + 2 - 2 = 23 - 2$$
$$3x = 21$$

We now divide both sides by 3, again to keep both sides equal:
$$\frac{3x}{3} = \frac{21}{3}$$
$$x = 7$$

Example 5.3 ▶

Simplify these expressions.

a $4a \times b$ **b** $9p \times 2$ **c** $3h \times 4i$

Leave out the multiplication sign and write the number to the left of the letters:

a $4a \times b = 4ab$ **b** $9p \times 2 = 18p$ **c** $3h \times 4i = 12hi$

Example 5.4 ▶

Simplify these expressions.

a $8x \div 2$ **b** $5m \div m$ **c** $9q \div 12q$

Set out each expression in a fraction style, and cancel the numerator and the denominator wherever possible. So:

a $\frac{8x}{2} = 4x$ **b** $\frac{5m}{m} = 5$ **c** $\frac{9q}{12q} = \frac{9}{12} = \frac{3}{4}$

Exercise 5A

1 Simplify the following expressions.

    a $h \times 4p$ **b** $4s \times t$ **c** $2m \times 4n$ **d** $5w \times 5x$

    e $b \times 9c$ **f** $3b \times 4c \times 2d$ **g** $4g \times f \times 3a$ **h** $4m \times 5p \times 3q$

2 Write each of these expressions in as simple a way as possible.

    a $4x \div 2$ **b** $12x \div 3$ **c** $20m \div 4$ **d** $36q \div 3$

    e $4m \div m$ **f** $16p \div p$ **g** $7q \div q$ **h** $5n \div n$

    i $16m \div 2m$ **j** $20k \div 10k$ **k** $36p \div 9p$ **l** $25t \div 5t$

    m $18p \div 12p$ **n** $16q \div 10$ **o** $15m \div 10m$ **p** $14t \div 6$

3 Find the pairs of expressions in each box that are equal to each other and write them down. The first one is done for you.

    | $a + b$ |
    | $b + a$ | $a + b = b + a$
    | ab |

a
| $m \times n$ |
| $m + n$ |
| mn |

b
| $p - q$ |
| $q - p$ |
| $-p + q$ |

c
| $a \div b$ |
| $b \div a$ |
| $\frac{a}{b}$ |

d
| $6 + x$ |
| $6x$ |
| $x + 6$ |

e
| $3y$ |
| $3 + y$ |
| $3 \times y$ |

4 Solve the following equations, making correct use of the equals sign.

a	$2x + 1 = 11$	**b**	$4x - 3 = 5$	**c**	$5x + 4 = 19$	**d**	$2x - 1 = 13$
e	$4x + 3 = 9$	**f**	$6x - 3 = 12$	**g**	$10x + 7 = 12$	**h**	$2x - 5 = 10$
i	$3x - 12 = 33$	**j**	$7x + 3 = 80$	**k**	$5x + 8 = 73$	**l**	$9x - 7 = 65$

5 Only some of the statements below are true. List those that are.

a $b + c = d + e$ is the same as $d + e = b + c$

b $a - b = 6$ is the same as $6 = a - b$

c $5x = x + 3$ is the same as $x = 5x + 3$

d $5 - 2x = 8$ is the same as $8 = 2x - 5$

e $ab - bc = T$ is the same as $T = ab - bc$

6 Show by substitution which of the following either are not true or may be true.

a $m(b + c) = mb + mc$ **b** $(m + n) \times (p + q) = mp + nq$

c $(m + n) \times (m - n) = (m \times m) - (n \times n)$ **d** $a(b + c) + d(b + c) = (a + d) \times (b + c)$

Extension **Work**

Show by substitution that the following equations are always true.

1 $\dfrac{1}{a} + \dfrac{1}{b} = \dfrac{a + b}{ab}$

2 $\dfrac{1}{a} \div \dfrac{1}{b} = \dfrac{b}{a}$

3 $\dfrac{a}{b} + \dfrac{c}{d} = \dfrac{ad + bc}{bd}$

4 $\dfrac{a}{10 - b} - \dfrac{a}{10 + b} = \dfrac{2ab}{100 - b^2}$

You could use a spreadsheet for this extension.

Like terms

5 apples + 3 apples can be simplified to 8 apples. Similarly, $5a + 3a$ can be simplified to $8a$. $5a$ and $3a$ are called **like terms**, which can be combined because they contain exactly the same letters.

5 apples + 3 bananas cannot be simplified. Similarly, $5a + 3b$ cannot be simplified. $5a$ and $3b$ are **unlike terms**, which cannot be combined.

Example 5.5 ▶

Simplifying:

a $5p - 2p = 3p$ **b** $5ab + 3ab = 8ab$

c $3x^2 + 6x^2 = 9x^2$ **d** $7y - 9y = -2y$ (because $7 - 9 = -2$)

e $-3u - 6u = -9u$ (because $-3 - 6 = -9$)   **f** $5a + 2a + 3b = 7a + 3b$

g $5p - 2p + 7y - 9y = 3p - 2y$ **h** $8t + 3i - 6t - i = 8t - 6t + 3i - i$
$= 2t + 2i$

Exercise 5B

1 Simplify the following expressions.

a	$5h + 6h$	**b**	$4p + p$	**c**	$9u - 3u$
d	$3b - 8b$	**e**	$-2j + 7j$	**f**	$-6r - 6r$
g	$2k + k + 3k$	**h**	$9y - y$	**i**	$7d - 2d + 5d$
j	$10i + 3i - 6i$	**k**	$2b - 5b + 6b$	**l**	$-2b + 5b - 7b$
m	$3xy + 6xy$	**n**	$4p^2 + 7p^2$	**o**	$5ab - 10ab$
p	$5a^2 + 2a^2 - 3a^2$	**q**	$4fg - 6fg - 8fg$	**r**	$6x^2 - 3x^2 - 5x^2$

2 Simplify the following expressions.

a	$6h + 2h + 5g$	**b**	$4g - 2g + 8m$	**c**	$8f + 7d + 3d$
d	$4x + 5y + 7x$	**e**	$6q + 3r - r$	**f**	$4 + 5s - 3s$
g	$c + 2c + 3$	**h**	$12b + 7 + 2b$	**i**	$7w - 7 + 7w$
j	$2bf + 4bf + 5g$	**k**	$7d + 5d^2 - 2d^2$	**l**	$6st - 2st + 5t$
m	$4s - 7s + 2t$	**n**	$-5h + 2i + 3h$	**o**	$4y - 2w - 7w$

3 Simplify the following expressions.

a	$9e + 4e + 7f + 2f$	**b**	$10u - 4u + 9t - 2t$	**c**	$b + 3b + 5d - 2d$
d	$4a + 5c + 3a + 2c$	**e**	$f + 2g + 3g + 5f$	**f**	$9h + 4i - 7h + 2i$
g	$7p + 8q - 6p - 3q$	**h**	$14j - 5k + 5j + 9k$	**i**	$4u - 5t - 6u + 7t$
j	$2s + 5t - 9t + 3s$	**k**	$5p - 2q - 7p + 3q$	**l**	$-2d + 5e - 4d - 9e$

4 Simplify the following expressions.

a	$x^2 + 5x + 2x^2 + 3x$	**b**	$5ab + 3a + 4ab + 7a$	**c**	$4y^2 - 4y + 3y^2 - 5y$
d	$8mn - 3n + 3mn + 2n$	**e**	$5t^2 - 8t - 2t^2 - 4t$	**f**	$3q^2 - 5q - 6q^2 + 3q$

Extension Work

1 Show that any three consecutive integers always multiply together to give a multiple of 6.

2 Prove that two consecutive integers multiplied together always give an even number. (*Hint:* Start with the first number as *n*.)

Expanding brackets and factorising

Expressions often have **brackets**. The terms in the brackets can be multiplied by the term outside. This is called **expanding** or **multiplying out** the bracket, and it removes the bracket.

- When a number or variable multiplies a bracket in this way, it multiplies every term inside the bracket.

- When a negative number or variable multiplies a bracket, it changes all the signs in the bracket.

- After expanding brackets, it may be possible to **simplify** the answer.

- Remember also that $ab = ba$.

The opposite to expanding is **factorising**. This puts the brackets back into an expression, with a term outside the brackets. You can always check your factorising by expanding again.

Example 5.6 ▷

Expanding:

a $4(2s - 3) = 8s - 12$

b $m(2n + 4) = 2mn + 4m$

Example 5.7 ▷

Expanding with negative numbers:

a $-2(x + y) = -2x - 2y$

b $-5(2d - 4e) = -10d + 20e$

c $-(2a + 4b) = -2a - 4b$

d $-(3x - 2) = -3x + 2$

Example 5.8 ▷

Expanding and simplifying:

a $3(2w + 3v) + 2(4w - v) = 6w + 9v + 8w - 2v = 14w + 7v$

b $4(u - 3t) - 2(4u - t) = 4u - 12t - 8u + 2t = -4u - 10t$

Example 5.9 ▷

Factorise:

a $6p + 12$ **b** $ab - 8b$

a Since 6 divides exactly into both $6p$ and 12, we take 6 outside the bracket:
$6p + 12 = 6(p + 2)$

b Since b divides exactly into both ab and $8b$, we take b outside the bracket:
$ab - 8b = b(a - 8)$

Exercise 5C

1 Expand the following brackets.

a $5(p + q)$ **b** $9(m - n)$ **c** $s(t + u)$

d $4(3d + 2)$ **e** $a(2b + c)$ **f** $3(5j - 2k)$

g $e(5 + 2f)$ **h** $10(13 - 5n)$ **i** $6(4g + 3h)$

2 Expand the following brackets.

a $-(a + b)$ **b** $-(q - p)$ **c** $-(3p + 4)$

d $-(7 - 2x)$ **e** $-3(g + 2)$ **f** $-2(d - f)$

g $-5(2h + 3i)$ **h** $-4(6d - 3f)$ **i** $-3(-2j + k)$

3 Expand and simplify the following expressions.

a $3w + 2(w + x)$ **b** $7(d + f) - 2d$ **c** $4h + 5(2h + 3s)$

d $12x + 4(3y + 2x)$ **e** $2(2m - 3n) - 8n$ **f** $16p + 3(3q - 4p)$

g $8h - (3h + 2k)$ **h** $12 - (3e - 4)$ **i** $4a - (5b - 6a)$

4 Expand and simplify the following expressions.

   a $4(a + b) + 2(a + b)$ **b** $3(2i + j) + 5(3i + 4j)$

   c $6(5p + 2q) + 3(3p + q)$ **d** $5(d + f) + 3(d - f)$

   e $7(2e + t) + 2(e - 3t)$ **f** $2(3x - 2y) + 6(2x + y)$

5 Expand and simplify the following expressions.

   a $5(m + n) - (3m + 2n)$ **b** $8(g + 3h) - 2(2g + h)$

   c $7(d + 2e) - 3(2d - 3e)$ **d** $6(2 - 3x) - 3(2 - 5x)$

6 Factorise the following.

   a $3x^2 + 9$ **b** $2ab - 6$ **c** $8ab + 3a$

   d $4x^2 - 10$ **e** $3a - 4ab$ **f** $6ab + 5b$

   g $5mn + 3m$ **h** $10pq + 5$ **i** $8mp - 3m$

Extension Work

1   Mandy was asked to factorise $6ab + 12abc$. She wrote $2(3ab + 6abc)$, $3(2ab + 4abc)$, $a(6b + 12bc)$, $b(6a + 12ac)$. She then wrote the full factorisation, which is $6ab(1 + 2c)$.

2   Write down the answer to the factorisation of the following.

   a $4a + 12ab$ **b** $6ab - 9b$

   c $8mn - 6mp$ **d** $100t + 20mt$

3   Prove that $a(b + c) + b(a + c) + c(a + b)$ always equals $2(ab + bc + ac)$.

Using algebra with shapes

Example 5.10

Find:

a   the perimeter.

b   the area of the rectangle in the simplest expanded form.

$k + 3$

p

a   The perimeter is:

    $2(k + 3) + 2p$ or $2(k + 3 + p) = 2k + 2p + 6$

b   The area is:

    $p(k + 3) = pk + 3p$

Example 5.11 ▶ Find the area of the shape in the simplest expanded form.

First, split the shape into two parts
A and B as shown.

    Shape A has area xy cm².
    Shape B has base $8 - y$ cm.
    So the area is:
    $2(8 - y) = 16 - 2y$ cm²

The total area is $xy + 16 - 2y$ cm².

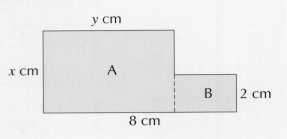

Exercise 5D

(1) Find the length of the perimeter of each of the following shapes in the simplest expanded form.

a
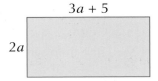
3a + 5
2a

b
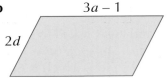
3a – 1
2d

c
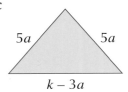
5a   5a
k – 3a

d
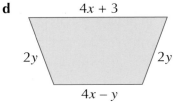
4x + 3
2y   2y
4x – y

e
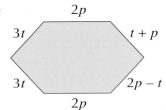
2p
3t   t + p
3t   2p – t
2p

f
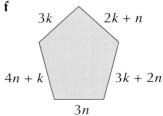
3k   2k + n
4n + k   3k + 2n
3n

(2) What is the total area of each of the following shapes?

a
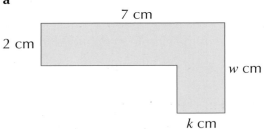
7 cm
2 cm
w cm
k cm

b
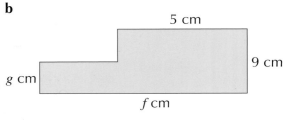
5 cm
g cm
9 cm
f cm

(3) Look at the shape below.

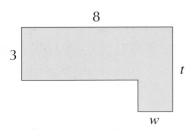
8
3
t
w

It can be split into two rectangles in two different ways as shown.

i   **ii**

a   Use **i** to write an expression for the area of the whole shape.

b   Use **ii** to write an expression for the area of the whole shape.

c   Show that the expressions in **a** and **b** are equal to each other.

4   The diagram shows a shape split into three rectangles in two different ways.

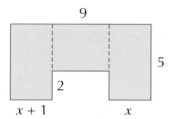 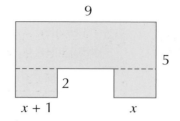

a   Work out the area of each rectangle in both cases.

b   Show that both ways give the same total area.

5   Look at the diagram below.

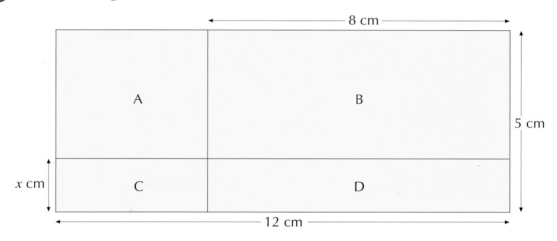

a   Calculate the area of each small rectangle A, B, C, D in the simplest expanded form.

b   Calculate the area of the large rectangle.

c   Show that the sum of the areas of the small rectangles equals the area of the large rectangle.

6   The expression in each box is made by adding the expressions in the two boxes it stands on. Copy the diagrams and fill in the missing expressions.

a

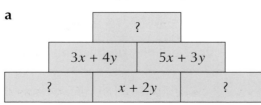

b

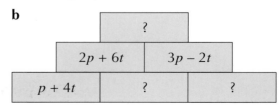

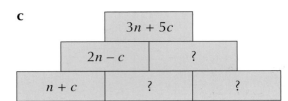

c

3n + 5c

2n − c	?

n + c	?	?

d

6a + 4b

?	4a + b

?	2a − b	?

Extension Work

1 Use a spreadsheet to verify that $3a + 3b$ is always the same as $3(a + b)$.

	A	B	C	D
1				

Put any number in A	Put any number in B	Put in the formula 3*A1 + 3*B1	Put in the formula 3*(A1 + B1)

Copy the formulae from C1 and D1 down to about C20 and D20. Put a variety of numbers in each row of columns A and B. Check that for any type of number, negative and decimal, the value in cell C equals the value in cell D for each row.

2 Use a spreadsheet to verify that $(a + b)(a − b)$ is always the same as $a^2 − b^2$.

Index notation with algebra

You can save time by writing $5 \times 5 \times 5$ as 5^3, using raised **index** notation to form **powers**. In the same way, $m \times m \times m$ can be written as m^3.

Look at the following examples of **multiplying** powers:

$$m^2 \times m^3 = (m \times m) \times (m \times m \times m) = m \times m \times m \times m \times m = m^5$$
$$t^1 \times t^2 = t \times (t \times t) = t \times t \times t = t^3$$
$$k^3 \times k^4 = (k \times k \times k) \times (k \times k \times k \times k) = k \times k \times k \times k \times k \times k \times k = k^7$$

Notice that:

$$m^2 \times m^3 = m^{2+3} = m^5$$
$$t^1 \times t^2 = t^{1+2} = t^3$$
$$k^3 \times k^4 = k^{3+4} = k^7$$

When multiplying powers of the same variable, add the indices:

$$x^A \times x^B = x^{A+B}$$

Look at the following examples of **dividing** powers:

$$m^6 \div m^2 = \frac{m^6}{m^2} = \frac{m \times m \times m \times m \times m \times m}{m \times m} = m^{6-2} = m^4$$

$$t^4 \div t = \frac{t^4}{t} = \frac{t \times t \times t \times t}{t} = t^{4-1} = t^3$$

When dividing powers of the same variable, subtract the indices:

$$x^A \div x^B = \frac{x^A}{x^B} = x^{A-B}$$

Example 5.12 ▷

Simplifying:

a $x \times x = x^2$

b $4m \times 3m = 12mm = 12m^2$

c $2a \times 3a \times 5a = 30aaa = 30a^3$

Example 5.13 ▷

Simplifying:

a $2m^3 \times 5m = 2 \times 5 \times m^3 \times m = 10m^{3+1} = 10m^4$

b $m^5 \div m^3 = \dfrac{m^5}{m^3} = m^{5-3} = m^2$

c $8t^7 \div 4t^2 = \dfrac{8t^7}{4t^2} = 2t^{7-2} = 2t^5$

Example 5.14 ▷

Expanding and simplifying:

a $3m(2m - 4n) = 6m^2 - 12mn$

b $a(a + 4b) - b(2a - 5b) = a^2 + 4ab - 2ba + 5b^2$
$$= a^2 + 2ab + 5b^2$$

Exercise 5E

1   Write the following expressions using index form.

    a $a \times a \times a$ **b** $r \times r \times r \times r \times r$

    c $b \times b \times b \times b \times b \times b \times b \times b$ **d** $4a \times 3a$

    e $2g \times 3g \times 2g$ **f** $9k \times 4 \times 2k \times k \times 3k$

2   **a**   Write $f + f + f + f + f$ as briefly as possible.

    b   Write $w \times w \times w \times w$ as briefly as possible.

    c   Show the difference between $5j$ and j^5.

3   Expand the following brackets.

    a $d(d + 1)$ **b** $a(4a - 3)$ **c** $p(4 + p)$

    d $w(6 - 3w)$ **e** $f(3f + g)$ **f** $u(2u - 3s)$

4   Expand and simplify the following expressions.

    a $d(d + h) + h(2h + d)$ **b** $m(3m + 7n) + n(2m - 4n)$

    c $e(5e + 4f) - f(2e + 3f)$ **d** $y(4x - 2y) + x(7y + 5x)$

    e $k(4k - 2t) - t(3k + 7t)$ **f** $j(j + 7r) - r(2r - 9j)$

5   Expand and simplify the following expressions.

    a $4d^2 + d(2d - 5)$ **b** $a(a + 1) + a(2a + 3)$

    c $t(3t + 5) + t(2t - 3)$ **d** $w(5w + 4) - w(2w + 3)$

    e $u(5u - 3) - u(3u - 1)$ **f** $d(2d - 5) - d(7 - 3d)$

6 Expand and simplify the following.

a $x(x^3 + 3) + x^2(5 + x)$ 　　　　　　　　b $3y(4y - 5) + y^2(y + 3)$

c $4m(m^2 - 1) + m^2(4 - m)$ 　　　　　　d $5t^2(8 - t) + 2t(3t^2 - 5t)$

7 Simplify the following.

a $m^5 \times m^3$ 　　b $t^4 \times t$ 　　c $3k^2 \times 2k^4$ 　　d $4w^5 \times 3w$

e $x^6 \div x^2$ 　　f $n^5 \div n$ 　　g $10y^2 \div 2y$ 　　h $16m^5 \div 2m^3$

8 Factorise the following.

a $y^2 + 3y$ 　　b $2x^2 + 3x$ 　　c $3m^3 - 5m$ 　　d $2ab - b^2$

e $5p^2 - 10$ 　　f $x^3 + 3x^2$ 　　g $3m^2 - 2m$ 　　h $7k^3 + 3kp$

Extension **Work**

Use a spreadsheet to investigate the statement:

'The formula $P = n^2 - n + 11$ generates prime numbers for all values of n.'

LEVEL BOOSTER

4
I can simplify algebraic expressions.
I can solve simple equations.
I can simplify algebraic expressions by collecting like terms.

5
I know the equivalence of algebraic expressions.
I can solve equations with two operations.
I can expand a bracket.
I can write algebraic expressions in a simpler form using index notation.

6
I can expand a bracket with a negative sign outside.
I can expand and simplify expressions with more than one bracket.
I can simplify algebraic expressions using index notation.

7
I can factorise simple expressions.
I can use index laws to simplify expressions.

1 *2006 Paper 1*

Write the correct operations (+ or − or × or ÷) in these statements.

$$a \ldots a = 0 \qquad a \ldots a = 1 \qquad a \ldots a = 2a \qquad a \ldots a = a^2$$

2 *2006 Paper 1*

Solve this equation.

$$3y + 14 = 5y + 1$$

3 *2004 Paper 2*

Look at these expressions.

$$5y - 8 \qquad\qquad 3y + 5$$

first expression   second expression

What value of y makes the two expressions equal?

Show your working.

4 *2005 Paper 2*

Write these expressions as simply as possible.

$$3k \times 2k \qquad \frac{9k^2}{3k}$$

5 *2006 Paper 2*

Here are the rules for an algebra grid.

Use these rules to complete the algebra grids below.

Copy the grids and write your expressions as simply as possible.

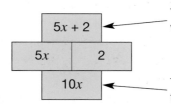

This value is the **sum** of the values in the middle row.

This value is the **product** of the values in the middle row.

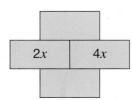 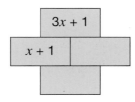 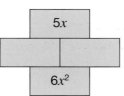

6 *2007 Paper 1*

Work out the values of m and n.

$$5^8 \times 5^4 = 5^m \qquad \frac{5^8}{5^4} = 5^n$$

CHAPTER 6

Geometry and Measures **2**

This chapter is going to show you

- The definition of a circle and the names of its parts
- How to use the formulae for the circumference and the area of a circle
- How to calculate the surface area and the volume of prisms
- How to convert imperial units to metric units

What you should already know

- How to draw circles given the radius
- The metric units for area and volume
- How to calculate areas of two-dimensional shapes
- How to calculate the surface area and volume of a cuboid

The circle

A circle is a set of points equidistant from a **centre** O.

Make sure that you know all the following terms for different parts of a circle.

Circle

×O

Circumference The distance around the circle; a special name for the perimeter of a circle.

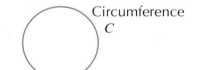

Circumference
C

Arc A part of the circumference.

Arc

Radius The distance from the centre to the circumference. The plural is radii.

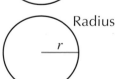

Radius
r

Diameter The distance from side to side passing through the centre; the greatest width of a circle.

The diameter *d* is twice the radius *r*:

$$d = 2r$$

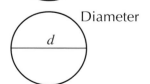

Diameter
d

Chord A line which cuts the circle into two parts.

Chord

Tangent A line that touches the circle at a single point on the circumference.

Tangent

Segment   An area of the circle enclosed by a chord and an arc.

Segment

Sector   An area of the circle enclosed by two radii and an arc.

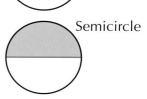
Sector

Semicircle Half a circle; the area of the circle enclosed by a diameter and an arc.

Semicircle

How can you measure the circumference of a circle?

Is there a relation between the diameter and the circumference?

The following exercise will show you.

Exercise 6A

This activity looks at the relation between the diameter and the circumference of a circle.

For the activity you will need compasses, a 30 cm ruler and a piece of string about 40 cm long.

Copy the following table and draw circles with the given radii.

Measure the circumference of each circle by using the string, and complete the table. Calculate the last column to one decimal place.

Radius r (cm)	Diameter d (cm)	Circumference C (cm)	$C \div d$
1			
1.5			
2			
2.5			
3			
3.5			
4			
4.5			
5			
5.5			
6			

What do you notice about the last column?

Can you say how the circumference is related to the diameter?

Write down what you have found out in your book.

Extension **Work**

1   How can you find the centre of a circle that you cannot cut out?
    (*Hint:* Draw chords.)

2   Draw a circle on paper and cut it out. Draw a thin sector on the circle
    and cut it out. Make a cone with the remaining larger sector. What
    happens as you make the size of the removed sector larger?

Circumference of a circle

In Exercise 6A, you should have found that the **circumference** C of a circle with **diameter**
d is given approximately by the formula $C = 3d$.

In fact the number by which you have to multiply the diameter to get a more accurate
circumference is slightly larger than 3.

Over the centuries mathematicians have tried to find this number. It is a special number
for which we use the Greek letter π (pronounced **pi**). The value of π cannot be written
down exactly as a fraction or a decimal, so we have to use an approximation for it. The
approximations commonly used are:

$\pi = \frac{22}{7}$ (as a fraction)

$\pi = 3.14$ (as a decimal to two decimal places)

$\pi = 3.141\ 592\ 654$ (on a scientific calculator)

π has been calculated to millions of decimal places, using computers to do the
arithmetic. So far no repeating pattern has ever been found.

To 30 decimal places $\pi = 3.141\ 592\ 653\ 589\ 793\ 238\ 462\ 643\ 383\ 270$

Look for the $\boxed{\pi}$ key on your calculator.

We can now write the formula for calculating the circumference C of a circle with
diameter d as:

$C = \pi d$

The diameter is twice the **radius**, so we also have:

$C = \pi d = \pi \times 2r = 2\pi r$

Example 6.1 ▷ Calculate the circumference of the following circles. Give your answers to one
decimal place.

a

b

a $d = 8$ cm
    So, $C = \pi d = \pi \times 8 = 25.1$ cm (to 1 decimal place)

b $r = 6.4$ m, so $d = 12.8$ m
    $C = \pi d = \pi \times 12.8 = 40.2$ m (to 1 decimal place)

Exercise 6B

In this exercise take π = 3.14 or use the ⟨π⟩ key on your calculator.

1 Calculate the circumference of each of the following circles. Give your answers to one decimal place.

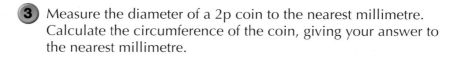

a **5 cm** b **12 mm** c **2.3 m** d **1.5 cm** e **3.8 m**

2 The Big Wheel at a theme park has a diameter of 40 m. How far would you travel in one complete revolution of the wheel? Give your answer to the nearest metre.

3 Measure the diameter of a 2p coin to the nearest millimetre. Calculate the circumference of the coin, giving your answer to the nearest millimetre.

4 The diagram shows the dimensions of a running track at a sports centre. The bends are semicircles.

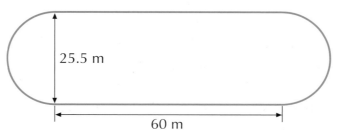

25.5 m

60 m

Calculate the distance round the track, giving your answer to the nearest metre.

5 The Earth's orbit can be taken to be a circle with a radius of approximately 150 million kilometres.

Calculate the distance the Earth travels in one orbit of the Sun. Give your answer to the nearest million kilometres.

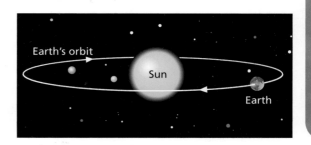

6 Calculate the perimeter of the following semicircular shape, giving your answer to one decimal place.

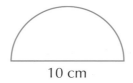

10 cm

7

1   In the following shapes, all the curves are semicircles.

Calculate the perimeter of each shape:

   i   using a calculator and giving your answer to one decimal place.

   ii   using $\pi = \frac{22}{7}$ and giving your answer as a mixed number.

a 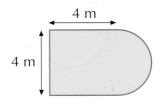   b   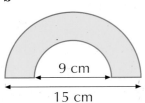   c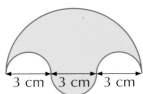

2   The distance round a circular running track is 400 m. Calculate the radius of the track, giving your answer to the nearest metre.

3   a   'How I wish I could calculate pi exactly' is a mnemonic to remember π to seven decimal places. A mnemonic is an aid to remember facts. Can you see how this one works?

Look on the Internet to find other mnemonics for π, or make one up yourself.

   b   Look on the Internet to find the world record for the most number of decimal places that has been calculated for π so far.

Area of a circle

The circle shown has been split into 16 equal sectors. These have been placed together to form a shape that is roughly rectangular.

As the circle is split into more and more sectors which are placed together, the resulting shape eventually becomes a rectangle. The area of this rectangle will be the same as the area of the circle.

The length of the rectangle is half the circumference C of the circle and the width is the radius r of the circle. So the area of the rectangle is given by:

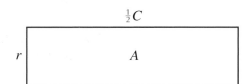

$$A = \tfrac{1}{2}C \times r$$
$$= \tfrac{1}{2} \times 2 \times \pi \times r \times r$$
$$= \pi \times r \times r$$
$$= \pi r^2$$

So the formula for the area A of a circle with radius r is $A = \pi r^2$.

Example 6.2 ▶ Calculate the area of the following circles. Give your answers to one decimal place.

a

4 cm

b

6.2 m

a $r = 4$ cm
So, $A = pr2 = p ¥ {}^42 = 16p = 50.3$ c^{m}2 (to 1 decimal place)

b $d = 6.2$ m, so $r = 3.1$ m
$A = \pi r^2 = \pi \times 3.1^2 = 9.61\pi = 30.2$ m² (to 1 decimal place)

Different calculators work in different ways. For example, the following may be the calculator keys needed for part **a**:

$$\boxed{\pi} \quad \boxed{\times} \quad \boxed{4} \quad \boxed{x^2} \quad \boxed{=}$$

Other calculators may require you to use the $\boxed{x^2}$ key first.

Note that the answers could also be left in terms of π to give: **a** 16π **b** 9.61π
This may be necessary when a calculator is not allowed.

Exercise 6C

In this exercise take $\pi = 3.14$ or use the $\boxed{\pi}$ key on your calculator.

1 Calculate the area of each of the following circles. Give your answers to one decimal place.

a 3 cm   **b** 12 mm   **c** 1.8 m   **d** 2.1 cm   **e** 6.7 m

2 Calculate the area of a circular tablemat with a diameter of 16 cm. Give your answer to the nearest square centimetre.

3 Measure the diameter of a 1p coin to the nearest millimetre. Calculate the area of one face of the coin, giving your answer to the nearest square millimetre.

4 Calculate the area of the sports ground shown. The bends are semicircles. Give your answer to the nearest square metre.

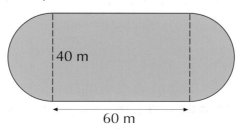

40 m

60 m

5 The minute hand on a clock has a length of 11 cm. Calculate the area swept by the minute hand in one hour. Give your answer in terms of π.

6 Calculate the area of the semicircular protractor shown, giving your answer to one decimal place.

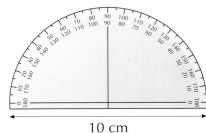

10 cm

Extension Work

1 Calculate the area of each of the following shapes. Give your answers to one decimal place.

a

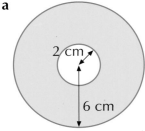

2 cm

6 cm

b

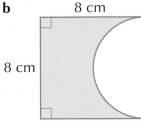

8 cm

8 cm

c

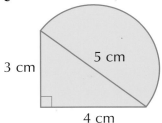

5 cm

3 cm

4 cm

2 A circular lawn has an area of 100 m². Calculate the radius of the lawn, giving your answer to one decimal place.

3 A circular disc has a circumference of 20 cm. Calculate the area of the disc, giving your answer to one decimal place.

4 Show that the formula for the area A of a circle with diameter d can also be written as:

$$A = \frac{\pi d^2}{4}$$

Surface area and volume of prisms

The following are the metric units for area, volume and capacity that you need to know. Also given are the conversions between these units.

Area	Volume	Capacity
10 000 m² = 1 hectare (ha)	1 000 000 cm³ = 1 m³	1 m³ = 1000 litres
10 000 cm² = 1 m²	1000 mm³ = 1 cm³	1000 cm³ = 1 litre
100 mm² = 1 cm²		1 cm³ = 1 ml

The unit symbol for litres is the letter l. In books, to avoid confusion with 1 (one), the full unit name 'litres' may be used instead of the symbol.

Example 6.3 ▶

Convert: **a** 72 000 cm² to m² **b** 0.3 cm³ to mm³ **c** 4500 cm³ to litres

a 72 000 cm² = 72 000 ÷ 10 000 = 7.2 m²

b 0.3 cm³ = 0.3 × 1000 = 300 mm³

c 4500 cm³ = 4500 ÷ 1000 = 4.5 litres

Prisms

A prism is a three-dimensional (3-D) shape which has exactly the same two-dimensional (2-D) shape all the way through it.

This 2-D shape is the **cross-section** of the prism.

The shape of the cross-section depends on the type of prism, but it is always the same for a particular prism.

The volume V of a prism is found by multiplying the area A of its cross-section by its length l:

$V = Al$

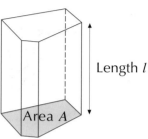

Length l

Area A

Example 6.4 ▶

Calculate: **a** the total surface area and

b the volume of the triangular prism shown.

a The total surface area is composed of two equal right-angled triangles and three different rectangles. The area of one triangle is:

$$\frac{4 \times 3}{2} = 6 \text{ cm}^2$$

The sum of the areas of the three rectangles is:

$(3 \times 10) + (4 \times 10) + (5 \times 10) = 120 \text{ cm}^2$

So the total surface area is:

$(2 \times 6) + 120 = 132 \text{ cm}^2$

b The cross-section is a right-angled triangle with an area of 6 cm². So the volume is given by:

area of cross-section × length = $6 \times 10 = 60 \text{ cm}^3$

Exercise 6D

1 Calculate **i** the total surface area and **ii** the volume of each of the following prisms.

a

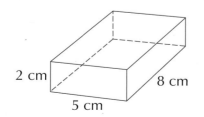

2 cm 8 cm 5 cm

b

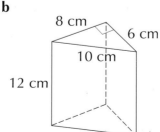

8 cm 6 cm 10 cm 12 cm

c

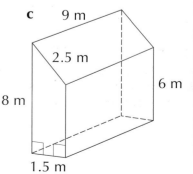

9 m 2.5 m 6 m 8 m 1.5 m

2 Convert the following.

    a   0.83 hectares to m²   **b**   730 mm² to cm²

    c   1 500 000 cm³ to m³   **d**   3.7 m³ to litres

3 The section of pencil shown is a hexagonal prism with a cross-sectional area of 60 mm² and a length of 140 mm.

    a   Calculate the volume of the pencil in cubic millimetres.

    b   Write down the volume of the pencil in cubic centimetres.

4 The biscuit tin shown is an octagonal prism with a cross-sectional area of 450 cm² and a height of 8 cm. Calculate the volume of the tin.

5 The diagram shows the cross-section of a swimming pool along its length. The pool is 20 m wide.

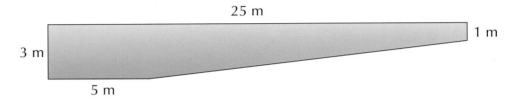

    a   Calculate the area of the cross-section of the pool.

    b   Find the volume of the pool.

    c   How many litres of water does the pool hold when it is full?

6 Andy is making a solid concrete ramp for wheelchair access to his house. The dimensions of the ramp are shown on the diagram.

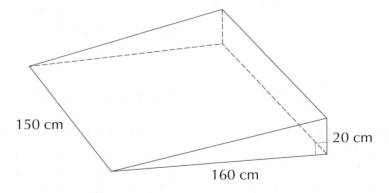

    a   Calculate the volume of the ramp, giving your answer in cubic centimetres.

    b   What volume of concrete does Andy use? Give your answer in cubic metres.

Extension Work

Volume of a cylinder

The cross-section of a cylinder is a circle with radius r.

The area of the cross-section is $A = \pi r^2$.

If the height of the cylinder is h, then the volume V of the cylinder is given by the formula:

$$V = \pi r^2 \times h = \pi r^2 h$$

1 Calculate the volume of each of the following cylinders, giving your answers to three significant figures:

a 5 cm / 4 cm

b 12 m / 2 m

2 Ask your teacher for some cylindrical objects. Calculate the volume of each, using the most appropriate units.

Imperial units

In Britain we now use the metric system of units, but people still prefer to use the imperial system in certain cases, as the examples show.

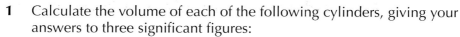

I need to order 3 pints of milk

The distance to London is 256 miles

My height is 5' 7"

The recipe requires ½ lb of butter

The following imperial units are still used and it is useful to be familiar with them.

Imperial units of length	Imperial units of mass	Imperial units of capacity
12 inches (in) = 1 foot (ft) 3 feet = 1 yard (yd) 1760 yards = 1 mile (mi)	16 ounces (oz) = 1 pound (lb) 14 pounds = 1 stone (st) 2240 pounds = 1 ton	8 pints (pt) = 1 gallon (gal)

Example 6.5

Express 5 ft 6 in in inches.

5 ft = 5 × 12 = 60 in

So 5 ft 6 in = 60 + 6 = 66 in

Example 6.6 ▷ Express 100 lb in stones and pounds.

100 lb ÷ 14 = 7 st with 2 lb left over

So 100 lb = 7 st 2 lb

Rough metric equivalents of imperial units

Sometimes you need to be able to convert from imperial units to metric units by using suitable approximations. It is useful to know the following rough metric equivalents of imperial units. If better accuracy is required, the exact conversion factors should be used. The symbol ≈ means 'is approximately equal to'.

Units of length	Units of mass	Units of capacity
1 inch ≈ 2.5 centimetres 1 yard ≈ 1 metre 5 miles ≈ 8 kilometres	1 ounce ≈ 30 grams 1 pound ≈ 500 grams	$1\frac{3}{4}$ pints ≈ 1 litre 1 gallon ≈ 4.5 litres

Example 6.7 ▷ Approximately how many kilometres are there in 20 miles?

5 miles ≈ 8 kilometres

So 20 miles ≈ 4 × 8 = 32 kilometres

Example 6.8 ▷ Approximately how many gallons are there in 18 litres?

4.5 litres ≈ 1 gallon

So 18 litres ≈ 18 ÷ 4.5 = 4 gallons

Exercise 6E

1. Express each of the following in the units given in brackets.

   a 6 ft 2 in (in)   b 22 yd (ft)   c 2 lb 10 oz (oz)

   d 6 st 5 lb (lb)   e $3\frac{1}{2}$ gal (pt)

2. Express each of the following in the units given in brackets.

   a 30 in (ft and in)   b 20 ft (yd and ft)   c 72 oz (lb and oz)

   d 35 lb (st and lb)   e 35 pt (gal and pt)

3. How many inches are there in:

   a a yard?   b a mile?

4. How many ounces are there in:

   a a stone?   b a ton?

5. Convert each of the following imperial quantities into the metric quantity given in brackets.

   a 6 in (cm)   b 10 yd (m)   c 25 mi (km)

   d 8 oz (g)   e $1\frac{1}{2}$ lb (g)   f 7 pt (litres)

   g 8 gal (litres)

6 Convert each of the following metric quantities into the imperial quantity given in brackets.

 a 30 cm (in) **b** 200 m (ft) **c** 80 km (mi) **d** 150 g (oz)
 e 3 kg (lb) **f** 6 litres (pt) **g** 54 litres (gal)

 7 Pièrre is on holiday in England and he sees this sign near to his hotel. Approximately how many metres is it from his hotel to the beach?

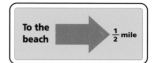

 8 Mike is travelling on a German autobahn and he sees this road sign. He knows it means that the speed limit is 120 kilometres per hour. What is the approximate speed limit in miles per hour?

 9 Steve needs 6 gallons of petrol to fill the tank of his car. The pump only dispenses petrol in litres. Approximately how many litres of petrol does he need?

10 A metric tonne is 1000 kg. Approximately how many pounds is this?

 11 Anne's height is 5 ft 6 in. She is filling in an application form for a passport and needs to know her height in metres. What height should she enter on the form?

Extension Work

1 Working in pairs or groups, draw up a table to show each person's height and weight in imperial and in metric units.

2 Other imperial units are less common, but are still used in Britain. For example:
 • furlongs to measure distance in horse racing
 • fathoms to measure the depth of sea water
 • nautical miles to measure distance at sea

Use reference material or the Internet to find metric approximations for these units. Can you find other imperial units for measuring length, mass and capacity that are still in use?

3 How long is 1 million seconds? Give your answer in days, hours, minutes and seconds.

LEVEL BOOSTER

5 I can use a calculator to convert between imperial units and metric units.

6 I can use the appropriate formulae to calculate the circumference and the area of a circle.

7 I can calculate the surface area and the volume of a prism.

6

1 *2001 Paper 2*

A trundle wheel is used to measure distances.

Imran makes a trundle wheel, of diameter 50 cm.

   a   Calculate the circumference of Imran's trundle wheel. Show your working.

   b   Imran uses his trundle wheel to measure the length of the school car park.

       His trundle wheel rotates 87 times. What is the length of the car park, to the nearest metre?

2 *2000 Paper 2*

The diagram shows a circle and a square.

   a   The radius of the circle is 12 mm.

       What is the **area** of the circle to the nearest mm²?

   b   The **ratio** of the area of the **circle** to the area of the **square** is **2 : 1**

       What is the area of the square to the nearest mm²?

   c   What is the side length of the square?

12 mm

not drawn accurately

3 *2007 Paper 1*

Kevin is working out the **area** of a circle with **radius 4**.

He writes: Area = π × 8

Explain why Kevin's working is **wrong**.

4

4 *2002 Paper 2*

The drawing shows two cuboids that have the same volume:

Cuboid A   **Cuboid B**

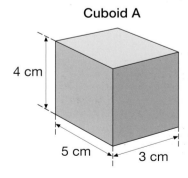

4 cm

5 cm   3 cm

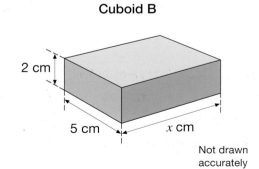

2 cm

5 cm   *x* cm

Not drawn accurately

   a   What is the volume of cuboid A?

       Remember to state your units.

   b   Work out the value of the length marked x in Cuboid B.

5 *1999 Paper 1*

    a   What is the volume of this prism?

        You must show each step in your working.

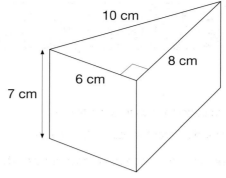

Not drawn accurately

    b   Prisms A and B have the same cross-sectional area.

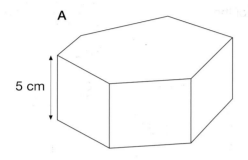

Not drawn accurately

        Copy and complete the table:

	Prism A	Prism B
Height	5 cm	3 cm
Volume	200 cm³	…… cm³

6   2007 Paper 2

    One face of a prism is made from 5 squares.

    Each square has side length 3 cm.

    Work out the volume of the prism.

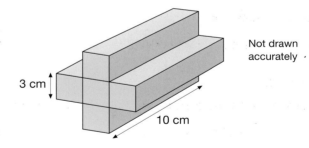

Not drawn accurately

7   *2007 Paper 2*

    This shaded shape is made using **two semicircles.**

    One semicircle had a diameter of **20 cm.**

    The other has a diameter of **30 cm.**

    Calculate the **perimeter** of the shaded shape.

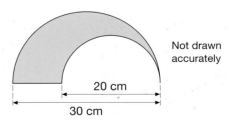

Not drawn accurately

This chapter is going to show you

- How to draw mapping diagrams from functions
- How to identify a function from inputs and outputs
- Special features of a linear graph
- How to show and find average speed on a distance–time graph

What you should already know

- How to use a function
- How to plot coordinates
- How to calculate with negative numbers

Linear functions

A **function** is a rule that changes a number into another number. In this chapter, functions involve any of the following operations:

Addition	Subtraction	Multiplication	Division

The functions in this chapter are **linear**. This means that they do not contain powers. Later you will meet functions that do contain powers.

Functions can be illustrated using **mapping** diagrams, as shown in Example 7.1.

Example 7.1 ▷ Draw a mapping diagram to illustrate the function:
$$x \rightarrow 2x + 3$$

Draw two number lines as shown:

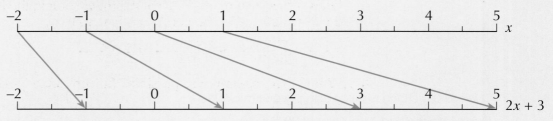

The top line is for the starting points or **inputs**. The arrows show how the function $x \rightarrow 2x + 3$ **maps** its inputs to its **outputs** on the bottom line. The arrowheads point to the outputs. So:
$$-2 \rightarrow -1$$
$$-1 \rightarrow 1$$
$$0 \rightarrow 3$$
$$1 \rightarrow 5$$

The diagram shows only part of an infinitely long pair of number lines with infinite mappings.

Exercise 7A

1 a Using two number lines from −5 to 10, draw mapping diagrams to illustrate the following functions.

    i $x \rightarrow x + 2$

    ii $x \rightarrow 2x + 1$

    iii $x \rightarrow x - 2$

    iv $x \rightarrow 2x - 1$

b In each of your mapping diagrams from **a**, draw the lines from −1.5, 0.5 and 1.5.

2 a Using number lines from −5 to 15, draw mapping diagrams to illustrate the following functions.

    i $x \rightarrow 3x + 1$

    ii $x \rightarrow 4x - 1$

    iii $x \rightarrow 2x + 5$

    iv $x \rightarrow 3x - 2$

b In each of your mapping diagrams from **a**, draw the lines from −0.5, 1.5 and 2.5.

3 Write down the similarity between all the mapping diagrams of functions like:

$x \rightarrow x + 2$ $x \rightarrow x + 1$ $x \rightarrow x + 5$ $x \rightarrow x + 7$

4 a Using number lines from 0 to 10, draw a mapping diagram of the function $x \rightarrow 2x$. Leave plenty of space above your diagram.

b Extend the line joining the two zeros upwards. Then extend all the other arrows backwards to meet this line.

c Repeat the above for the mapping $x \rightarrow 3x$. Does this also join together at a point on the line joining the zeros?

d Can you explain why this works for all similar functions?

Extension **Work**

1 a Draw a mapping diagram to show arrows joining the inputs and just the final outputs for the combined function:

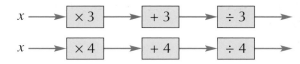

b Write down, as simply as possible, the combined function in the form:

$x \rightarrow Ax + B$

2 Repeat the instructions in **1a** and **b** for:

$$x \longrightarrow \boxed{\times 3} \longrightarrow \boxed{+ 3} \longrightarrow \boxed{\div 3} \longrightarrow$$

$$x \longrightarrow \boxed{\times 4} \longrightarrow \boxed{+ 4} \longrightarrow \boxed{\div 4} \longrightarrow$$

3 Explain what you notice about the results in **1** and **2**.

Finding functions from inputs and outputs

Any **function** will have a particular set of outputs for a particular set of inputs. If we can find some outputs and inputs, then we can find the function.

Example 7.2 ▷

State the function that maps the inputs $\{-1, 0, 1, 2, 3\}$ to $\{-1, 3, 7, 11, 15\}$.

Notice that for each integer increase in the inputs, the outputs increase by 4. This suggests that part of the function is:

$$\boxed{\times 4}$$

The input 0 maps to 3. Hence the function uses:

$$\boxed{+ 3}$$

This leads to the function:

$x \rightarrow 4x + 3$

A quick check shows that this does map 1 to 7, and 2 to 11. This confirms that the function is correct.

Inverse functions

The **inverse** of a function maps the outputs of the function back to the inputs.

Example 7.3 ▷

Function $x \rightarrow x + 3$ has inverse $x \rightarrow x - 3$. This can be shown with some example inputs:

function	inverse
$x \rightarrow x + 3$	$x \rightarrow x - 3$
$2 \rightarrow 5$	$5 \rightarrow 2$
$8 \rightarrow 11$	$11 \rightarrow 8$

Here the function maps the input 2 to the output 5. Then the inverse function takes the 5 as its input and maps it to its output 2. This is the original input.

Example 7.4 ▷

Function $x \rightarrow 4x$ has inverse $x \rightarrow \frac{x}{4}$:

function	inverse
$x \rightarrow 4x$	$x \rightarrow \frac{x}{4}$
$2 \rightarrow 8$	$8 \rightarrow 2$
$5 \rightarrow 20$	$20 \rightarrow 5$

Most functions are more complicated. To find their inverses, we have to think of their operations as building bricks and work back from output to input.

Example 7.5 ▷ Find the inverse of the function $x \rightarrow 4x + 3$.

This function is built up as:

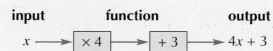

input	function	output

We now reverse the path, call the new input x, and invert each operation to find the inverse function:

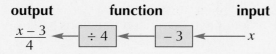

output	function	input

Check:

function	inverse
$x \rightarrow 4x + 3$	$x \rightarrow \dfrac{x - 3}{4}$
$5 \rightarrow 23$	$23 \rightarrow 5$
$7 \rightarrow 31$	$31 \rightarrow 7$

Exercise 7B

1 State the function that maps the following inputs to their outputs.

a $\{-1, 0, 1, 2, 3\} \longrightarrow \{4, 5, 6, 7, 8\}$

b $\{-1, 0, 1, 2, 3\} \longrightarrow \{-2, -1, 0, 1, 2\}$

c $\{-1, 0, 1, 2, 3\} \longrightarrow \{-1, 1, 3, 5, 7\}$

d $\{-1, 0, 1, 2, 3\} \longrightarrow \{3, 5, 7, 9, 11\}$

e $\{-1, 0, 1, 2, 3\} \longrightarrow \{2, 5, 8, 11, 14\}$

2 What are the functions that generate the following mixed outputs from the given mixed inputs? (*Hint:* Put the numbers in sequence first.)

a $\{2, 5, 3, 0, 6, 4\} \longrightarrow \{6, 8, 9, 3, 7, 5\}$

b $\{5, 9, 6, 4, 10, 8\} \longrightarrow \{15, 17, 12, 16, 11, 13\}$

c $\{5, 1, 8, 4, 0, 6\} \longrightarrow \{5, 13, 15, 3, 19, 11\}$

d $\{3, 1, 7, 5, 8, 2\} \longrightarrow \{9, 1, 13, 5, 15, 3\}$

e $\{9, 5, 10, 6, 3, 7\} \longrightarrow \{16, 10, 28, 19, 31, 22\}$

3 For each of the functions **a–f**:

i find the output for the input $\{0, 1, 2, 3\}$.

ii find the inverse function.

iii check that the inverse function maps the output from **i** back to $\{0, 1, 2, 3\}$.

a	$x \rightarrow 2x + 3$	**b**	$x \rightarrow 3x + 4$
c	$x \rightarrow 3x - 2$	**d**	$x \rightarrow 4x - 1$
e	$x \rightarrow 5x + 3$	**f**	$x \rightarrow 5x - 4$

4 **a** Find the inverse function of $x \rightarrow 10 - x$.

b What do you notice about your answer to **a**?

c This function is called a 'self-inverse'. Can you explain why?

d Write down five more self-inverse functions.

When two functions are combined, the output of the first becomes the input of the second. The combined function is treated as one function.

Investigate the following statements to find out which you think are true.

1   Two addition functions always combine to give a single addition function.

2   Two multiplication functions always combine to give a single multiplication function.

3   Changing the order of two combined functions makes no difference to the result.

Graphs of functions

There are different ways to write functions. For example, the function:

$x \rightarrow 4x + 3$

can also be written as:

$y = 4x + 3$

The inputs are x and the outputs are y.

Functions written in this way are called **equations**. The equation form is simpler for drawing graphs.

Every function has a graph associated with it. The graph is plotted against **axes** using ordered pairs or **coordinates** of the function. The graph of a linear function or equation is a straight line.

Example 7.6

Draw a graph of the function:

$y = 3x + 1$

First, we draw up a table of simple values for x:

x	−2	−1	0	1	2	3
$y = 3x + 1$	−5	−2	1	4	7	10

Then we plot each point on a grid, and join up all the points.

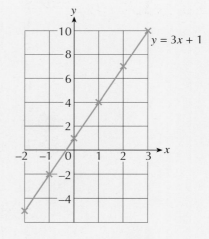

The line has an infinite number of other coordinates too. *All* of these obey the same rule of the function, that is $y = 3x + 1$. Choose any points on the line that have not been plotted and show that this is true: for example, (1.5, 5.5), (8, 25).

Sometimes a function is expressed in a different way, such as:

$$2y + 3x = 12$$

Example 7.7 ▶

Draw the graph of $2y + 3x = 12$.

We need to find at least three points to determine the straight line.

Two easy points to find are when $x = 0$ and $y = 0$:

when $x = 0$, $2y = 12$; so $y = 6$ and $(0, 6)$ is a point
when $y = 0$, $3x = 12$; so $x = 4$ and $(4, 0)$ is a point

A useful third point for x or y is about halfway between 0 and the higher value just found. So here we could try $x = 3$ or $y = 3$ or both:

when $x = 3$, $2y + 9 = 12$; so $2y = 3$ and $(3, 1.5)$ is a point
when $y = 3$, $6 + 3x = 12$; so $x = 2$ and $(2, 3)$ is a point

There are now sufficient points to draw the line as shown.

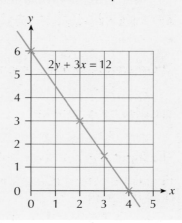

Exercise 7C

1 a Complete the table below for the function $y = 4x + 1$.

x	−2	−1	0	1	2	3
$y = 4x + 1$			1			

b Draw a grid with its x-axis from −2 to 3 and y-axis from −7 to 13.

c Use the table to help draw, on the grid, the graph of the function $y = 4x + 1$.

2 a Complete the table below for the function $y = 4x − 1$.

x	−2	−1	0	1	2	3
$y = 4x − 1$			−1			

b Draw a grid with its x-axis from −2 to 3 and y-axis from −9 to 11.

c Use the table to help draw, on the grid, the graph of the function $y = 4x − 1$.

3 a Complete the table below for the functions shown.

x	−2	−1	0	1	2	3
y = 2x + 5	1					11
y = 2x + 3		1			7	
y = 2x + 1			1	3		
y = 2x − 1			−1	1		
y = 2x − 3		−5			1	

b Draw a grid with its x-axis from −2 to 3 and y-axis from −7 to 11.

c Draw the graph for each function in the table.

d What two properties do you notice about each line?

e Use the properties you have noticed to draw the graphs of the functions below.

    i $y = 2x + 2.5$ **ii** $y = 2x − 1.5$

4 a Complete the table below for the functions shown.

x	−2	−1	0	1	2	3
y = 3x + 4	−2					13
y = 3x + 2		−1			8	
y = 3x			0	3		
y = 3x − 2			−2	1		
y = 3x − 4		−7			2	

b Draw a grid with its x-axis from −2 to 3 and y-axis from −10 to 13.

c Draw the graph for each function in the table.

d What two properties do you notice about each line?

e Use the properties you have noticed to draw the graphs of the functions below.

    i $y = 3x + 2.5$ **ii** $y = 3x − 2.5$

5 By finding at least three suitable points, draw the graph of the function $4y + 2x = 8$.

6 By finding at least three suitable points, draw the graph of the function $3y + 4x = 24$.

Extension Work

Draw the graphs of:

    $y = 0.5x − 2$ and $y = 0.5x + 2$

Now draw, without any further calculations, the graphs of:

    $y = 0.5x − 1$ and $y = 0.5x + 3$

Gradient of a straight line

The **gradient** or steepness of a straight line is defined as:

the increase in the y coordinate for an increase of 1 in the x coordinate

Examples of gradients:

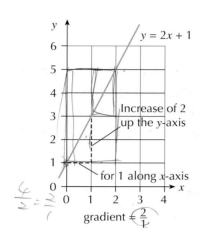

gradient $= \frac{2}{1}$

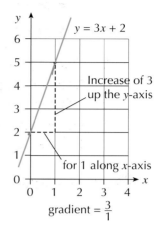

gradient $= \frac{3}{1}$

For any linear or straight-line equation of the form $y = mx + c$, you might have found the following from the previous exercise:

m is the gradient of the line

$y = mx + c$

c is the intercept of the line on the y-axis

The **intercept** c is where the line cuts the y-axis. It is the value of y when $x = 0$. It is sometimes called the constant.

Example 7.8 ▷

The diagram shows the graph of $y = 2x + 3$.

The gradient is $m = 2$.

The intercept is $c = 3$.

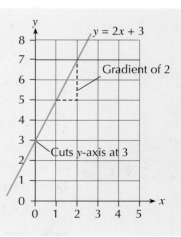

Exercise 7D

1 State the gradient of each of the following lines.

a 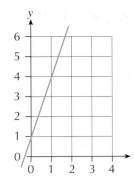   **b** 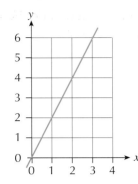   **c** 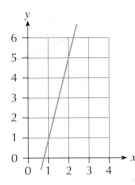   **d**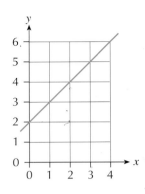

2 State the equation of the straight line with:

  a   a gradient of 3 passing through the y-axis at $(0, 5)$.

  b   a gradient of 2 passing through the y-axis at $(0, 7)$.

  c   a gradient of 1 passing through the y-axis at $(0, 4)$.

  d   a gradient of 7 passing through the y-axis at $(0, 15)$.

3 For each of the equations **a–f**:

  i   write down the gradient.

  ii   write down the intercept on the y-axis.

  iii   sketch a graph without plotting points.

      a $y = 2x + 1$ **b** $y = 3x - 4$ **c** $y = 4x + 1$

      d $y = 5x - 3$ **e** $y = x + 2$ **f** $y = 0.5x + 2$

4 For each of the following lines:

  i   find the gradient.

  ii   write down the coordinates of where the line crosses the y-axis.

  iii   write down the equation of the line.

a 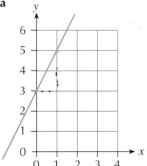   **b** 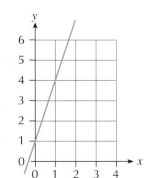   **c** 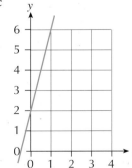   **d**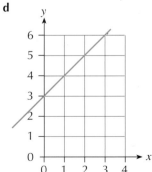

Find the equations of the graphs that pass through the following points.

Hint: Plot each pair of points on a coordinate grid. Work out the gradient and extend the line to cross the *y*-axis if necessary.

1 (0, 3) and (1, 4)

2 (0, 2) and (1, 5)

3 (1, 2) and (2, 3)

4 (1, 3) and (2, 7)

5 (2, 3) and (4, 7)

6 (3, 5) and (5, 11)

Real-life graphs

Graphs are all around us. They are found in newspapers, in advertisements, on TV, and so on. They usually involve relationships between data.

When you draw graphs from data, you have to plot coordinates to identify the line or lines. The axes must be labelled and marked accurately.

Distance–time graphs

A distance–time graph or **travel graph** uses data to describe a journey.

On a distance–time graph, a straight line shows **average speed**:

$$\text{Average speed} = \frac{\text{distance travelled}}{\text{time taken}}$$

Example 7.9 ▶

The graph shows an example of a journey.

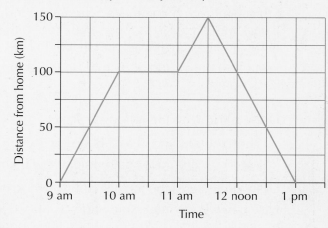

The following describe the stages in the journey:

- between 9 and 10 am, the average speed was 100 km/h (outward)

- between 10 and 11 am, the average speed was zero (stopped)

- between 11 and 11.30 am, the average speed was 100 km/h (outward)

- between 11.30 am and 1 pm, the average speed was 100 km/h (returning)

Example 7.10 ▷ I set off from home to pick up a dog from the vet. I travelled $1\frac{1}{2}$ hours at an average speed of 60 km/h. It took me 30 minutes to get the dog settled into my car. I then travelled back home at an average speed of 40 km/h as I did not want to jolt the dog. Draw a distance–time graph of the journey.

The key coordinates (time, distance from home) are:

● start from home at (0, 0)

● arrive at the vets at $(1\frac{1}{2}, 90)$ $(60 \times 1\frac{1}{2} = 90$ km)

● set off from the vet at (2, 90)

● arrive back home at $(4\frac{1}{4}, 0)$ $(90 \div 40 = 2\frac{1}{4}$ h)

Then plot the points and draw the graph:

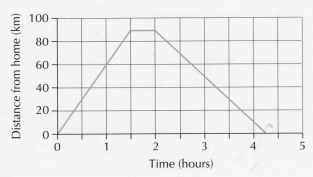

Exercise 7E

1 a Draw a grid with the following scale:

horizontal: time, 0 to 5 hours, at 1 cm to 30 min

vertical: distance from home, 0 to 100 km, at 1 cm to 20 km

b Draw on the grid the travel graph that shows the following:

I travelled from home to Manchester Airport, at an average speed of 50 km/h. It took me 2 hours. I stopped there for 30 minutes, and picked up Auntie Freda. I brought her straight back home, driving this time at an average speed of 40 km/h.

c I set off to the airport at 9 am. Use the graph to determine what time I arrived back home.

2 a Draw a grid with the following scale:

horizontal: time, 0 to 2 hours, at 1 cm to 20 min

vertical: distance from home, 0 to 60 km, at 1 cm to 10 km

b Draw on the grid the travel graph showing the following:

Elise travelled to meet Ken who was 60 km away. She left home at 11 am and travelled the first 40 km in 1 hour. She stopped for 30 minutes to buy a present, and then completed her journey in 20 minutes.

c What was Elise's average speed over the last 20 minutes?

3 a Draw a grid with the following scale:

horizontal: time, 0 to 60 minutes, at 1 cm to 5 min

vertical: depth, 0 to 200 cm, at 2 cm to 50 cm

b A swimming pool, 2 m deep, was filled with water from a hose. The pool was empty at the start and the depth of water in the pool increased at the rate of 4 cm/min. Complete the table below, showing the depth of water after various times.

Time (min)	0	10	25	40	50
Depth (cm)					

c Draw a graph to show the increase in depth of water against time.

4 Draw a graph for the depth of water in the same swimming pool if the water was poured in with a different hose that filled the pool more quickly, at the rate of 5 cm/min.

5 A different swimming pool that contained water was emptied by a pump at the rate of 30 gal/min. It took 3 hours for the pool to be emptied.

a Complete the following table that shows how much water is in the pool.

Time (min)	0	30	60	90	120	150	180
Water left (gal)	5400						

b Draw a graph to show the amount of water left in the pool against time.

Extension **Work**

At 11 am, Billy and Leon set off towards each other from different places 32 km apart. Billy cycled at 20 km/h and Leon walked at 5 km/h.

Draw distance–time graphs of their journeys on the same grid to find out:

1 the time at which they meet.

2 the time at which they are 12 km apart.

LEVEL BOOSTER

5
I can complete a mapping diagram to represent a linear function.

6
I can find the linear function that connects two sets of data.

I can complete a table of values for a linear relationship and use this to draw a graph of the relationship.

I can calculate the gradient of a straight line drawn on a coordinate grid and can distinguish between a positive and a negative gradient.

I can draw and interpret graphs that describe real-life situations.

I can plot a straight-line graph using the gradient–intercept method.

7
I can find an inverse function using a flow diagram.

I can plot graphs of the form $ax + by = c$.

I can find the equation of a line using the gradient–intercept method.

National Test questions

1 *2002 Paper 2*

I went for a walk.

The distance–time graph shows information about my walk.

Write out the statement below that describes my walk:

   I was walking faster and faster.

   I was walking slower and slower.

   I was walking north-east.

   I was walking at a steady speed.

   I was walking uphill.

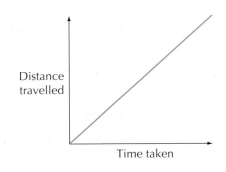

2 *2002 Paper 1*

The graph shows a straight line.
The equation of the line is $y = 3x$.

Does the point (25, 75) lie on the straight line $y = 3x$?

Explain how you know.

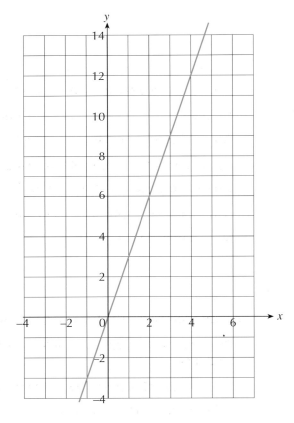

3 *2004 Paper 2*

Kali uses a running machine to keep fit.

The simplified distance–time graph shows how she used the machine during one run.

Use the graph to answer these questions.

a Between 0930 and 0940, what was her speed in **kilometres per hour**?

b Throughout the run, for how many **minutes** did she travel at this speed?

c At 0940, she increased her speed.

By how many kilometres per hour did she increase her speed?

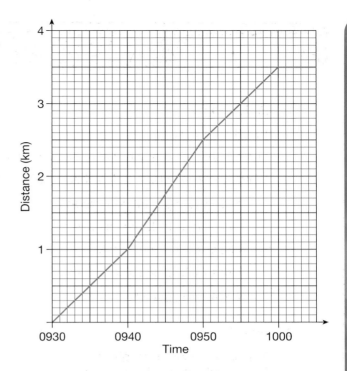

4 *2005 Paper 1*

The graph shows the straight line with equation $y = 3x - 4$.

a A point on the line $y = 3x - 4$ has an **x-coordinate of 50**.

What is the y-coordinate of this point?

b A point on the line $y = 3x - 4$ has a **y-coordinate of 50**.

What is the x-coordinate of this point?

c Is the point $(-10, -34)$ on the line $y = 3x - 4$?

Show how you know.

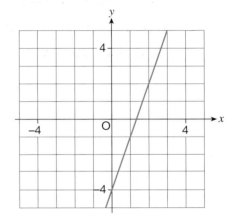

5 *2007 Paper 2*

The graph shows a straight line with **gradient 1**.

a On a copy of the graph, draw a different straight line with gradient 1.

b The equation of another straight line is $y = 5x + 20$.

Write down the missing number.

The straight line $y = 5x + 20$ passes through (0, __).

c A straight line is parallel to the line with equation $y = 5x + 20$.

It passes through the point (0, 10).

What is the equation of this straight line?

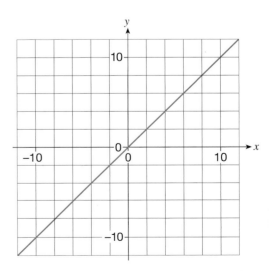

FM The M25

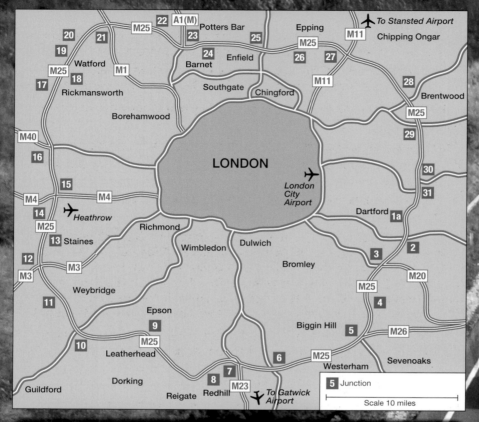

The M25 motorway is an orbital motorway, 117 miles long, that encircles London.

Construction of the first section began in 1973. Construction of the M25 continued in stages until its completion in 1986.

For most of its length, the motorway has six lanes (three in each direction), although there are a few short stretches which are four-lane and perhaps one-sixth is eight-lane, around the south-western corner. The motorway was widened to 10 lanes between junctions 12 and 14, and 12 lanes between junctions 14 and 15, in November 2005. The Highways Agency has plans to widen almost all of the remaining stretches of the M25 to eight lanes.

It is one of Europe's busiest motorways, with 205 000 vehicles a day recorded in 2006 between junctions 13 and 14 near London Heathrow Airport. This is, however, significantly fewer than the 257 000 vehicles a day recorded in 2002 on the A4 motorway at Saint-Maurice, in the suburbs of Paris, or the 216 000 vehicles a day recorded in 1998 on the A 100 motorway near the Funkturm in Berlin.

The road passes through several counties. Junctions 1–5 are in Kent, 6–14 in Surrey, 15–16 are in Buckinghamshire, 17–24 are in Hertfordshire, 25 in Greater London, 26–28 in Essex, 29 in Greater London and 30–31 in Essex.

Use the information on the left to help you answer these questions.

1 Look at the map of the M25.

  a How many other motorways intersect with the M25?

  b How many junctions are on the M25?

2 Use the scale shown.

  a The nearest point of the M25 to the centre of London is Potters Bar. Approximately how far from the centre of London is this?

  b The furthest point of the M25 from the centre of London is near junction 10. Approximately how far from the centre of London is this?

3 In 2008 approximately $\frac{2}{5}$ of the M25 was illuminated at night. How many miles is this?

4 The original design capacity of the M25 was 65 000 vehicles a day.

  a By how many vehicles per day does the busiest stretch exceed the design capacity?

  b Approximately how many vehicles a year use the M25 at its busiest point?

5 There are three airports near to the M25 – Heathrow, Gatwick and Stansted. From Stansted to Heathrow via the M25 (anti-clockwise) is 67 miles. From Heathrow to Gatwick (anti-clockwise) is 43 miles. From Gatwick to Stansted (anti-clockwise) is 73 miles. A shuttle bus drives from Stansted and calls at Heathrow and Gatwick then returns to Stansted. It does this four times a day. How far does it travel altogether?

6 The legal speed limit on the M25 is 70 mph. Assuming no hold ups how long would it take to drive around the M25 at the legal speed limit? Answer in hours and minutes.

  Distance = speed × time

7 Five miles is approximately equal to eight kilometres. How long, to the nearest kilometre, is the M25?

8 The longest traffic jam on the M25 was 22 miles long. What percentage of the total length was the length of the jam?

9 This table shows the lengths of the three longest orbital motorways in the world and the length of the M60, which is the only other orbital motorway in Britain.

City	Country	Road	Length (miles)
Berlin	Germany	B-10	122
London	England	M25	117
Cincinnati	USA	I-275	84
Manchester	England	M60	35

The formula for the radius of a circle given the circumference is $r = \dfrac{C}{2\pi}$

10 Near to Heathrow Airport what is the average number of vehicles using the M25 per hour each day? Give your answer to the nearest 100 vehicles.

  a Assuming the M25 is a circle with a circumference of 117 miles what would the radius be?

  b Making the same assumption, calculate the radii of the other orbital roads.

This chapter is going to show you

- How to multiply and divide by powers of 10
- How to round numbers to one or two decimal places
- How to check calculations by approximations
- How to use a calculator efficiently

What you should already know

- How to multiply and divide by 10, 100 and 1000
- How to round to the nearest 10, 100 and 1000
- How to use brackets and memory keys on a calculator
- How to use standard column methods for the four operations

Powers of 10

The nearest star, Proxima Centauri, is 40 653 234 200 000 kilometres from Earth. An atom is 0.000 000 000 1 metres wide.

When dealing with very large and very small numbers it is easier to **round** them and work with **powers of 10**. You will meet this later when you do work on standard form.

In this section you will multiply and divide by powers of 10 and round numbers to one or two decimal places.

Example 8.1

Multiply and divide:

a 0.937 **b** 2.363 **c** 0.002 81 by **i** 10 **ii** 10^4

a i $0.937 \times 10 = 9.37$, $0.937 \div 10 = 0.0937$
   ii $0.937 \times 10^4 = 9370$, $0.937 \div 10^4 = 0.000 093 7$

b i $2.363 \times 10 = 23.63$, $2.363 \div 10 = 0.2363$
   ii $2.363 \times 10^4 = 23 630$, $2.363 \div 10^4 = 0.000 236 3$

c i $0.002 81 \times 10 = 0.0281$, $0.002 81 \div 10 = 0.000 281$
   ii $0.002 81 \times 10^4 = 28.1$, $0.002 81 \div 10^4 = 0.000 000 281$

Example 8.2

Multiply and divide:

a 6 **b** 50 **c** 7.8 by **i** 0.1 **ii** 0.01

a i $6 \times 0.1 = 0.6$, $6 \div 0.1 = 60$ **ii** $6 \times 0.01 = 0.06$, $6 \div 0.01 = 600$
b i $50 \times 0.1 = 5$, $50 \div 0.1 = 500$ **ii** $50 \times 0.01 = 0.5$, $50 \div 0.01 = 5000$
c i $7.8 \times 0.1 = 0.78$, $7.8 \div 0.1 = 78$ **ii** $7.8 \times 0.01 = 0.078$, $7.8 \div 0.01 = 780$

Example 8.3 ▸ Work out:

  a 0.00737×10^2 **b** $54.1 \div 10^3$

  Round the answers to two decimal places.

  a $0.00737 \times 10^2 = 0.737$
     0.737 is 0.74 to two decimal places.

  b $54.1 \div 10^3 = 0.0541$
     0.0541 is 0.05 to two decimal places.

Exercise 8A

1 Multiply the numbers below by: **i** 10   **ii** 10^2
    a 5.3   **b** 0.79   **c** 24   **d** 5.063   **e** 0.003

2 Divide the numbers below by: **i** 10   **ii** 10^3
    a 83   **b** 4.1   **c** 457   **d** 6.04   **e** 34 781

3 Write down the answers to the following.
    a 3.1×10 **b** 6.78×10^2 **c** 0.56×10^3 **d** $34 \div 10^3$
    e $823 \div 10^2$ **f** $9.06 \div 10^3$ **g** 57.89×10^2 **h** $57.89 \div 10^2$
    i 0.038×10^3 **j** $0.038 \div 10$ **k** 0.05×10^5 **l** $543 \div 10^5$

4 Multiply the numbers below by: **i** 0.1   **ii** 0.01:
    a 4.5   **b** 56.2   **c** 0.04   **d** 400   **e** 0.7

5 Divide the numbers below by: **i** 0.1   **ii** 0.01:
    a 6.3   **b** 300   **c** 7   **d** 81.3   **e** 29

6 Calculate the following.
    a 6.34×100 **b** $47.3 \div 100$ **c** 66×1000 **d** $2.7 \div 1000$
    e $3076 \times 10\,000$ **f** $7193 \div 10\,000$ **g** 9.2×0.1 **h** $0.64 \div 0.1$
    i 0.84×0.01 **j** $8.71 \div 0.01$ **k** 3.76×10^2 **l** $2.3 \div 10^3$
    m 0.09×10^5 **n** $3.09 \div 10^3$ **o** 2.35×10^2 **p** $0.01 \div 10^4$

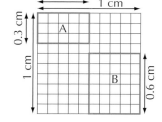

7 This grid represents a 1 cm × 1 cm square that has been split into 100 equal smaller squares. Give all your answers to the questions below in centimetres.
    a What is the area of each small square?
    b How many small squares are there inside rectangle A, and what is its area?
    c Use your answer to **b** to write down the answer to 0.3×0.5.
    d Rectangle B has an area of 0.3 cm². Use this fact and the diagram to write down the answer to $0.3 \div 0.6$.

8 Round these numbers to: **i** one decimal place.   **ii** two decimal places.
    a 4.722   **b** 3.097   **c** 2.634   **d** 1.932   **e** 0.784
    f 0.992   **g** 3.999   **h** 2.604   **i** 3.185   **j** 3.475

9 Multiply the numbers below by: **i** 10   **ii** 10²

    a 0.4717   **b** 2.6345   **c** 0.0482

    Round each answer to one decimal place.

10 Divide the numbers below by: **i** 10   **ii** 10²

    a 12.34   **b** 136.71   **c** 10.05

    Round each answer to one decimal place.

Extension | Work

1 Write down the answers to:

    a 5×10 **b** 70×10 **c** 0.8×10 **d** 6.3×10

2 Write down the answers to:

    a $5 \div 10$ **b** $70 \div 10$ **c** $0.8 \div 10$ **d** $6.3 \div 10$

3 Write down the answers to:

    a $5 \div 0.1$ **b** $70 \div 0.1$ **c** $0.8 \div 0.1$ **d** $6.3 \div 0.1$

4 Write down the answers to:

    a 5×0.1 **b** 70×0.1 **c** 0.8×0.1 **d** 6.3×0.1

5 Explain the connection between the answers to the above problems, particularly the connection between multiplying by 10 and dividing by 0.1.

6 What is a quick way to calculate $73 \div 0.01$?

Large numbers

Example 8.4 ▷

Write down in words the two numbers shown in the table below.

	10⁶	10⁵	10⁴	10³	10²	10	1
a	6	0	5	8	7	0	2
b	1	7	0	0	0	5	6

Consider the numbers in blocks of three digits, that is:

    6   058   702

    1   700   056

In words, the numbers are:

a   Six million, fifty-eight thousand, seven hundred and two

b   One million, seven hundred thousand, and fifty-six

Example 8.5 ▷

The United Kingdom is said to have a population of 61 million. What is the largest and smallest population this could mean?

As the population is given to the nearest million, the actual population could be as much as half a million either way. So the population is between $60\frac{1}{2}$ million and $61\frac{1}{2}$ million, or 60 500 000 and 61 500 000.

Example 8.6

a The bar chart shows the annual profit for a large company over the previous five years. Estimate the profit each year.

b The company chairman says, 'Profit in 2008 was nearly 50 million pounds.' Is the chairman correct?

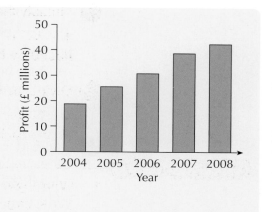

a The profit was:

in 2004, about 19 million pounds
in 2005, about 25 million pounds
in 2006, about 31 million pounds
in 2007, about 39 million pounds
in 2008, about 43 million pounds

b The chairman is wrong, as in 2008 the profit was nearer 40 million pounds.

Exercise 8B

1 Write the following numbers in words.

a 3 452 763   **b** 2 047 809   **c** 12 008 907   **d** 3 006 098

2 Write the following numbers using figures.

a Four million, forty-three thousand, two hundred and seven
b Nineteen million, five hundred and two thousand, and thirty-seven
c One million, three hundred and two thousand, and seven

3 The bar chart shows the population of some countries in the European Community (the actual figures may vary). Estimate the population of each country.

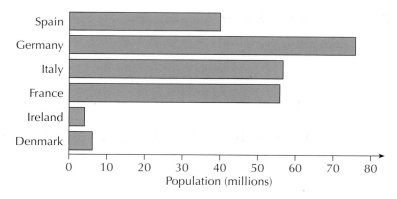

4 Round the following numbers to: **i** the nearest ten thousand. **ii** the nearest hundred thousand. **iii** the nearest million.

a 3 547 812   **b** 9 722 106   **c** 3 042 309   **d** 15 698 999

FM **5** There are 2 452 800 people out of work. The government says, 'Unemployment is just over two million'. The opposition says, 'Unemployment is still nearly three million'. Who is correct and why?

6 There are 8 million people living in London. What are the highest and lowest figures that the population of London could be?

7 a Copy this list of powers of 10. Write the missing powers of 10 in the boxes.

10^6 10^5 10^4 10^3 10^2 10^1 $10^\square$ $10^\square$ $10^\square$ $10^\square$ $10^\square$

b Use a calculator to work out, or write down, these numbers in full. The first two have been done.

   i $10^4 = 10\,000$ **ii** $10^{-1} = 0.1$ **iii** $10^2 = \dots$

   iv $10^{-2} = \dots$ **v** $10^{-4} = \dots$ **vi** $10^0 = \dots$

8 Standard form is a way of writing large numbers in a more manageable form. For example, 3.1×10^6 means $3.1 \times 1\,000\,000 = 3\,100\,000$, and $4.54 \times 10^9 = 4\,540\,000\,000$.

Write these standard form numbers in full.

  a 2.9×10^7 **b** 3.56×10^5 **c** 1.17×10^8 **d** 2.2×10^6

  e 9.5×10^8 **f** 8.3×10^6 **g** 2.31×10^{10} **h** 5.04×10^5

Extension **Work**

The common prefixes for units are 'kilo', as in kilogram (1000 grams), 'centi', as in centilitre (one-hundredth of a litre), etc.

This table gives the main prefixes and their equivalent powers.

Prefix	giga	mega	kilo	centi	milli	micro	nano	pico
Power	10^9	10^6	10^3	10^{-2}	10^{-3}	10^{-6}	10^{-9}	10^{-12}

For example, $7\,000\,000\,000$ grams would be 7 gigagrams, although this is more likely to be written as 7 kt, which is 7 kilotonnes.

1 Write the following quantities in a simpler form using words.

  a   0.004 grams   **b**   8 000 000 watts   **c**   0.75 litres

2 Use the Internet or a reference book to find out the common abbreviations for the prefixes in the table. For example, the abbreviation for 'kilo' is k, as in 6 kg.

3 Use the Internet or a reference book to find out how far light travels in 1 nanosecond.

Estimations

Example 8.7   Estimate the answers to:

  a   12% of 923   **b** $\dfrac{11.2 + 53.6}{18.7 - 9.6}$ **c** $324 \div 59$

  a   Round to 10% of $900 = 90$

  b   Round to $\dfrac{10 + 50}{20 - 10} = \dfrac{60}{10} = 6$

  c   Round to $300 \div 60 = 5$

Example 8.8 ▷ For each question, one of the answers given in the brackets is correct. Without using a calculator, choose the answer and give reasons for your choice.

a √18 (4.24, 5.24, 6.24)   **b** 6 ÷ 0.7 (5.8, 8.6, 65)

c 29 × 45 (905, 1250, 1305)

a √18 must be between √16 and √25, so 4.24 is the best choice.

b 6 ÷ 0.7 must be bigger than 6, but not as large as 65, so 8.6 is the best choice.

c The answer is bigger than 30 × 40 ≈ 1200, but must end in 9 × 5 = ?5, so 1305 is the best answer.

Exercise 8C

1 Estimate the value the arrow is pointing at in each of these.

a   0.7   3.7   b   0   6.3   c   −20   10

2 Estimate the answers to the following.

a	23% of 498	**b**	√40	**c**	6.72^2	**d**	523 × 69
e	$\frac{1}{3}$ of 320	**f**	1.75 × 16	**g**	0.072 × 311	**h**	287 × 102
i	$\frac{18.3 - 5.2}{10.7 + 8.6}$	**j**	$\frac{178 \times 18}{21}$	**k**	$\frac{39.2 \times 17.5}{12.1 \times 5.8}$	**l**	$\frac{29.3^2}{17.8 - 5.9}$
m	0.082 × 0.61	**n**	0.69 ÷ 0.09	**o**	$(0.052)^2$	**p**	74% of 442

3 Pick out the answer given in brackets that is the most appropriate for the calculations shown and justify your choice.

a √20 (3.5, 4.5, 5.5)   **b** 49 × 57 (2793, 2937, 3033)

c 454 × 0.46 (150, 210, 280)   **d** 8.7 ÷ 0.01 (8, 87, 870)

e 7.07^2 (48, 50, 52)   **f** 44 × 99 (3456, 4356, 5346)

4 Using estimates, write which of these statements is likely to be correct.

a The mean of 34, 56, 71, 82, 95 is between 40 and 90.

b In the most recent election 46% voted Labour, 37% voted Conservative and 16% voted for other parties (46% + 37% + 16% = 99%).

c $(5.2915)^2 = 38$

d $7 \times \frac{23}{5} = 23.2$

e Eight packets of crisps at 47p per packet costs £4.14.

Extension Work

1 Without working out areas or counting squares, explain why the area of the square shown must be between 36 and 64 grid squares.

2 Now calculate the area of the square.

3 Using an 8 × 8 grid, draw a square with an area of exactly 50 grid squares.

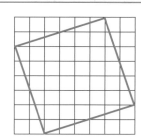

Working with decimals

Example 8.9 Round the following numbers to: **i** two decimal places.   **ii** three decimal places.

   a   8.2625   **b**   0.087 63   **c**   3.6989

   a   8.2625 = 8.26 (2 dp) = 8.263 (3 dp)

   b   0.087 63 = 0.09 (2 dp) = 0.088 (3 dp)

   c   3.6989 = 3.70 (2 dp) = 3.699 (3 dp)

Example 8.10 Calculate the area of the following shapes, giving your answers to one decimal place.

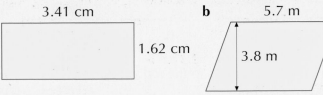

a 3.41 cm   1.62 cm   **b** 5.7 m 3.8 m

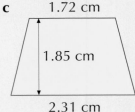

c 1.72 cm   1.85 cm   2.31 cm

   a   Area of a rectangle = length × width
        = 3.41 × 1.62 = 5.5242 = 5.5 cm² (1 dp)

   b   Area of a parallelogram = base × height
        = 5.7 × 3.8 = 21.66 = 21.7 m² (1 dp)

   c   Area of a trapezium = half × (sum of parallel sides) × distance between them
        = 0.5 × (1.72 + 2.31) × 1.85 = 3.727 75 = 3.7 cm² (1 dp)

Exercise 8D

1 Round the numbers below to: **i** two decimal places.   **ii** three decimal places.

a 4.5682	**b** 8.7028	**c** 11.4239	**d** 42.7985
e 19.879 36	**f** 12.0969	**g** 23.9071	**h** 7.0505
i 7.2599	**j** 19.3008	**k** 6.0699	**l** 12.8539

2 Use a calculator to work out the following, then round the answers to two decimal places.

a $1 \div 55$	**b** $1 \div 17$	**c** $2 \div 17$	**d** $3 \div 17$
e $\sqrt{456}$	**f** $5 \div 63$	**g** 5.287^2	**h** $\sqrt{3.54^2 + 2.61^2}$

3 There are 1000 grams in a kilogram. Calculate the mass of the following shopping baskets (work in kilograms).

   a   3.2 kg of apples, 454 g of jam, 750 g of lentils, 1.2 kg of flour

   b   1.3 kg of sugar, 320 g of strawberries, 0.65 kg of rice

4 In an experiment a beaker of water has a mass of 1.104 kg. The beaker alone weighs 0.125 kg. What is the mass of water in the beaker?

5 A rectangle is 2.35 m by 43 cm. What is its perimeter (in metres)?

6 A piece of string is 5 m long. Pieces of length 84 cm, 1.23 m and 49 cm are cut from it. How much string is left (in metres)?

7 A large container of oil contains 20 litres. Over five days the following amounts are poured from the container:

2.34 litres, 1.07 litres, 0.94 litres, 3.47 litres, 1.2 litres

How much oil is left in the container?

8 Calculate the area of the following shapes, giving your answers to one decimal place.

a
4.07 cm

2.34 cm

b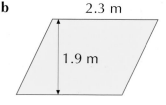
2.3 m

1.9 m

c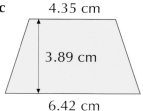
4.35 cm

3.89 cm

6.42 cm

9 π (pi) is a number that is used in calculating areas and circumferences of circles. It cannot be found exactly, but many people have tried to find a simple fraction or calculation for giving the value of π to several decimal places.

The value of π to nine decimal places is 3.141 592 654. Use your calculator to evaluate the following approximations to π and round them to two, three and four decimal places.

a $22 \div 7$ **b** $377 \div 120$ **c** $355 \div 113$

d Which do you think is the best approximation?

Extension Work

Much as fractions and decimals show the same thing, centimetres and millimetres both show lengths. The first length shown on the rule below, AB, can be given as 1.6 cm, 16 mm or $1\frac{3}{5}$ cm.

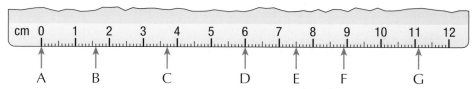

Write the distances shown:

i in centimetres as a decimal.   **ii** in millimetres.   **iii** in centimetres as a fraction.

1 AC   **2** BD   **3** CE   **4** DE   **5** EF   **6** EG

Efficient calculations

 It is important that you know how to use your calculator. You should be able to use the basic functions (×, ÷, +, −) and the square, square root and brackets keys. You have also met the memory and sign-change keys. This exercise introduces the fraction and power keys.

Example 8.11 ▷

Use a calculator to work out:

a $(1\frac{3}{10} - \frac{4}{5}) \times \frac{3}{4}$

b $\dfrac{1\frac{2}{5} + 1\frac{1}{4}}{2\frac{1}{2} - 1\frac{7}{8}}$

a Using the fraction button $\blacksquare\!\!/\!\!\blacksquare$ and the arrows ◀ ▲ ▶ ▼, type in the calculation as:

[ ] [SHIFT] [$\blacksquare\!\!/\!\!\blacksquare$] [1] [▶] [3] [▼] [1] [0] [▶] [−] [$\blacksquare\!\!/\!\!\blacksquare$] [4] [▼] [5] [ )] [×] [$\blacksquare\!\!/\!\!\blacksquare$] [3] [▼] [4] [=]

The display should show $\frac{3}{8}$. Note that the way this is keyed in may be different on your calculator.

b Using brackets and the fraction buttons gives an answer of $4\frac{6}{25}$ (may also display as $\frac{106}{25}$).

To convert from an improper fraction ($\frac{106}{25}$) to a mixed number ($4\frac{6}{25}$), press [SHIFT] [S↔D] .

Example 8.12 ▷

Use a calculator to work out:

a 5^6 b $\sqrt[3]{729}$ c $\sqrt{19.5^2 - 7.5^2}$

a Using the power button, [$x^\blacksquare$], the answer should be 15 625.

b This can be keyed in as:

[SHIFT] [$x^\blacksquare$] [3] [▶] [7] [2] [9] [=]

The answer is 9. Make sure you can use your calculator to find this answer.

c Using the square root, bracket and square keys the answer should be 18. For example, the following are two ways to key the problem in to the calculator:

or
[√] [( ] [1] [9] [.] [5] [x^2] [−] [7] [.] [5] [x^2] [ )] [=]
[( ] [1] [9] [.] [5] [x^2] [−] [7] [.] [5] [x^2] [ )] [√] [=]

Exercise 8E

1 Use the bracket and/or memory keys on your calculator to work out each of these.

a $\dfrac{38.7 - 23.1}{3.82 + 1.38}$ b $\sqrt{4.1^2 - 0.9^2}$ c $9.75 \div (3.2 - 1.7)$

2 Use the fraction key on your calculator to work out each of these (give your answer as a mixed number or a fraction in its simplest form).

a $\frac{1}{8} + \frac{3}{5} + \frac{3}{16}$ b $1\frac{2}{3} + 2\frac{2}{9} - \frac{5}{6}$ c $\frac{3}{8} \times \frac{4}{15} \div \frac{4}{5}$

d $(2\frac{1}{5} + 3\frac{3}{4}) \times 2\frac{1}{7}$ e $\dfrac{2\frac{1}{4} - 1\frac{2}{7}}{1\frac{1}{2} + 1\frac{1}{14}}$ f $\dfrac{4\frac{3}{5} - 3\frac{2}{3}}{3\frac{3}{8} - 1\frac{4}{5}}$

g $(1\frac{3}{4})^2$ h $\sqrt{3\frac{11}{16} - 1\frac{7}{16}}$ i $(2\frac{2}{3} + 1\frac{1}{8}) \div \frac{7}{8}$

6

3 Use the power, cube and cube root keys on your calculator to work out each of these (round your answers to one decimal place if necessary).

a 4^6

b 2.3^3

c $\sqrt[3]{1331}$

d $\sqrt{3^4 + 4^3}$

e 2^{10}

f $4 \times (5.78)^3$

g 3×7.2^2

h $(3 \times 7.2)^2$

i $\sqrt{8.9^2 - 3.1^2}$

4 A time given in hours and minutes can be put into a calculator as a fraction. For example, 3 hours and 25 minutes is $3\frac{25}{60}$, which is entered as:

Using the fraction button on your calculator and remembering that $\frac{1}{3}$ hour = 20 minutes, $\frac{1}{5}$ hour = 12 minutes, and so on, do the following time problems (give your answers in hours and minutes).

a   Add 2 hours and 25 minutes to 3 hours and 55 minutes.

b   Subtract 1 hour 48 minutes from 3 hours 24 minutes.

c   Multiply 1 hour 32 minutes by 5.

d   You can also use the ○'" button to input time so 3 ○'" 2 5 displays as 3°25′0″. Repeat parts **a**, **b** and **c** using this button.

5 Most square roots and cube roots cannot be given as an exact value, so we have to approximate them. The following are a selection of square roots and cube roots of whole numbers. You do not know if the number is a square root or a cube root. Use your calculator to find out if it is a square root or a cube root, and the number for which it is either of these (**a** and **b** are done for you below).

a   1.414 21

b   2.154 43

c   3.419 95

d   2.236 07

e   4.472 14

f   1.442 25

g   2.289 43

h   5.477 23

a $1.414\,21^2 = 1.999\,990$, so $\sqrt{2} \approx 1.414\,21$

b $2.154\,43^3 = 9.999\,935$, so $\sqrt[3]{10} \approx 2.154\,43$

Extension **Work**

On your calculator you may have a key or a function above a key marked x^{-1}.

Find out what this key does. For example, on some calculators you can key:

$\underset{x!}{3 \; \text{SHIFT} \; x^{-1}}$ and the display shows 6,

and you can key:

$\underset{x!}{7 \; \text{SHIFT} \; x^{-1}}$ which gives a display of 5040.

Similarly, investigate what the key marked x^{-1} does.

Multiplying and dividing decimals

Example 8.13 ▷

Work out:

a 8.6×6.5 **b** 1.43×3.4

a Firstly, estimate the answer, that is $9 \times 6 = 54$. This problem is done using a box method, breaking the two numbers into their whole number and fractions. Each are multiplied together and the totals added:

×	8	0.6
6	48	3.6
0.5	4	0.3

Sum of multiplications

$$\begin{array}{r} 48 \\ 4 \\ 3.6 \\ 0.3 \\ \hline 55.9 \end{array}$$

The answer is 55.9.

b Firstly, estimate the answer, that is $1.5 \times 3 = 4.5$, to show where the decimal point will be. This problem is then done using standard column methods without decimal points:

$$\begin{array}{r} 143 \\ \times\ \ 34 \\ \hline 572 \\ 4290 \\ \hline 4862 \end{array}$$

The position of the decimal point is shown by the estimate, and so the answer is 4.862.

Note that the number of decimal points in the answer is the same as in the original problem, that is $1.\underline{43} \times 3.\underline{4} = 4.\underline{862}$.

Example 8.14 ▷

Work out:

a $76.8 \div 16$ **b** $156 \div 2.4$

a Firstly, estimate the answer, that is $80 \div 16 = 5$.
Now consider the problem as $768 \div 16$:

$$\begin{array}{rl} 768 & \\ -\ 640 & (40 \times 16) \\ \hline 128 & \\ -\ \ 64 & (4 \times 16) \\ \hline 64 & \\ -\ \ 64 & (4 \times 16) \\ \hline 0 & (48 \times 16) \end{array}$$

The position of the decimal point is shown by the estimate, and so the answer is 4.8.

b Firstly, estimate the answer, that is $150 \div 3 = 50$.
Now consider the problem as $1560 \div 24$:

$$\begin{array}{rl} 1560 & \\ -\ 960 & (40 \times 24) \\ \hline 600 & \\ -\ 480 & (20 \times 24) \\ \hline 120 & \\ -\ 120 & (5 \times 24) \\ \hline 0 & (65 \times 24) \end{array}$$

The position of the decimal point is shown by the estimate, and so the answer is 65.

As you become used to this method of division, you can start to take away larger 'chunks' each time. For example, in **b** you could take away 60×24 instead of 40×24 and then 20×24. This will improve your mental multiplication too!

Exercise 8F

1 Without using a calculator, and using any other method you are happy with, work out the following.

a	6.3×9.4	**b**	5.8×4.5	**c**	2.7×2.7	**d**	1.4×12.6
e	0.78×2.5	**f**	1.26×3.5	**g**	2.58×6.5	**h**	0.74×0.22

2 Without using a calculator, and using any other method you are happy with, work out the following.

a	$78.4 \div 14$	**b**	$7.92 \div 22$	**c**	$24 \div 3.2$	**d**	$12.6 \div 3.6$
e	$143 \div 5.5$	**f**	$289 \div 3.4$	**g**	$57 \div 3.8$	**h**	$10.8 \div 0.24$

3 Roller ball pens cost £1.23 each. How much will 72 pens cost?

4 Number fans cost 65p each. How many can be bought for £78?

Extension Work

The box method can be used to do quite complicated decimal multiplications. For example, 2.56×4.862 can be worked out as follows:

$\times$	**4**	**0.8**	**0.06**	**0.002**	**Sum of row**
2	8	1.6	0.12	0.004	9.724
0.5	2	0.4	0.03	0.001	2.431
0.06	0.24	0.048	0.0036	0.000 12	0.291 72
				Total	12.446 72

Use the box method to calculate 1.47×2.429.

Check your answer with a calculator.

LEVEL BOOSTER

5
I can round numbers to one decimal place.
I can use bracket, square and square root keys on a calculator.
I can add and subtract decimals up to two decimal places.
I can multiply and divide decimals up to two decimal places.

6
I can multiply and divide by powers of 10.
I can approximate decimals when solving numerical problems.

7
I can round numbers to one significant figure.
I can make estimates by rounding numbers to one significant figure.
I can multiply and divide decimals by writing them as equivalent problems involving integers.

1 *2002 Paper 1*

a The number 6 is halfway between 4.5 and 7.5.

What are the missing numbers below?

The number 6 is halfway between 2.8 and …

The number 6 is halfway between −12 and …

b Work out the number that is halfway between 27 × 38 and 33 × 38.

FM **2** *2002 Paper 2*

A company sells and processes films of two different sizes.
The tables show how much the company charges.

Film size: 24 photos	
Cost of each film	£2.15
Postage	Free
Cost to print film	£0.99
Postage of each film	60p

Film size: 36 photos	
Cost of each film	£2.65
Postage	Free
Cost to print film	£2.89
Postage of each film	60p

I want to take 360 photos. I need to buy the film, pay for the film to be printed and pay for the postage.

a Is it cheaper to use all films of 24 photos or all films of 36 photos?

b How much cheaper is it?

3 *2006 Paper 1*

Copy these multiplication grids and write in the missing numbers.

×	8	
9	72	
−6		30

×	0.2	
3		1.2
		6

4   *2005 Paper 1*

A three-digit number is **multiplied** by a two-digit number.

How many digits could the answer have?

Write the minimum number and the maximum number of digits that the answer could have.

You **must** show your working.

FM Taxes

There are two types of taxes – direct tax and indirect tax.

Direct tax is tax taken directly from what you earn, for example Income tax.

Indirect tax is tax taken from what you spend, for example VAT.

Direct tax

Income tax

Each person has a tax allowance. This is the amount they are allowed to earn without paying income tax.

Tax rates

Basic rate: First £36 000 of taxable pay is taxed at the rate of 20%.

Higher rate: Earnings above this amount are taxed at the rate of 40%.

Example 1

Mr Gallagher's tax allowance is £5435.

He earns £25 000.

His taxable pay is £25 000 – £5435 = £19 565

So his income tax is:

Basic rate: 20% of £19 565 = £3913

Example 2

Mrs Senior's tax allowance is £5435.

She earns £70 000.

Her taxable pay is £70 000 – £5435 = £64 565

So her income tax is:

Basic rate: 20% of £36 000 = £7200

Higher rate: 40% of (£64 565 – £36 000)
= 40% of 28 565 = £11 426

So her total income tax is £18 626

Indirect tax

VAT

Value added tax is charged at three different rates on goods and services.

Standard rate (17.5%)

You pay VAT on most goods and services in the UK at the standard rate.

Reduced rate (5%)

In some cases, a reduced rate of VAT is charged, for example children's car seats and domestic fuel or power.

Zero rate (0%)

There are some goods on which you do not pay any VAT, for example:

- Food
- Books, newspapers and magazines
- Children's clothes
- Special exempt items, such as equipment for disabled people

Example 3

Work out the 17.5% VAT charged on a bicycle costing £180 excluding VAT.

10% of £180 = £18

5% of £180 = £9

2.5% of £180 = £4.50

So 17.5% of £180 = £31.50

Use the information on taxes to answer these questions.

1 Hollie earnt £16 000 last year. This year she had a pay increase of 5%. How much does she earn now?

2 Miss Howe receives her gas bill. What is the rate of VAT that she will have to pay?

3 Mr Legg buys a wheelchair. What is the rate of VAT that he pays?

4 Bradley bought a new child seat. The cost was £90 excluding VAT.

a What rate of VAT is charged?

b Work out the total cost of the child seat including VAT.

5 Kerry bought a mobile phone. The cost was £260 excluding 17.5% VAT.

Work out the cost including VAT.

6 Mrs Pritchard earns £24 000. Her tax allowance is £6000. She pays tax on the rest at 20%.

a How much does she pay tax on?

b How much tax does she pay?

7 Miss France earns £14 000. Her tax allowance is £5600. She pays tax on the rest at 20%.

a How much does she pay tax on?

b How much does she earn after the tax is deducted?

8 Sohaib earns £5500. His tax allowance is £6200.

a Explain why he does not pay any tax.

b How much more can he earn before he has to pay tax?

9 Mr Key earns £80 000 as a locksmith. His tax allowance is £5500. He pays tax on the first £36 000 of taxable income at 20%. He then pays 40% tax on the remainder.

How much tax does he pay altogether?

10 Miss Spent earns £72 000. Her tax allowance is £9000. She pays tax on the first £36 000 of taxable income at 20%. She then pays 40% tax on the remainder.

How much does she earn after the tax is deducted?

This chapter is going to show you	**What you should already know**
<ul><li>How to recognise congruent shapes</li><li>How to transform 2-D shapes by combinations of reflections, rotations and translations</li><li>How to enlarge a shape by a negative scale factor</li><li>How to recognise planes of symmetry in 3-D shapes</li><li>How to solve problems using ratio</li></ul>	<ul><li>How to reflect a 2-D shape in a mirror line</li><li>How to rotate a 2-D shape about a point</li><li>How to translate a 2-D shape</li><li>How to enlarge a shape by a scale factor</li><li>How to recognise reflective symmetry in 2-D shapes</li><li>How to use ratio</li></ul>

Congruent shapes

All the triangles on the grid below are reflections, rotations or translations of triangle A. What do you notice about them?

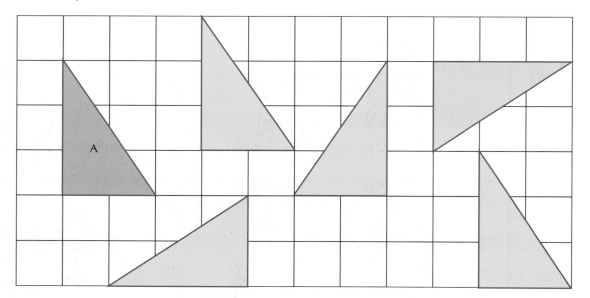

You should remember that the **image** triangles are exactly the same shape and size as the **object** triangle A.

Two shapes are said to be **congruent** if they are exactly the same shape and size. Reflections, rotations and translations all produce images that are congruent to the original object. For shapes that are congruent, all the corresponding sides and angles are equal.

Example 9.1 ▶ Which two shapes below are congruent?

a   b   c   d

Shapes **b** and **d** are exactly the same shape and size, so **b** and **d** are congruent.
Tracing paper can be used to check that two shapes are congruent.

Exercise 9A

1. For each pair of shapes below, state whether they are congruent or not (use tracing paper to help if you are not sure).

a   b   c

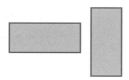
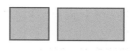
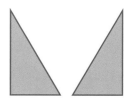

d   e   f

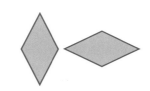
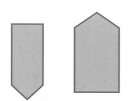
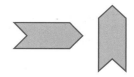

2. Which pairs of shapes on the grid below are congruent?

129

3 Which of the shapes below are congruent?

a   b   c   d

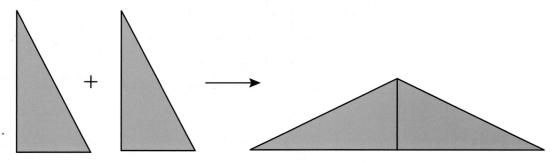

4 Two congruent right-angled triangles are placed together with two of their equal sides touching to make another shape (an isosceles triangle), as shown on the diagram below.

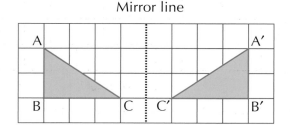

   a   How many different shapes can you make from the two triangles? To help, you can cut out the triangles from a piece of card.

   b   Repeat the activity using two congruent isosceles triangles.

   c   Repeat the activity using two congruent equilateral triangles.

Extension Work

The four-by-four pinboard is divided into two congruent shapes.

1   Use square-dotted paper to show the number of different ways this can be done.

2   Can you divide the pinboard into four congruent shapes?

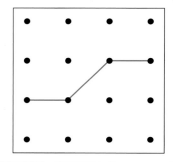

Combinations of transformations

The three single **transformations** you have met so far and the notation that we use to explain these transformations are shown below.

Reflection

Mirror line

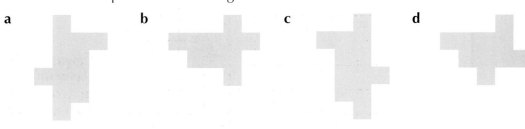

Triangle ABC is **mapped** onto triangle A'B'C' by a reflection in the mirror line. The object and the image are congruent.

Rotation

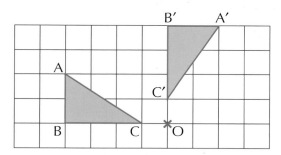

Triangle ABC is mapped onto triangle A′B′C′ by a rotation of 90° clockwise about the centre of rotation O. The object and the image are congruent.

Translation

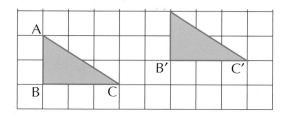

Triangle ABC is mapped onto triangle A′B′C′ by a translation of 5 units to the right, followed by 1 unit up. The object and the image are congruent.

The example below shows how a shape can be transformed by a combination of two of the above transformations.

Example 9.2

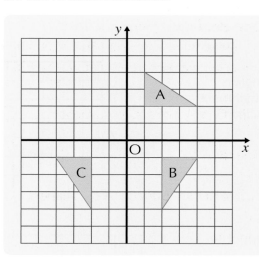

Triangle A is mapped onto triangle C by two combined transformations. Firstly, a rotation of 90° clockwise about the origin O maps A onto B. Secondly, a reflection in the y-axis maps B onto C. So triangle A is mapped onto triangle C by a rotation of 90° clockwise about the origin O, followed by a reflection in the y-axis.

Exercise 9B

Tracing paper and a mirror will be useful for this exercise.

1 Copy the diagram onto squared paper:

   a Reflect shape A in mirror line 1 to give shape B.

   b Reflect shape B in mirror line 2 to give shape C.

   c Describe the single transformation that maps shape A onto shape C.

Mirror line 1   Mirror line 2

2 Copy the diagram opposite onto squared paper.

  a Reflect shape A in the *x*-axis to give shape B.

  b Reflect shape B in the *y*-axis to give shape C.

  c Describe the single transformation that maps shape A onto shape C.

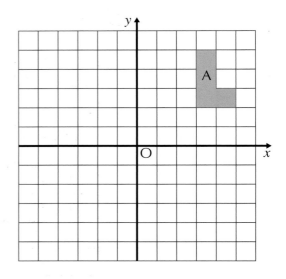

3 Copy the diagram opposite onto squared paper.

  a Rotate shape A 90° clockwise about the origin O to give shape B.

  b Rotate shape B 90° clockwise about the origin O to give shape C.

  c Describe the single transformation that maps shape A onto shape C.

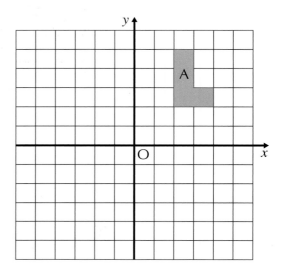

4 Copy the diagram opposite onto squared paper.

  a Translate shape A 3 units to the right, followed by 2 units up, to give shape B.

  b Translate shape B 4 units to the right, followed by 1 unit down, to give shape C.

  c Describe the single transformation that maps shape A onto shape C.

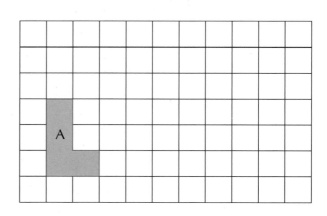

5 Copy the triangles A, B, C, D, E and F onto a square grid, as shown.

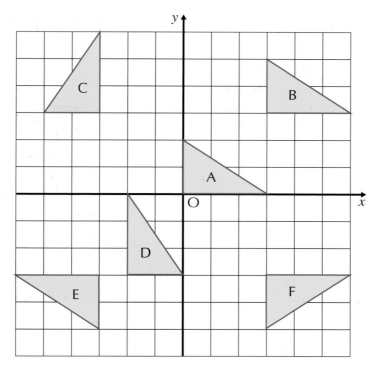

a Find a single transformation that will map:

    i A onto B   **ii** E onto F   **iii** B onto E   **iv** C onto B

b Find a combination of two transformations that will map:

    i A onto C   **ii** B onto F   **iii** F onto D   **iv** B onto E

c Find other examples of combined transformations for different pairs of triangles.

6 On squared paper, show how repeated reflections of a rectangle generate a tessellating pattern.

Extension Work

1 Copy the congruent 'T' shapes A, B, C and D onto a square grid, as shown.

Find a combination of two transformations that will map:

    a A onto B   **b** A onto C

    c A onto D   **d** B onto C

    e B onto D   **f** C onto D

2 Use ICT software, such as LOGO, to transform shapes by using various combinations of reflections, rotations and translations. Print out some examples and present them on a poster.

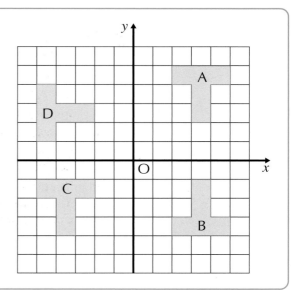

Enlargements

A pinhole camera projects an image of an object onto a screen. The image is inverted as it has been produced by a negative enlargement.

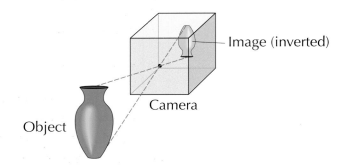

In the diagram below, triangle ABC is **enlarged** by a **scale factor** of 2 to give triangle A'B'C'.

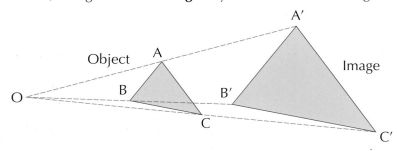

Lines called rays or guidelines are drawn from O through A, B, C to A', B', C'. Here the scale factor is given as 2. So OA' = 2 × OA, OB' = 2 × OB, OC' = 2 × OC. The sides of △A'B'C' are twice the corresponding sides of triangle ABC.

We say that **object** triangle ABC is enlarged by a **scale factor** of 2 about the **centre of enlargement** O to give **image** triangle A'B'C'.

The object and image are on the *same side* of O. The scale factor is positive. This is positive enlargement.

Under any enlargement, corresponding angles on the object and image are the same.

Negative enlargement

The diagram below shows object flag A enlarged by a scale factor of −2 to give image flag B.

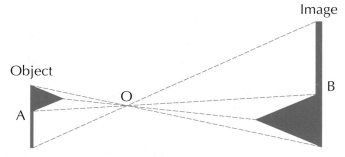

The size of the scale factor is 2 (ignoring the minus sign), so the lengths of the rays from O to flag B are double the lengths of the corresponding rays to flag A. The length of each line on flag B is double the corresponding line on flag A.

However, this time the image is inverted (upside-down) and on the *other side* of O because the scale factor is negative (it has a minus). This is negative enlargement.

Negative enlargement on a grid

When enlargement is on a grid, the principles are the same. The grid may or may not have coordinate axes, and the centre of enlargement may be anywhere on the grid.

The grid means that you may not need to draw rays to find the image points.

Example 9.3 ▶ Enlarge △XYZ by a scale factor of –2 about the centre of enlargement O.

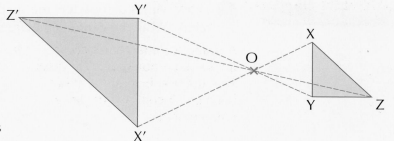

- Draw rays from points X, Y, Z to O.
- Measure their lengths and multiply by 2.
- Continue the rays beyond O by these new lengths to give points X′, Y′ and Z′.
- Join these points to give △X′Y′Z′.

△XYZ has been enlarged by a scale factor of –2 about the centre of enlargement O to give △X′Y′Z′.

Example 9.4 ▶ Enlarge △ABC on the coordinate grid by a scale factor of –3 about the origin (0, 0).

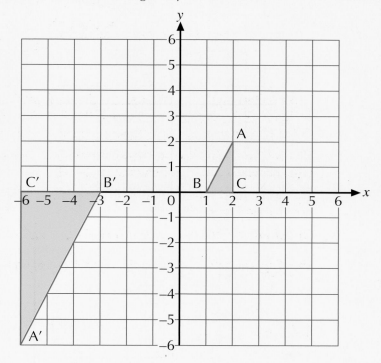

- Draw rays, or count grid units in the *x* and *y* directions, from points A, B, C to the origin.
- Multiply the ray lengths or *x*, *y* units by 3.
- Continue beyond the origin by these new lengths or units to give points A′, B′, C′.
- Join these points to give △A′B′C′.

△ABC has been enlarged by a scale factor of –3 about the origin (0, 0) to give △A′B′C′.

If a negative enlargement is about the *origin* of a grid, as in this case, the coordinates of the image shape are the coordinates of the object shape multiplied by the negative scale factor. So here:

object coordinates:	A(2, 2)	B(1, 0)	C(2, 0)
image coordinates:	A′(–6, –6)	B′(–3, 0)	C′(–6, 0)

Exercise 9C

1. Draw copies of (or trace) the shapes below and enlarge each one by the given scale factor about the centre of enlargement O.

   a   scale factor −2   **b**   scale factor −3   **c**   scale factor −2

2. Copy the diagrams below onto a coordinate grid and enlarge each one by the given scale factor about the origin (0, 0).

   a   scale factor −2   **b**   scale factor −2   **c**   scale factor −3

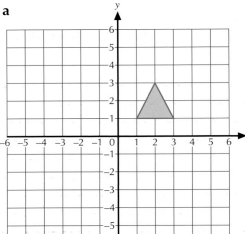 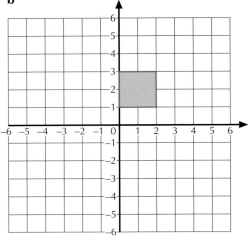

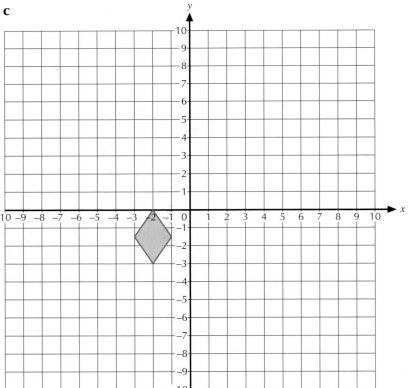

3 Copy the diagram shown onto a coordinate grid.

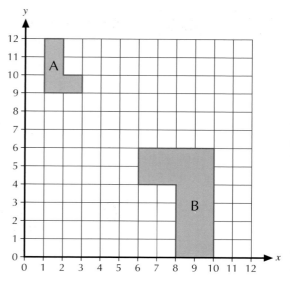

a Shape A is mapped onto shape B by an enlargement. What is the scale factor of the enlargement?

b By adding suitable rays to your diagram, find the coordinates of the centre of enlargement.

c Shape A can also be mapped onto shape B by a combination of a rotation followed by an enlargement. Carefully describe these two transformations.

4 Copy the diagram shown onto centimetre squared paper.

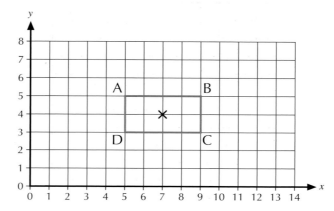

a Enlarge the rectangle ABCD by a scale factor of −3 about the point (7, 4). Label the rectangle A'B'C'D'.

b Write down the coordinates of A', B', C', D'.

c **i** Write down the lengths of AB and A'B'.
   ii Write down the ratio of the two sides in its simplest form.

d **i** Write down the perimeters of ABCD and A'B'C'D'.
   ii Write down the ratio of the two perimeters in its simplest form.

e **i** Write down the areas of ABCD and A'B'C'D'.
   ii Write down the ratio of the two areas in its simplest form.

Extension **Work**

1 Working in pairs or groups, design a poster to show how the 'stick person' shown can be enlarged by different negative scale factors about any convenient centre of enlargement.

2 Use reference books or the Internet to explain how each of the following uses negative enlargements.
   a A camera   **b** The eye

3 Use ICT software, such as Logo, to enlarge shapes by different negative scale factors and with different centres of enlargement.

Planes of symmetry

A **plane** is a flat surface.

All the two-dimensional (2-D) shapes you have met so far have plane surfaces. These 2-D shapes can have line symmetry.

Three-dimensional (3-D) shapes or **solids** can have plane symmetry.

A **plane of symmetry** divides a solid into two identical parts. Each part is a reflection of the other.

Example 9.5 ▷ Draw diagrams to show the different planes of symmetry for the cuboid:

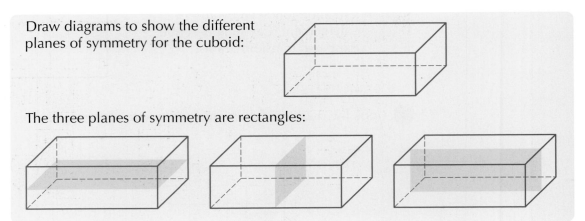

The three planes of symmetry are rectangles:

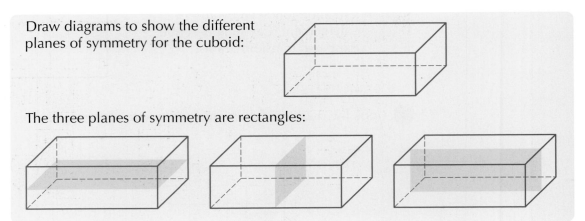

Exercise 9D

(1) Write down the number of planes of symmetry for each of the following 3-D shapes.

| a | Cube | b | Cuboid with two square faces | c | Square-based pyramid | d | Regular tetrahedron | e | Regular octahedron |

(2) Write down the number of planes of symmetry for each of the following regular prisms.

    a   Triangular prism   **b**   Pentagonal prism   **c**   Hexagonal prism

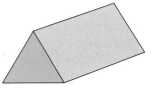 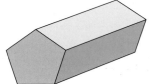 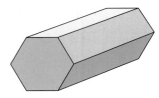

(3) A prism has an *n*-sided regular polygon as its cross-section. How many planes of symmetry does it have?

4 Draw sketches to show the different planes of symmetry for each of the following solids.

a 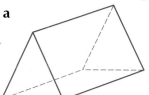 **b** 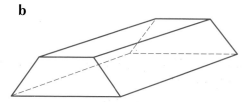 **c**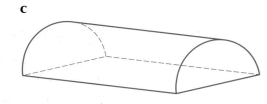

5 Draw sketches of some everyday objects that have one or more planes of symmetry. Below each sketch, write the number of planes of symmetry of the object.

6 Four cubes can be arranged to make the following different solids. Write down the number of planes of symmetry for each.

a 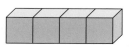   **b** 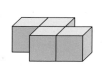   **c** 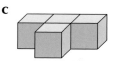   **d**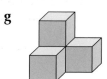

e   **f**   **g**   **h**

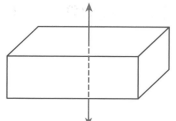

Extension Work

1 Draw separate diagrams to show all the planes of symmetry for a cube.

2 *Axes of symmetry*

The diagram shows an axis of symmetry for a cuboid. The cuboid has rotation symmetry of order 2 about this axis.

a Draw diagrams to show the other two axes of symmetry for the cuboid. What is the order of rotational symmetry about each of these axes?

b How many different axes of symmetry can you find for a cube?

3 Use reference books or the Internet to find the number of planes of symmetry for more complex 3-D shapes.

Shape and ratio

Ratio can be used to compare **lengths**, **areas** and **volumes** of 2-D and 3-D shapes, as the following examples show.

Example 9.6

A ———— B   C ——————————————————— D
   12 mm   4.8 cm

To find the ratio of the length of the line segment AB to the length of the line segment CD, change the measurements to the smaller unit and then simplify the ratio. So the ratio is 12 mm : 4.8 cm = 12 mm : 48 mm = 1 : 4. Remember that ratios have no units in the final answer.

Example 9.7 ▷

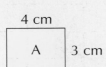

4 cm

A | 3 cm

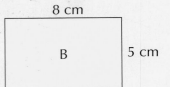

8 cm

B | 5 cm

Find the ratio of the area of rectangle A to the area of rectangle B, giving the answer in its simplest form.

The ratio is 12 cm² : 40 cm² = 3 : 10

Example 9.8 ▷

2 cm

2 cm

2 cm

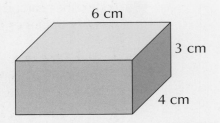

6 cm

3 cm

4 cm

Find the ratio of the volume of the cube to the volume of the cuboid, giving the answer in its simplest form.

The ratio is 8 cm³ : 72 cm³ = 1 : 9

Exercise 9E

1 Express each of the following ratios in its simplest form.

   a 10 mm : 25 mm   **b** 2 mm : 2 cm   **c** 36 cm : 45 cm

   d 40 cm : 2 m   **e** 500 m : 2 km

2 For the two squares shown, find each of the following ratios, giving your answers in their simplest form.

A | 2 cm

6 cm

B | 6 cm

   a The length of a side of square A to the length of a side of square B

   b The perimeter of square A to the perimeter of square B

   c The area of square A to the area of square B

3 Three rectangles A, B and C are arranged as in the diagram. The ratio of the length of A to the length of B to the length of C is 3 cm : 6 cm : 9 cm = 1 : 2 : 3.

   a Find each of the following ratios in the same way, giving your answers in their simplest form.

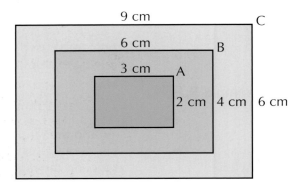

9 cm   C

6 cm   B

3 cm   A

2 cm | 4 cm | 6 cm

     i The width of A to the width of B to the width of C

     ii The perimeter of A to the perimeter of B to the perimeter of C

     iii The area of A to the area of B to the area of C

   b Write down anything you notice about the three rectangles.

4 In the diagram, flag X is mapped onto flag Y by a reflection in mirror line 1. Flag X is also mapped onto flag Z by a reflection in mirror line 2.

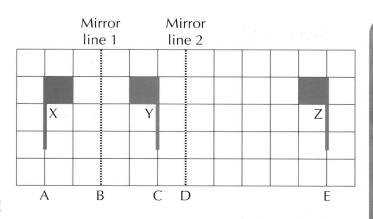

Find the ratio of each of the following lengths, giving your answers in their simplest form.

a AB : BC **b** AB : AE

c AC : AE **d** BD : CE

5 **a** Find the ratio of the area of the small square to the area of the surround, giving your answer in its simplest form.

b Express the area of the small square as a fraction of the area of the surround.

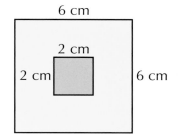

6 The dimensions of lawn A and lawn B are given on the diagrams.

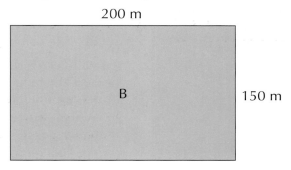

a Calculate the area of lawn A, giving your answer in square metres.

b Calculate the area of lawn B, giving your answer in:

    i square metres   **ii** hectares (1 hectare = 10 000 m²)

c Find the ratio of the length of lawn A to the length of lawn B, giving your answer in its simplest form.

d Find the ratio of the area of lawn A to the area of lawn B, giving your answer in its simplest form.

e Express the area of lawn A as a fraction of the area of lawn B.

7 The dimensions of a fish tank are given on the diagram.

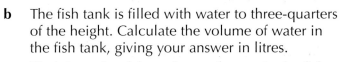

a Calculate the volume of the fish tank, giving your answer in litres (1 litre = 1000 cm³).

b The fish tank is filled with water to three-quarters of the height. Calculate the volume of water in the fish tank, giving your answer in litres.

c Find the ratio of the volume of water in the fish tank to the total volume of the fish tank, giving your answer in its simplest form.

7

1 For the three cubes shown, find each of the following ratios, giving your answers in their simplest form.

a **i** The length of an edge of cube A to the length of an edge of cube B
ii The length of an edge of cube A to the length of an edge of cube C

b **i** The total surface area of cube A to the total surface area of cube B
ii The total surface area of cube A to the total surface area of cube C

c **i** The volume of cube A to the volume of cube B
ii The volume of cube A to the volume of cube C

d Cube D has an edge length of k cm. Write down each of the following ratios.
i The length of an edge of cube A to the length of an edge of cube D
ii The total surface area of cube A to the total surface area of cube D
iii The volume of cube A to the volume of cube D

2 You will need a sheet each of A5, A4 and A3 paper for this activity. Measure the length and width of the sides of each sheet of paper to the nearest millimetre.

a What is the connection between the length and width of successive paper sizes?

b Find the ratio of the lengths for each successive paper size. Give your answer in the form 1 : n.

LEVEL BOOSTER

5 I know how to recognise congruent shapes.
I can reflect, rotate and translate a 2-D shape.
I can express a ratio, giving it in its simplest form.

6 I can transform 2-D shapes by using a combination of transformations.
I can solve problems using ratio.

7 I can enlarge a 2-D shape by a negative scale factor.
I can recognise planes of symmetry in 3-D shapes.

1 *2001 Paper 1*

Two parts of this square design are shaded black.
Two parts are shaded pink.

Show that the ratio of black to pink is 5 : 3.

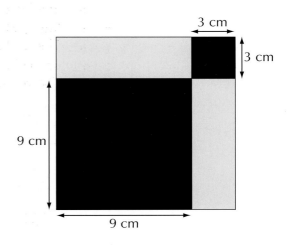

2 *2006 Paper 2*

The diagram shows a shaded rectangle.

It is divided into four smaller rectangles, labelled A, B, C and D.

The ratio of area **C** to area **B** is **1 : 2**.

Calculate area A.

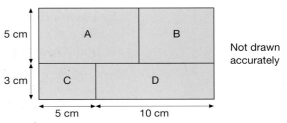

3 *2002 Paper 2* (adapted)

The grid shows an arrow.

Copy the arrow onto squared paper.
Draw an enlargement of scale factor
–2 of the arrow. Use point C as the
centre of enlargement.

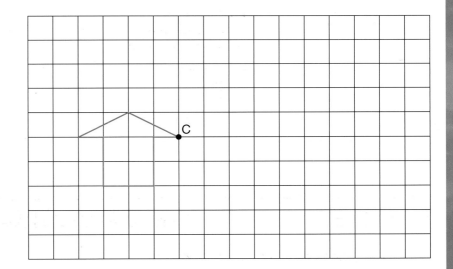

4 *2007 Paper 1*

A **square** of area **64 cm²** is cut to make two rectangles, A and B.

The ratio of **area A** to **area B** is **3 : 1**.

Work out the dimensions of rectangles A and B.

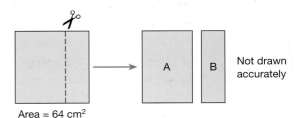

This chapter is going to show you

- How to solve more difficult equations
- How to substitute into a formula
- How to create your own expressions and formulae

What you should already know

- How to add, subtract and multiply negative numbers

Solving equations

The **equations** you are going to meet will contain an **unknown**, often written x. **Solving** an equation such as $5x - 3 = 27$ means finding the actual value of x. By carefully using the methods below, you can solve this sort of equation quickly and correctly every time.

Remember: you must always do the same to both sides of an equation.

Example 10.1

Solve the equation $5x - 3 = 27$.

Add 3 to both sides: $\quad 5x - 3 + 3 = 27 + 3$

$$5x = 30$$

Divide both sides by 5: $\quad \dfrac{5x}{5} = \dfrac{30}{5}$

$$x = 6$$

Example 10.2

Solve the equation $4(2z + 1) = 64$.

Expand the bracket: $\quad\quad\quad\quad 8z + 4 = 64$

Subtract 4 from both sides: $\quad 8z + 4 - 4 = 64 - 4$

$$8z = 60$$

Divide both sides by 8: $\quad\quad\quad\quad z = 7.5$

Exercise 10A

1 Solve the following equations.

a	$2x + 3 = 17$	**b**	$4x - 1 = 19$	**c**	$5x + 3 = 18$	**d**	$2y - 3 = 1$
e	$4z + 5 = 17$	**f**	$6x - 5 = 13$	**g**	$2 + 3x = 38$	**h**	$8 + 5x = 13$
i	$3 + 4m = 11$	**j**	$6 + 2n = 20$	**k**	$4 + 3x = 31$	**l**	$7 + 5x = 52$

2 Solve the following equations.

a	$2x + 5 = 12$	**b**	$2s - 3 = 10$	**c**	$2t + 3 = 14$	**d**	$2g - 5 = 12$
e	$4x + 3 = 13$	**f**	$4x - 5 = 13$	**g**	$4v + 9 = 39$	**h**	$4x - 3 = 11$
i	$6x - 1 = 8$	**j**	$6q + 5 = 26$	**k**	$6x + 7 = 34$	**l**	$6p - 8 = 37$

5

3 Solve the following equations. Start by expanding the brackets. The convention is to write the answer as it is said, with x on the left of the = sign: 'x equals 9' is written $x = 9$. If the equation has x on the right, you can reverse the equation before you start solving it, or after you have found x.

a $2(x + 3) = 16$ **b** $4(x - 1) = 16$ **c** $5(x + 3) = 20$

d $4(x + 1) = 12$ **e** $6(x - 5) = 18$ **f** $30 = 2(x + 9)$

g $2(3x + 1) = 14$ **h** $4(2x - 1) = 36$ **i** $5(2x + 3) = 55$

j $4(3x + 5) = 32$ **k** $6(4x - 5) = 42$ **l** $110 = 10(2x + 9)$

4 Joe got very mixed up with his homework. Here are his answers. In each case:
  i write down where he has gone wrong.   **ii** solve the equation correctly.

a $5x + 3 = 12 = 9 = \frac{5}{9}$ **b** $3x - 7 = 8 = 1 = 3$

c $4x + 5 = 11 = 16 = 4$ **d** $6x - 3 = 12 = 9 = 1.5$

e $4(x + 7) = 60$ **f** $3(x - 4) = 18$
  $4x + 7 = 60 = 53$ $3x - 4 = 18 = 14$
  $x = 47$ $x = 11$

g $5(2x + 3) = 17$ **h** $4(3x - 7) = 32$
  $10x + 15 = 17 = 2$ $12x - 7 = 32 = 39$
  $x = 5$ $x = 5$

i $3(6x + 1) = 30$ **j** $2(4x - 3) = 14$
  $18x + 3 = 30 = 27$ $8x - 6 = 14 = 8$
  $x = 9$ $x = 1$

5 Sheehab solved some of his equations as shown below.

  Solve: $4(2x + 1) = 64$
  Divide both sides by 4: $2x + 1 = 16$
  Subtract 1 from each side: $2x = 15$
  Divide both sides by 2: $x = 7.5$

  Solve the following equations in the same way as Sheehab.

  a $2(3x + 1) = 38$ **b** $4(5x - 3) = 68$ **c** $3(4x + 5) = 63$

6 Solve the following equations in two different ways:
  i by first expanding the bracket.   **ii** by first dividing both sides by a number.
  a $5(3x - 2) = 95$ **b** $4(6x + 3) = 96$ **c** $2(3x - 4) = 25$

Extension   Work

In the diagram shown, the contents of any two adjacent boxes are added together to give the contents of the box above them.

1 There are three consecutive integers from left to right in the boxes at the bottom.

  a Use algebra to find the integers in the bottom boxes that give the top box a total of 40. (*Hint:* Start with x as shown in the bottom left box.)

  b Write down all the integers between 50 and 60 (inclusive) that cannot appear in the top box.

2 There are now three consecutive *even* integers in the boxes at the bottom.

  a Use algebra to find the integers in the bottom boxes that give the top box a total of 40.

  b Write down all the integers between 80 and 100 (inclusive) that cannot appear in the top box.

Equations involving negative numbers

The equations that you met in the last lesson all had solutions that were positive numbers. This lesson will give you practice at solving equations involving **negative** numbers.

Example 10.3 ▶

Solve the equation $5x + 11 = 1$.

Subtract 11 from each side: $5x + 11 - 11 = 1 - 11$

$$5x = -10$$

Divide both sides by 5: $\dfrac{5x}{5} = \dfrac{-10}{5}$

$$x = -2$$

Example 10.4 ▶

Solve the equation $-5x = 10$.

Divide both sides by -5: $\dfrac{-5x}{-5} = \dfrac{10}{-5}$

$$x = -2$$

Example 10.5 ▶

Solve the equation $8 - 3x = 20$.

Subtract 8 from each side: $8 - 3x - 8 = 20 - 8$

$$-3x = 12$$

Divide both sides by -3: $\dfrac{-3x}{-3} = \dfrac{12}{-3}$

$$x = -4$$

Exercise 10B

1 Solve the following equations.

a $2x + 3 = 1$	**b** $3x + 5 = 2$	**c** $2x + 9 = 5$	**d** $3h + 8 = 2$
e $3d + 4 = 19$	**f** $5x + 25 = 10$	**g** $4x + 15 = 3$	**h** $2x + 13 = 5$
i $2 = 3x + 11$	**j** $6n + 3 = 15$	**k** $12 = 5r + 27$	**l** $9x + 30 = 3$

2 Solve the following equations.

a $13 + 2x = 5$	**b** $6 + 3j = 21$	**c** $15 + 4x = 7$	**d** $24 + 5x = 4$
e $27 + 4x = 31$	**f** $9 + 2s = 15$	**g** $22 + 3x = 28$	**h** $18 + 5x = 3$
i $33 + 4p = 9$	**j** $1 + 2x = 17$	**k** $12 = 24 + 3x$	**l** $2 = 17 + 5y$

3 Solve the following equations.

a $3x + 6 = -12$	**b** $4x - 2 = -10$	**c** $3x + 1 = 16$	**d** $2x - 4 = -12$
e $4j + 3 = -13$	**f** $2k - 7 = -1$	**g** $2x + 9 = -39$	**h** $3x - 2 = -11$
i $6x - 2 = -8$	**j** $2m + 6 = -26$	**k** $31 = 5x + 6$	**l** $3x - 10 = -37$

4 Solve the following equations.

a $-4x = 20$	**b** $-10x = 20$	**c** $-2x = -12$	**d** $-6x = 54$
e $-7x = 42$	**f** $9 = -3x$	**g** $-9x = 99$	**h** $8 = -2x$
i $-x = 13$	**j** $-5x = -20$		

5 Solve the following equations.

a $15 - 2x = 19$ **b** $11 - 3x = 14$ **c** $15 - 4x = 27$ **d** $29 - 5x = 14$

e $15 - 4e = 3$ **f** $13 - 2x = 23$ **g** $20 - 3x = 29$ **h** $16 - 5x = 36$

i $20 = 40 - 4f$ **j** $10 = 16 - 2w$

6 Solve the following equations.

a $2(x + 3) = 4$ **b** $4(x - 5) = -8$ **c** $5(x + 3) = 5$

d $4(x + 5) = 8$ **e** $6(z - 5) = -36$ **f** $10(y + 9) = 20$

g $3(t - 11) = -15$ **h** $21 = 7(x + 5)$ **i** $44 = 4(3 - 2x)$

7 Solve the following equations.

a $2(3x + 1) = -10$ **b** $4(2x - 1) = -28$ **c** $5(2x + 3) = 5$

d $4(3x + 5) = 8$ **e** $-26 = 2(4d - 5)$ **f** $10(2a + 9) = 230$

g $3(5v - 11) = 27$ **h** $7(2x + 5) = -7$ **i** $27 = 3(7 - 2x)$

8 Victoria has made a mistake somewhere in her working for each of the equations shown. Can you spot on which line the error occurs and work out the correct solution to each one?

a
$$18 - 3x = 30$$
$$18 - 3x + 3x = 30 + 3x$$
$$18 = 30 + 3x$$
$$18 + 30 = 30 + 3x - 30$$
$$48 = 3x$$
$$\frac{48}{3} = \frac{3x}{3}$$
$$x = 16 \quad \times$$

b
$$4 - 5x = 24$$
$$4 + 5x - 4 = 24 - 4$$
$$5x = 20$$
$$\frac{5x}{5} = \frac{20}{5}$$
$$x = 4 \quad \times$$

c
$$5(x + 10) = 5$$
$$5x + 10 = 5$$
$$5x + 10 - 10 = 5 - 10$$
$$5x = -5$$
$$\frac{5x}{5} = \frac{-5}{5}$$
$$x = -1 \quad \times$$

d
$$5(4x + 7) = -5$$
$$\frac{5(4x + 7)}{5} = \frac{-5}{5}$$
$$4x + 7 = -1$$
$$4x + 7 - 7 = -1 - 7$$
$$4x = -8$$
$$\frac{4x}{4} = \frac{-8}{4}$$
$$x = 2 \quad \times$$

Extension **Work**

1 The following equations each have two possible solutions, one where x is positive, and one where x is negative. Use a spreadsheet to help you find the solutions to each equation by trial and improvement.

a $x(x + 5) = 24$ **b** $x(x - 4) = 12$

2 Use a spreadsheet to help you solve $x(x + 8) = -12$ by trial and improvement. There are two answers, both negative, one greater than -4, the other less than -4.

Equations with unknowns on both sides

Sometimes the **unknown** is on both sides of an equation. You need to add or subtract terms in order to create an equation with the unknown on one side only.

Example 10.6 ▷

Solve the equation $5x - 4 = 2x + 14$.

Subtract $2x$ from both sides: $5x - 4 - 2x = 2x + 14 - 2x$

$$3x - 4 = 14$$

Add 4 to both sides: $3x - 4 + 4 = 14 + 4$

$$3x = 18$$

Divide both sides by 3: $\dfrac{3x}{3} = \dfrac{18}{3}$

$$x = 6$$

Example 10.7 ▷

Solve the equation $4x + 2 = 7 - x$.

Add x to each side: $4x + 2 + x = 7 - x + x$

$$5x + 2 = 7$$

Subtract 2 from both sides: $5x + 2 - 2 = 7 - 2$

$$5x = 5$$

Divide each side by 5: $\dfrac{5x}{5} = \dfrac{5}{5}$

$$x = 1$$

Exercise 10C

1 Solve the following equations.

   a $2x = 4 + x$ **b** $3x = 12 - x$ **c** $4x = x - 15$ **d** $5x = 12 + x$

   e $3x = 19 + 2x$ **f** $5x = 16 - 3x$ **g** $4x = 14 + 2x$ **h** $5x = 2x - 15$

   i $7x = 12 + 4x$ **j** $6x = 15 + 9x$ **k** $5x = 12 + 2x$ **l** $9x = 30 + 12x$

2 Solve the following equations.

   a $5x - 3 = x - 15$ **b** $4x + 5 = x + 20$ **c** $6x + 4 = x + 14$

   d $4x - 2 = 2x + 8$ **e** $5x - 3 = 2x + 9$ **f** $8x - 6 = 3x - 16$

   g $2x - 5 = 6x - 9$ **h** $7x - 10 = 3x - 2$ **i** $4x - 6 = 9x - 21$

3 Solve the following equations.

   a $4x + 3 = 9 + x$ **b** $8x + 5 = 19 + x$ **c** $5x + 4 = x - 12$

   d $6x - 4 = 12 - 2x$ **e** $7x - 3 = 17 + 2x$ **f** $4x - 5 = 7 + 2x$

   g $7 - 5x = 2x - 14$ **h** $5 + 4x = 11 + 2x$ **i** $7 + 3x = 15 + 7x$

4 Solve the following equations. Begin by expanding the brackets.

   a $2(x + 3) = 14 + x$ **b** $3(2x + 5) = 25 + x$ **c** $5(3x - 4) = 12 + 7x$

   d $6x - 4 = 2(4 + 2x)$ **e** $9x - 3 = 3(2x - 8)$ **f** $8x - 10 = 2(3 + 2x)$

   g $2(5x + 7) = 3(7 + x)$ **h** $3(8 + 4x) = 4(9 + 2x)$ **i** $2(7x - 6) = 3(1 + 3x)$

   j $3(2x - 1) = 5(x - 1)$

5 Solve the following equations.

a $\dfrac{2x + 1}{x + 5} = 1$

b $\dfrac{5x + 3}{x + 6} = 2$

c $\dfrac{10x - 1}{2x + 5} = 3$

Extension **Work**

1 The product of three consecutive numbers is 13 800. Use a spreadsheet to help you find the three consecutive numbers.

2 The product of three consecutive even numbers is 63 840. Use a spreadsheet to help you find the sum of the three consecutive even numbers.

Substituting into expressions

Replacing the letters or **variables** in an expression by numbers is called **substitution**. Substituting different numbers will give an expression different values. You need to be able to substitute negative numbers as well as positive numbers into expressions.

Example 10.8 ▷

Calculate the value of $5x + 7$ when: **i** $x = 3$ **ii** $x = -4$

i When $x = 3$, $5x + 7 = 5 \times 3 + 7 = 22$

ii When $x = -4$, $5x + 7 = 5 \times (-4) + 7 = -20 + 7 = -13$

Exercise 10D

1 Write down the value of each expression for each value of x below.

		i		**ii**		**iii**	
a	$3x + 5$	$x = 3$		$x = 7$		$x = -1$	
b	$4x - 2$	$x = 4$		$x = 5$		$x = -3$	
c	$8 + 7x$	$x = 2$		$x = 6$		$x = -2$	
d	$93 - 4x$	$x = 10$		$x = 21$		$x = -3$	
e	$x^2 + 3$	$x = 4$		$x = 5$		$x = -3$	
f	$x^2 - 7$	$x = 6$		$x = 2$		$x = -10$	
g	$21 + 3x^2$	$x = 7$		$x = 3$		$x = -5$	
h	$54 - 2x^2$	$x = 3$		$x = 5$		$x = -1$	
i	$5(3x + 4)$	$x = 5$		$x = 4$		$x = -2$	
j	$3(5x - 1)$	$x = 3$		$x = 2$		$x = -6$	

2 If $a = 2$ and $b = 3$, find the value of each of the following.

a $3a + b$

b $a - 3b$

c $3(b + 4a)$

d $5(3b - 2a)$

e $b - (a - 2b)$

f $ab - 2(3a - 4b)$

3 If $c = 5$ and $d = -2$, find the value of each of the following.

a $2c + d$

b $6c - 2d$

c $2(3d + 7c)$

d $4(3c - 5d)$

e $c + (d - 2c)$

f $cd - 3(2c - 3d)$

4 If $e = 4$ and $f = -3$, find the value of each of the following:

    a $e^2 + f^2$ **b** $e^2 - f^2$ **c** $ef + 3e^2 - 2f^2$

    d $e(4f^2 - e^2)$ **e** $f^2 - (5f + e)$ **f** $e^2 - (2e + f)$

5 If $g = 6$, $h = -4$ and $j = 7$, find the value of each of the following:

    a $gh + j$ **b** $g - hj$ **c** ghj

    d $(g + h)(h + j)$ **e** $gh - hj + gj$ **f** $g(h + j) - h(g - j)$

6 What values of n can be substituted into n^2 that give n^2 a value less than 1?

7 What values of n can be substituted into $(n - 4)^2$ that give $(n - 4)^2$ a value less than 1?

8 What values of n can be substituted into $\frac{1}{n}$ that give $\frac{1}{n}$ a value less than 1?

9 Find at least five different expressions that give the value 10 when $x = 2$ is substituted into them.

Extension **Work**

Use a spreadsheet to find three solutions to the equation:

$$n^3 - 18n^2 - 100n + 1800 = 0$$

(*Hint:* The solutions all lie between −20 and +20.)

Substituting into formulae

Formulae occur in all sorts of situations, often when converting between two types of quantity. Some examples are converting between degrees **Celsius** and degrees **Fahrenheit**, or between different currencies such as from pounds (£) to euros (€).

Example 10.9 ▷

The formula for converting a temperature C in degrees Celsius (°C) to a temperature F in degrees Fahrenheit (°F) is:

$$F = \frac{9C}{5} + 32$$

Convert 35°C to °F.

Substituting $C = 35$ into the formula gives:

$$F = \frac{9 \times 35}{5} + 32 = 63 + 32 = 95$$

So 35 °C = 95 °F

Example 10.10 ▶

The formula for the area A of a triangle with base length b and height h is given by $A = \frac{1}{2}bh$.

Calculate the base length b of a triangle whose area is 14 cm² and whose height is 7cm.

Substitute the values that you know into the formula:

$14 = \frac{1}{2} \times b \times 7$

Rearrange to get the unknown b by itself on one side:

$14 \div 7 = \frac{1}{2} \times b \times 7 \div 7$

$2 = \frac{1}{2} \times b$

$2 \times 2 = \frac{1}{2} \times b \times 2$

$b = 4$

So the base is 4cm long.

Exercise 10E

1 If $A = 180(n - 2)$, find A when: **i** $n = 7$ **ii** $n = 12$

2 If $V = u + ft$:
  a find V when: **i** $u = 40, f = 32$ and $t = 5$ **ii** $u = 12, f = 13$ and $t = 10$
  b find u when: $V = 5, f = 1$ and $t = 2$

3 If $D = \frac{M}{V}$:
  a find D when: **i** $M = 28$ and $V = 4$ **ii** $M = 8$ and $V = 5$
  b find M when: $D = 7$ and $V = 3$

 4 A magician charges £25 for every show he performs, plus an extra £10 per hour spent on stage. The formula for calculating his charge is $C = 10t + 25$, where C is the charge in pounds and t is the length of the show in hours.

  a How much does he charge for a show lasting:
     i 1 hour?   **ii** 3 hours?   **iii** $2\frac{1}{2}$ hours?
  b The magician charges £30 for one of his shows. How long did the show last?

 5 The following formula converts a temperature C in degrees Celsius (°C) to a temperature F in degrees Fahrenheit (°F) .

$F = 1.8C + 32$

  a Convert each of these temperatures to degrees Fahrenheit:
     i 45 °C   **ii** 40 °C   **iii** 65 °C   **iv** 100 °C
  b Convert each of these temperatures to degrees Celsius:
     i 50 °F   **ii** 59 °F   **iii** 41 °F   **iv** 23 °F

6 If $N = h(A^2 - B^2)$, find N when: **i** $h = 7, A = 5$ and $B = 3$ **ii** $h = 15, A = 4$ and $B = 2$

7 If $V = hr^2$, find V when: **i** $h = 5$ and $r = 3$ **ii** $h = 8$ and $r = 5$

8 The volume V of the cuboid shown is given by the formula:

$$V = abc$$

The surface area S of the cuboid is given by the formula:

$$S = 2ab + 2bc + 2ac$$

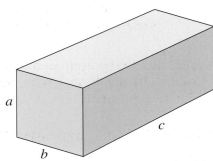

a Find: **i** the volume   **ii** the surface area
when $a = 3$ m, $b = 4$ m and $c = 5$ m.

b Find: **i** the volume   **ii** the surface area
when $a = 3$ cm and a, b and c are all the same length.

iii What name is given to this cuboid?

9 The triangle numbers are given by the following formula:

$$T = \frac{n(n + 1)}{2}$$

The first triangle number is found by substituting $n = 1$ into the formula, which gives

$$T = 1 \times \frac{(1 + 1)}{2} = 1$$

a Find the first 10 triangle numbers.

b Find the 99th triangle number.

10 If $\frac{1}{F} = \frac{1}{U} - \frac{1}{V}$, calculate:

i F when $U = 4$ and $V = 5$ **ii** V when $F = 2$ and $U = 3$

11 If $\frac{1}{T} = \frac{1}{A} + \frac{1}{B}$, calculate:

i T when $A = 3$ and $B = 2$ **ii** A when $T = 2$, $B = 8$

Extension   Work

Use a spreadsheet to help you find three different solutions to the equation:

$$n^3 - 3n^2 - 18n + 40 = 0$$

(*Hint:* The solutions all lie between -10 and $+10$.)

Creating your own expressions and formulae

The last lesson showed you some formulae that could be used to solve problems. In this lesson you will be given problems and have to write down your own formulae to help solve them.

You will need to choose a letter to represent each variable in a problem, and use these when you write the formula. Usually these will be the first letters of the words they represent, for example V often represents volume and A is often used for area.

Example 10.11

Find a formula for the sum S of any three consecutive whole numbers.

Let the smallest number be n.
The next number is $n + 1$ and the biggest number is $n + 2$.
So $S = n + (n + 1) + (n + 2)$
$S = n + n + 1 + n + 2$
$S = 3n + 3$

Example 10.12

How many months are there in: **i**   5 years?   **ii** t years?

There are 12 months in a year, so:

i   in 5 years there will be $12 \times 5 = 60$ months

ii   in t years there will be $12 \times t = 12t$ months

Exercise 10F

1. Using the letters suggested, construct a simple formula in each case.

   a   The sum S of three numbers a, b and c.

   b   The product P of two numbers x and y.

   c   The difference D between the ages of two people, the elder being a years old and the younger b years old.

   d   The sum S of four consecutive integers, the lowest of which is n.

   e   The number of days D in W weeks.

   f   The average age A of three boys whose ages are m, n and p years.

2. Juno is now 13 years old.

   a   How many years old will she be in t years' time?

   b   How many years old was she m years ago?

3. A car travels at a speed of 30 mph. How many miles will it travel in:

   a   2 hours?   **b** t hours?

4. How many grams are there in:

   a   5 kg?   **b** x kg?

5 How many minutes are there in m hours?

6 Write down the number that is half as big as b.

7 Write down the number that is twice as big as t.

8 If a boy runs at b miles per hour, how many miles does he run in k hours?

9 Write a formula for the cost C in pence of the following.

    a   6 papers at q pence each

    b k papers at 35 pence each

    c k papers at q pence each

10 A boy is b years old and his mother is 6 times as old.

    a   Write the mother's age in terms of b.

    b   Write both their ages in 5 years' time in terms of b.

    c   Find the sum S of their ages in y years' time, in terms of b and y.

11 Mr Speed's age A is equal to the sum of the ages of his three sons. The youngest son is aged x years, the eldest is 10 years older than the youngest, and the middle son is 4 years younger than the eldest. Write a formula for Mr Speed's age.

12 **a**   A man is now three times as old as his daughter. Write a formula with two variables to show this.

    b   In 10 years' time, the sum of their ages will be 76 years. Write a second formula to show this, using the same two variables.

    c   Substitute the formula from **a** into the formula from **b** to find the daughter's age now.

    d   How old was the man when his daughter was born?

13 A group of pupils had to choose between playing football and playing badminton. The number of pupils that chose football was three times the number that chose badminton. The number of players for each game would be equal if 12 pupils who chose football were asked to play badminton. Find the total number of pupils.

14 Find three consecutive odd numbers for which the sum is 57. Let the first odd number be n.

John wanted to build a cuboid with a volume of approximately 1000 cm³.
The length had to be three times greater than the width. The height had to be
5 cm less than the width. Find the width, length and height of the cuboid.

Use a spreadsheet to help you.

LEVEL BOOSTER

5
I can solve linear equations where the solution may be fractional or negative.
I can substitute positive and negative numbers into algebraic expressions.
I can substitute positive and negative numbers into formulae.
I can devise an algebraic formula to represent a simple relationship.

6
I can solve linear equations containing brackets where the solution may be fractional or negative.
I can solve equations with the unknown value on both sides.
I can substitute positive and negative numbers into formulae.

7
I can solve equations containing algebraic fractions.
I can use a spreadsheet to solve cubic equations.
I can substitute positive and negative numbers into fractional formulae.
I can set up formulae and equations to represent complex situations.

National Test questions

1 *2002 Paper 2*

Look at these equations:

$$3a + 6b = 24$$

$$2c - d = 3$$

a Use the equations above to work out the value of the expressions below.
The first one is done for you. Copy and complete the others.

$8c - 4d = \underline{\quad 12 \quad}$

i $a + 2b = \underline{\qquad}$

ii $d - 2c = \underline{\qquad}$

b Use one or both of the equations above to write an expression that has a value of 21.

2 *2003 Paper 1*

Solve these equations.

Show your working.

$$3t + 4 = t + 13 \qquad 2(3n + 7) = 8$$

3 *2005 Paper 2*

I think of a number.

I multiply this number by **8**, the subtract **66**.
The result is twice the number that I was thinking of.

What is the number I was thinking of?

4 *2007 Paper 1*

Solve this equation.

$$2(2n + 5) = 12$$

 5 *2004 Paper 2*

Doctors sometimes use this formula to calculate how much medicine to give a child.

$$c = \frac{ay}{12+y}$$

c is the correct amount for a child, in ml
a is the amount for an adult, in ml
y is the age of the child, in years

(a) A child who is **4 years old** needs some medicine.
The amount for an adult is **20 ml.**

Use the formula to work out the correct amount for this child.
You **must** show your working.

(b) Another child needs some medicine.
The amount for an adult is **30 ml.**

The correct amount for this child is **15 ml.**
How old is this child? Show your working.

6 *2006 Paper 2*

You can find the approximate volume of a tomato by using this formula:

$$V = \frac{1}{6}d^2h$$

V is the volume,
d is the diameter,
h is the height.

The diameter and the height of a tomato are both **3.5 cm.**

What is the approximate volume of this tomato in cm³?

FM **7** *2007 Paper 2*

I am going to use a wooden beam to support a load.

cross-section

The cross-section of the beam is a rectangle.

The formula below gives the greatest load, M kg, that a beam of this length can support.

M=kg

$M = 5d^2w$ where d is the depth of the beam in cm,
w is the width of the beam in cm.

I can place the cross-section of the beam in two different ways.

In which way will the beam be able to support the greater load?

Also, calculate and write down the difference in kilograms.

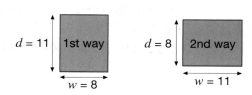

$d = 11$ 1st way

$w = 8$

$d = 8$ 2nd way

$w = 11$

This chapter is going to show you

- How to write questions for a questionnaire
- How to collect data
- How to use two-way tables
- How to construct statistical diagrams for discrete data
- When to use range, mean, median and mode
- How to construct stem-and-leaf diagrams
- How to compare two sets of data
- How to analyse data

What you should already know

- How to interpret data from tables, graphs and charts
- How to find mode, median, mean and range for small data sets
- How to write a short report of a statistical survey
- How to design a data-collection sheet

Statistical surveys

In the picture the teenagers are carrying out a **survey** about healthy eating. Do you think that their results will be fair if they only interview people who are buying burgers? How can they collect the **data** and make sure that many different opinions are obtained? How many people do you think they should ask?

Example 11.1 ▶ Here are some questions that might be used in a survey. Give a reason why each question is not very good and then write a better question.

a How old are you?

b Do you eat lots of fruit or vegetables?

c Don't you agree that exercise is good for you?

d If you go to a sports centre with your friends and you want to play badminton, do you usually play a doubles match or do you just practise?

a This is a personal question. If you want to find out about the ages of people, use answer boxes and group several ages together.

☐ 0–15 ☐ 16–30 ☐ 31–45 ☐ 46–50 ☐ More than 50

b This question is asking about two different items, so the answers may be confusing. It may be awkward to answer with a yes or a no. It is better to separate fruit and vegetables in the survey. You can then ask about the quantity eaten, for example how many pieces of fruit per week.

c This question is trying to force you to agree. It is a leading question. A better question would be, 'Is exercise good for you?' You could then limit people to answers such as 'very' and 'not at all'.

d This question is too long. There is too much information, which makes it difficult to answer. It should be split up into several smaller questions.

Exercise 11A

FM Choose one of the following statements for a statistical survey. For the statement chosen:
- Write a testable hypothesis based on the statement.
- Write three or four questions for a questionnaire to test the hypothesis.
- Decide how you will record the data you collect.
- Collect information from at least 30 people.

1 Girls spend more on clothes than boys.

2 Old people use libraries more than teenagers.

3 People who holiday abroad one year, tend to stay in Britain the following year.

4 Pupils who enjoy playing sports eat healthier foods.

5 More men wear glasses than women.

6 Families eat out more than they used to.

Extension **Work**

Take each problem statement from the exercise and write down how you would collect the data required. For example, would you collect the data using a questionnaire or by carrying out an experiment, or would you collect the data from books, computer software or the Internet? Also, write a short report or list on the advantages and disadvantages of each method of data collection.

Stem-and-leaf diagrams

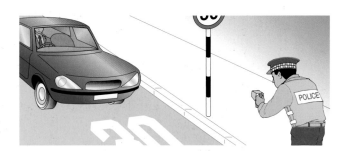

The speeds of vehicles in a 30 mph limit are recorded. The speeds are sorted into order and put into a **stem-and-leaf diagram** as shown. The slowest speed is 23 mph. The fastest speed is 45 mph. How can you tell this from the stem-and-leaf diagram?

```
2 | 3 7 7 8 9 9
3 | 1 2 3 5 5 5 7 9
4 | 2 2 5            Key: 2 | 3 means 23 miles per hour
```

How many cars are breaking the speed limit?

Example 11.2 ▷ A teacher asked 25 pupils how many pieces of homework they were given in one week. The results are shown in the stem-and-leaf diagram:

```
0 | 1 1 2 2 2 2 3 5 7 7 7 8 9
1 | 0 0 1 1 1 2 4 4 5 6
2 | 1 3
```
Key: 1 | 2 means 12 homeworks

Use the stem-and-leaf diagram to find:

a   the median   **b**   the range   **c**   the mode

a   The median is the middle value. As there are 25 pupils, the middle value is the 13th. So the median is 9 homeworks.

b   The range is the difference between the biggest and the smallest values. The biggest value (most homeworks) is 23, and the smallest value (least homeworks) is 1. So the range is 23 − 1 = 22 homeworks.

c   The mode is the value that occurs the most. So the mode is 2 homeworks.

Example 11.3 ▷ A hospital clinic records the number of patients seen each day. Here are some results:

141   132   128   145   137   138   140   149   131   143
139   125   126   142   132   129   127   134   130

a   Put the results into a stem-and-leaf diagram (remember to show a key).

Find:

b   the median   **c**   the range   **d**   the mode

a
```
12 | 5 6 7 8 9
13 | 0 1 2 2 4 7 8 9
14 | 0 1 2 3 5 9
```
Key: 12 | 5 means 125 patients

b   As there are 19 pieces of data the middle is the 10th, so the median is 134 patients.

c   The most patients seen is the last value, 149, and the least patients seen is the first value, 125. So the range is 149 − 125 = 24 patients.

d   Only one value, 132, occurs more than once. So the mode is 132 patients.

Exercise 11B

1   15 sales people have a competition to find out who sells the most items in one day. Here are the results:

```
1 | 2 2 3 7 7
2 | 1 4 4 4 5 5 6
3 | 0 2 5
```
Key: 1 | 2 means 12 items

a   How many items did the winner sell?   **b**   What is the mode?
c   Find the range.   **d**   Work out the median.

6

2 35 Year 8 pupils are asked to estimate how many text messages they send on their mobile phones each week. Their replies are put into a stem-and-leaf diagram.

```
0 | 5 5 6 7 8 8
1 | 0 0 0 0 0 1 1 4 4
1 | 8 9 9 9
2 | 0 0 1 3 3 3 4
2 | 5 6 7
3 | 0 0 4
3 | 5 6 6                    Key: 0 | 5 means 5 text messages
```

Work out the following.

a The mode   **b** The smallest estimate   **c** The range   **d** The median

3 A farmer records the number of animals of each type on his farm. There are six types of animal. His results are shown in the stem-and-leaf diagram.

```
5 | 2 6 8
6 | 5 9
7 | 5            Key: 5 | 2 represents 52 animals of one type
```

a He has more sheep than any other type of animal. How many sheep does he have?

b How many animals has he altogether?

c Explain why a stem-and-leaf diagram may not be the best way to represent these data.

4 The ages of 30 people at a disco are as shown.

32	12	47	25	23	23	17	36	42	17
31	15	24	49	19	31	23	34	36	45
47	12	39	11	26	23	22	38	48	17

a Put the ages into a stem-and-leaf diagram (remember to show a key).

b State the mode.

c Work out the range.

5 A survey is carried out into the maximum speeds, in miles per hour, of a range of cars. Here are the results:

```
101   98    107   123   131   102   112   115   126   99    120   97
93    88    122   149   130   136   116   129   130   104   118
```

a Put the speeds into a stem-and-leaf diagram (remember to show a key).

b Work out the median speed.

c Work out the range.

Extension Work

Obtain your own data. These could be from the Internet or from a textbook on another subject. Alternatively, you could use some of the data collected for Exercise 11A. Make sure they are suitable for stem-and-leaf use.

Produce a brief summary of your data. Use a stem-and-leaf diagram to present the information.

Interpreting graphs and diagrams

In this section you will learn how to **interpret** graphs and diagrams, and how to **criticise** statements made about the data that they contain.

Example 11.4 ▷ The diagram shows how a group of pupils say they spend their time per week.

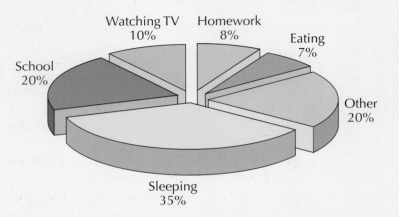

Matt says, 'The diagram shows that pupils spend too much time at school and doing homework'. Give two arguments to suggest that this is not true.

The diagram represents a group of pupils, so the data may vary for individual pupils. It could also be argued, for example, that pupils spend longer watching TV than doing homework.

Exercise 11C

1 A journey is shown on the distance–time graph. Chris says that the total distance travelled is 60 km. Explain why Chris is incorrect.

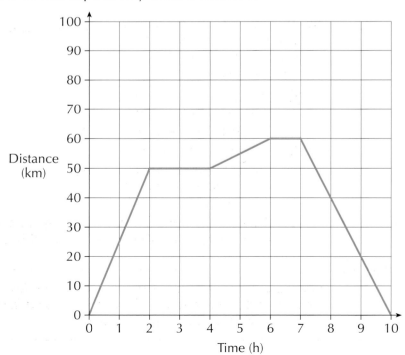

7

2 The results of a junior school throwing competition are shown in the bar chart.

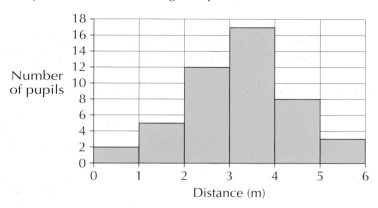

a Alex says, 'The longest throw was 5.4 metres'. Could she be correct? Explain your answer.

b Ben says, 'The median throw was between 2 and 3 metres'. Could he be correct? Explain your answer.

c Becky says, 'The range of the throws is 6 metres'. Explain why she is incorrect.

3 The pie chart shows how crimes were committed in a town over a month.

a It is claimed that most crime involves theft. Explain why this is incorrect.

b Write down two statements using the information in the pie chart.

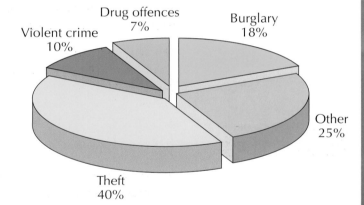

4 The table shows information about the animal populations on four small farms in the years 1995 and 2000.

a Which farm has increased the number of animals between 1995 and 2000?

b Which farm has shown the largest decrease in animal population from 1995 to 2000?

Farm	Animal population 1995	Animal population 2000
A	143	275
B	284	241
C	86	75
D	102	63
Total	615	654

c A newspaper headline says that farm animal populations are increasing. Using the information in the table, criticise this headline.

Extension Work

Find a graph or chart from a newspaper. Write down the facts that the newspaper article is claiming that the graph or chart shows. Use different arguments, referring to the graph or chart, to cast doubt on the facts given.

Scatter graphs

A doctor records the size of the pupils of people's eyes and the brightness of the sunlight. He then plots the results on a graph. What can you tell about the connection between the brightness and the pupil size of the people?

Brightness

Pupil size

Example 11.5 ▷ Below are three scatter graphs. Describe the relationships in each graph.

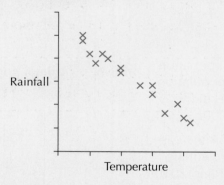

Rainfall

Temperature

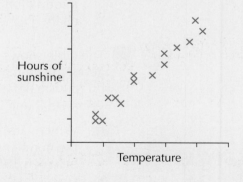

Hours of sunshine

Temperature

The first graph shows a **negative correlation**. Here, this means that the higher the temperature, the less the rainfall.

The second graph shows a **positive correlation**. Here, this means that the higher the temperature, the more hours of sunshine there are.

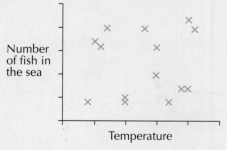

Number of fish in the sea

Temperature

The third graph shows **no correlation**. Here, this means that there is no connection between the temperature and the number of fish in the sea.

1 A survey is carried out to compare pupils' ages with the amount of money that they spend each week.

Age (years)	11	16	14	13	13	18	10	12	14	15
Amount spent	£3	£3.50	£6	£5	£6.50	£12	£2.50	£4	£8	£7.50

a   Plot the data on a scatter graph. Use the x-axis for age from 8 to 20 years, and use the y-axis for amount spent from £0 to £15.

b   Describe in words what the graph tells you and what sort of correlation there is.

2 The table shows how much time pupils spend watching television and how long they spend on homework per week.

Time watching TV (hours)	12	8	5	7	9	3	5	6	10	14
Time spent on homework (hours)	4	7	10	6	5	11	9	6	6	3

a   Plot the data on a scatter graph (take the axes as time spent on TV and homework, from 0 to 15 hours).

b   Describe in words what the graph tells you and what sort of correlation there is.

3 A car changes hands every year. The table shows the selling price and the age of the car.

Age (years)	1	2	3	4	5	6	7
Selling price	£10 000	£8300	£7500	£6000	£5300	£4200	£3400

a   Plot the data on a scatter graph. Use the x-axis for age from 0 to 10 years, and use the y-axis for price from £1000 to £11 000.

b   Describe in words what the graph tells you about the car's value as it gets older.

Extension Work

Put two columns in your exercise book. Write down pairs of events that have negative, positive or no correlation. In each case indicate the type of correlation.

Analysing data

Suppose that you want to put some **data** into the form of diagrams or tables. How do you choose which form to use? Ask yourself a few questions. Will my diagram be easy to understand? If I use a pie chart, will there be too many sectors? Am I comparing two sets of data?

Exercise 11E

FM **1** For each question below, write down whether the best way to collect data is by:
- Observation
- Questionnaire
- Controlled experiment
- Data from textbooks, newspapers or the Internet

a Do more men attend sports events than women?

b Does it always snow in December?

c Is a dice fair?

d Which soap powder is most popular?

e What percentage of 13-year-old children have mobile phones?

f How popular is a particular restaurant?

g How many people have had an illness in the past 2 months?

h Do Year 8 girls prefer Brad Pitt or Tom Cruise?

i How many people visit a shopping centre on a Sunday?

j How many lorries use a road between 8.00 am and 9.00 am?

FM **2** Now you are ready to analyse and write a report on the data that you collected for Exercise 11A.

Your report should consist of the following.
- A brief statement of what you expect to show: this is called a hypothesis
- A section that explains how you collected your data
- A copy of any questionnaires you may have used
- Completed data-collection sheets or tally charts
- Suitable diagrams to illustrate your data
- Calculated statistics, such as mean, median, mode and range
- A brief conclusion that refers back to your hypothesis

You may wish to use the following sorts of diagrams as you think appropriate: bar charts, pie charts, stem-and-leaf diagrams, scatter graphs.

Extension **Work**

The extension work is to finish writing up your report, including as much detail as possible using the guidelines given in this chapter.

LEVEL BOOSTER

6 I can use, collect and record continuous data.
I can construct pie charts.
I can draw conclusions from scatter graphs, and have a basic understanding of correlation.

7 I know how to generate a detailed solution to a given problem.
I can critically examine a mathematical diagram.

1 *2001 Paper 1*

There are 60 students in a school. 6 of these students wear glasses.

Wear glasses

Do not wear glasses

a The pie chart is not drawn accurately.

What should the angles be? Show your working.

b Exactly half of the 60 students in the school are boys.

From this information, is the percentage of boys in this school that wear glasses 5%, 6%, 10%, 20%, 50% or not possible to tell?

2 *2001 Paper 2*

A teacher asked two different classes: 'What type of book is your favourite?'

a Results from class A (total 20 pupils):

Draw a pie chart to show this information. Show your working and draw your angles accurately.

Type of book	Frequency
Crime	3
Non-fiction	13
Fantasy	4

b The pie chart on the right shows the results from all of class B.

Each pupil had only one vote.

The sector for non-fiction represents 11 pupils.

How many pupils are in class B?

Show your working.

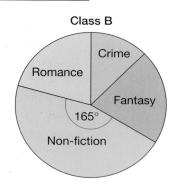

Class B

Crime
Romance
Fantasy
165°
Non-fiction

3 *2005 Paper 1*

Bumps are built on a road to slow cars down.

The stem-and-leaf diagrams show the speeds of 15 cars before and after the bumps were built.

Before						After					
2						2	3	4	4		
2	7	8				2	6	6	7	8	8	9
3	0	2	4			3	0	0	0	1	2
3	5	6	8	9		3	5				
4	1	3	4	4	4	4					
4	6					4					

Key:

2 | 3 means 23 miles per hour

a Copy the sentences below and use the diagrams to write in the missing **numbers**.

Before the bumps:

The maximum speed was … mph, and … cars went at more than 30 mph.

After the bumps:

The maximum speed was … mph, and … cars went at more than 30 mph.

b Show that the **median** speed fell by 10 mph.

4 *2007 Paper 1*

Chris read the first 55 numbers from a book of random numbers.

As he read each number he recorded it in the diagram below.

```
0 | 5  9  9  8  3  4  1
1 | 6  3  1  0  3
2 | 8  2
3 | 1  1  6  9  3
4 | 6  9  9  4  7  0
5 | 5  7  7  6
6 | 0  2  8  4  8  0  3  5
7 | 6  8  0  1  5  4
8 | 6  6  9  2  8  5  7
9 | 6  7  8  0  0
```

Key:

1 | 3 represents 13

a What was the **largest** number he recorded?

b Explain how Chris could change the diagram to make it easier for him to find the **median** of his data set.

5 *2006 Paper 1*

A teacher asked 21 pupils to estimate the height of a building in metres.

The stem-and-leaf diagram shows **all 21** results.

```
 6 | 5  9
 7 | 0  2  6  8  8
 8 | 3  3  5  7  7  9
 9 | 0  5  5  5
10 | 4  8
11 | 2  7
```

Key:

6 | 5 represents 6.5 m

a Show that the **range** of estimated heights was **5.2 m**.

b What was the **median** estimated height?

c The height of the building was **9.2 m**.

What **percentage** of the pupils **over-estimated** the height?

6 *2006 Paper 2*

Field voles are small animals that do not live for very long.

A scientist recorded data on **1000** of these voles that were born on the same day.

The graph shows how many voles were still alive after a number of weeks.

Use the graph to answer this question.

Estimate the probability that a field vole will live to be **at least 20** weeks old.

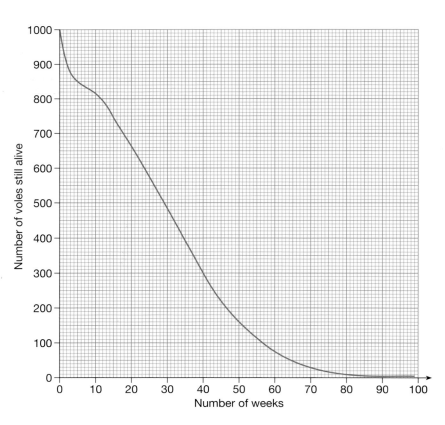

7 *2006 Paper 1*

Car tyres are checked for safety by measuring the tread.

The tread on a tyre and the distance travelled by that tyre were recorded for a sample of tyres. The scatter graph shows the results.

Tyres with a tread of **less than 1.6 mm** are illegal.

Suppose the government changes this rule to **less than 2.5 mm**.

a How many of these tyres would now be illegal?

b About **how many fewer kilometres** would you expect a tyre to last before it was illegal?

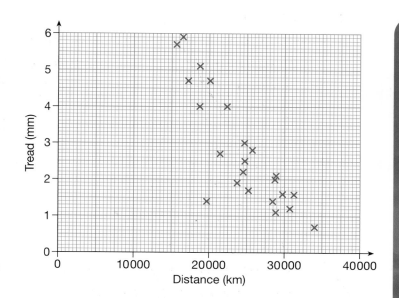

8 *2005 Paper 1*

A pupil investigated whether students who study more watch less television.

The scatter graph shows his results. The line of best fit is also shown.

a What type of correlation does the graph show?

b The pupil says the equation of the line of best fit is $y = x + 40$

Explain how you can tell that this equation is **wrong**.

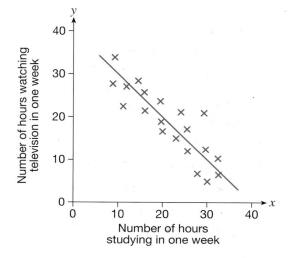

Football attendances

The Sheffield football teams have had various support over the years as they have moved in and out of the divisions. Below is a table comparing their attendances over the years 1989 to 2007.

Year	Sheffield Wednesday			Sheffield United		
	Level	Place	Attendance	Level	Place	Attendance
1989	1	15	20 035	3	2	12 279
1990	1	18	20 928	2	2	17 008
1991	2	3	26 196	1	13	21 609
1992	1	3	29 578	1	9	21 805
1993	1	7	27 264	1	14	18 985
1994	1	7	27 187	1	20	19 562
1995	1	13	26 596	2	8	14 408
1996	1	15	24 877	2	9	12 904
1997	1	7	25 714	2	5	16 675
1998	1	13	28 706	2	6	17 936
1999	1	12	26 745	2	8	16 258
2000	1	19	24 855	2	16	13 700
2001	2	17	19 268	2	10	17 211
2002	2	20	20 882	2	13	18 031
2003	2	21	20 327	2	3	18 073
2004	3	16	22 336	2	8	21 646
2005	3	5	23 100	2	8	19 594
2006	2	19	24 853	2	2	23 650
2007	2	9	23 638	1	18	30 512

Use this information to answer the questions.

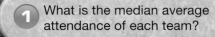

1 What is the median average attendance of each team?

2 What is the mean level played at by each team during these years?

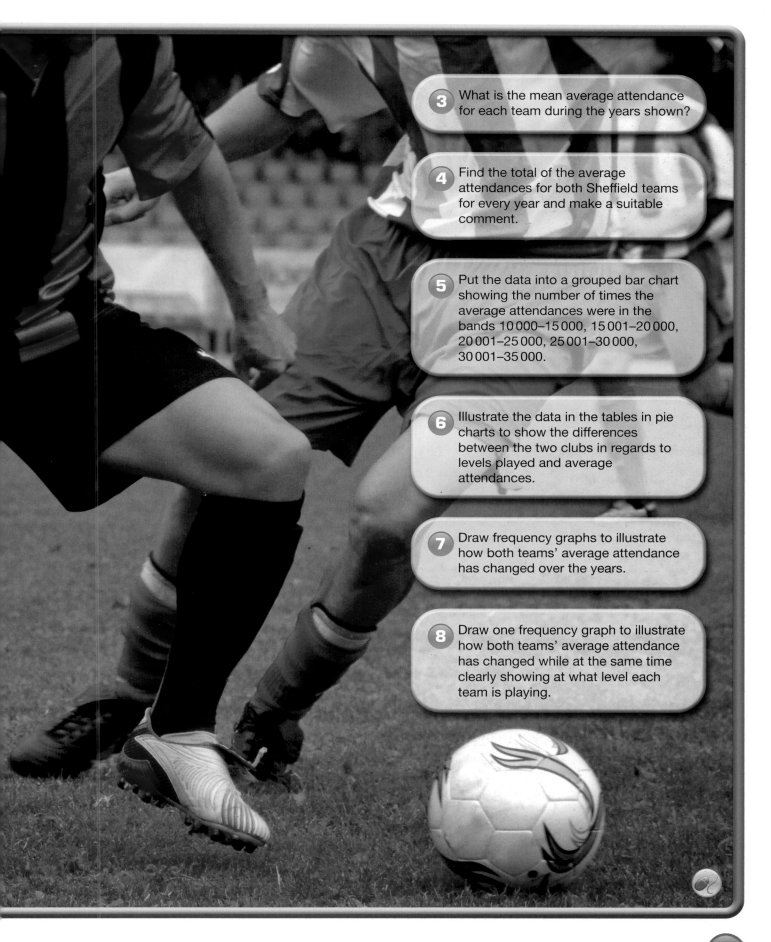

3 What is the mean average attendance for each team during the years shown?

4 Find the total of the average attendances for both Sheffield teams for every year and make a suitable comment.

5 Put the data into a grouped bar chart showing the number of times the average attendances were in the bands 10 000–15 000, 15 001–20 000, 20 001–25 000, 25 001–30 000, 30 001–35 000.

6 Illustrate the data in the tables in pie charts to show the differences between the two clubs in regards to levels played and average attendances.

7 Draw frequency graphs to illustrate how both teams' average attendance has changed over the years.

8 Draw one frequency graph to illustrate how both teams' average attendance has changed while at the same time clearly showing at what level each team is playing.

<table>
<tr><td>**This chapter is going to show you**</td><td>**What you should already know**</td></tr>
<tr><td>

- How to add and subtract fractions with any denominators
- How to use BODMAS with more complex problems
- How to solve problems using decimals, fractions, percentages and units of measurement

</td><td>

- How to add and subtract fractions with the same denominator
- How to find equivalent fractions
- How to use the four operations with decimals

</td></tr>
</table>

Fractions

This section recalls some of the rules you have already met about fractions.

Example 12.1

a How many sevenths are in 4 whole ones?

b How many fifths are in $3\frac{3}{5}$?

a There are 7 sevenths in a whole one, so there are $4 \times 7 = 28$ sevenths in 4 whole ones.

b There are $3 \times 5 = 15$ fifths in 3 whole ones, so there are $15 + 3 = 18$ fifths in $3\frac{3}{5}$.

Example 12.2

Write the following as mixed numbers.

a $\frac{48}{15}$ b The fraction of a kilometre given by 3150 metres

a $48 \div 15 = 3$ remainder 3, so $\frac{48}{15} = 3\frac{3}{15}$, which can cancel to $3\frac{1}{5}$.
Note: It is usually easier to cancel after the fraction has been written as a mixed number rather than before.

b 1 kilometre is 1000 metres, so the fraction is $\frac{3150}{1000} = 3\frac{150}{1000} = 3\frac{3}{20}$

Exercise 12A

1 Find the missing number in each of these fractions.

a $\frac{5}{3} = \frac{\square}{9}$

b $\frac{9}{8} = \frac{\square}{16}$

c $\frac{25}{9} = \frac{\square}{27}$

d $\frac{8}{5} = \frac{\square}{15}$

e $\frac{12}{7} = \frac{48}{\square}$

f $\frac{20}{9} = \frac{80}{\square}$

g $\frac{11}{6} = \frac{\square}{18}$

h $\frac{7}{2} = \frac{\square}{6}$

i $\frac{13}{3} = \frac{52}{\square}$

2 a How many sixths are in $3\frac{5}{6}$? **b** How many eighths are in $4\frac{1}{2}$?

c How many tenths are in $2\frac{2}{5}$? **d** How many ninths are in $5\frac{7}{9}$?

3 Write each mixed number in Question 2 as a top-heavy fraction in its simplest form.

4 Write each of the following as a mixed number in its simplest form.

a $\frac{14}{12}$ **b** $\frac{15}{9}$ **c** $\frac{24}{21}$ **d** $\frac{35}{20}$ **e** $\frac{28}{20}$ **f** $\frac{70}{50}$

g $\frac{28}{24}$ **h** $\frac{26}{12}$ **i** $\frac{44}{24}$ **j** $\frac{32}{10}$ **k** $\frac{36}{24}$ **l** $\frac{75}{35}$

5 Write these fractions as mixed numbers (cancel down if necessary).

a Seven thirds **b** Sixteen sevenths **c** Twelve fifths **d** Nine halves

e $\frac{20}{7}$ **f** $\frac{24}{5}$ **g** $\frac{13}{3}$ **h** $\frac{19}{8}$ **i** $\frac{146}{12}$ **j** $\frac{78}{10}$ **k** $\frac{52}{12}$ **l** $\frac{102}{9}$

6 Write the following fractions.

a The fraction of an hour given by the turn of the minute hand round a clock as it goes from:

    i 7:15 to 9:45 **ii** 8:25 to 10:10 **iii** 6:12 to 7:24

    iv 8:55 to 10:45 **v** 7:05 to 10:20 **vi** 9:36 to 11:24

b The fraction of a metre given by:

    i 715 cm **ii** 2300 mm **iii** 405 cm

    iv 580 cm **v** 1550 mm **vi** 225 cm

c The fraction of a kilogram given by:

    i 2300 g **ii** 4050 g **iii** 7500 g

    iv 5600 g **v** 1225 g **vi** 6580 g

Extension **Work**

A gallon is an imperial unit of capacity still in common use in the UK. There are 8 pints in a gallon. A litre is about $1\frac{3}{4}$ pints and a gallon is about $4\frac{1}{2}$ litres. Write the missing mixed numbers to make these statements true.

1 2 litres = ... pints **2** 10 pints = ... gallons **3** 5 gallons = ... litres

4 3 litres = ... pints **5** 3 gallons = ... litres **6** 20 pints = ... gallons

---

Adding and subtracting fractions

This section will give you more practice with adding and subtracting fractions.

Example 12.3 ▶

Work out:

a $\frac{3}{8} + 1\frac{1}{4}$ **b** $1\frac{7}{8} - \frac{3}{4}$

Previously, we used a fraction chart or line to do these. A fraction line is drawn below.

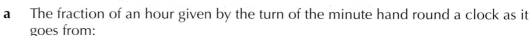

a Start at 0 and count on $\frac{3}{8}$, then 1 and then $\frac{1}{4}$ to give $\frac{3}{8} + 1\frac{1}{4} = 1\frac{5}{8}$.

b Start at $1\frac{7}{8}$ and count back $\frac{3}{4}$ to give $1\frac{7}{8} - \frac{3}{4} = 1\frac{1}{8}$.

When denominators are not the same, they must be made the same before the numerators are added or subtracted. To do this, we need to find the **lowest common multiple** (LCM) of the denominators.

Example 12.4

Work out:

a $\frac{2}{9} + \frac{1}{15}$ b $1\frac{9}{14} - \frac{5}{6}$

a   The LCM of 9 and 15 is 45, so the two fractions need to be written as forty-fifths:
$\frac{2}{9} + \frac{1}{15} = \frac{10}{45} + \frac{3}{45} = \frac{13}{45}$

b   The LCM of 14 and 6 is 42, so the two fractions need to be written as forty-seconds. The mixed number needs to be made into a top-heavy fraction.
$\frac{23}{14} - \frac{5}{6} = \frac{69}{42} - \frac{35}{42} = \frac{34}{42} = \frac{17}{21}$

Exercise 12B

① Work out the following. The eighths fraction line given earlier may help.

a $\frac{7}{8} + \frac{1}{4}$ b $1\frac{3}{8} + \frac{3}{4}$ c $2\frac{3}{4} + \frac{5}{8}$ d $\frac{3}{4} + 1\frac{1}{8} + 1\frac{3}{8}$

e $\frac{7}{8} - \frac{1}{4}$ f $2\frac{3}{8} - \frac{3}{4}$ g $2\frac{3}{4} - 1\frac{1}{8}$ h $1\frac{3}{8} + 1\frac{1}{2} - 1\frac{1}{4}$

② Convert the following fractions to equivalent fractions with a common denominator. Then work out the answer. Cancel down or write as a mixed number if appropriate.

a $\frac{1}{8} + \frac{3}{5}$ b $\frac{5}{7} + \frac{1}{4}$ c $\frac{3}{14} + \frac{3}{8}$ d $\frac{5}{9} + \frac{5}{6}$

e $\frac{5}{12} + \frac{3}{10}$ f $1\frac{3}{8} + \frac{1}{6}$ g $1\frac{7}{12} + \frac{1}{8}$ h $1\frac{3}{4} + 1\frac{1}{3} + \frac{5}{12}$

i $\frac{3}{5} - \frac{1}{8}$ j $\frac{5}{7} - \frac{1}{4}$ k $\frac{3}{14} - \frac{1}{4}$ l $\frac{5}{9} - \frac{1}{6}$

m $\frac{5}{12} - \frac{1}{10}$ n $1\frac{7}{8} - \frac{5}{14}$ o $1\frac{7}{12} - \frac{1}{8}$ p $1\frac{3}{4} + 1\frac{3}{14} - \frac{5}{8}$

③ A magazine has $\frac{1}{3}$ of its pages for advertising, $\frac{1}{12}$ for letters and the rest for articles.

a   What fraction of the pages is for articles?

b   If the magazine has 120 pages, how many are used for articles?

④ A survey of pupils showed that $\frac{1}{5}$ of them walked to school, $\frac{2}{3}$ came by bus and the rest came by car.

a   What fraction came by car?

b   If there were 900 pupils in the school, how many came by car?

⑤ A farmer plants $\frac{2}{7}$ of his land with wheat and $\frac{3}{8}$ with maize. The rest is used for cattle.

a   What fraction of the land is used to grow crops?

b   What fraction is used for cattle?

Extension **Work**

Consider the series $\frac{1}{2} + \frac{1}{4} + \frac{1}{8} + \frac{1}{16} + \frac{1}{32} + \frac{1}{64} + \frac{1}{128}$ … If we write down the first term, then add the first two terms, then add the first three terms, we obtain the series $\frac{1}{2}, \frac{3}{4}, \frac{7}{8},$ …

a   Continue this sequence for another four terms.

b   What total will the series reach if it continues for an infinite number of terms?

c   Repeat with the series $\frac{1}{3} + \frac{1}{9} + \frac{1}{27} + \frac{1}{81} + \frac{1}{243} + \frac{1}{729} + \frac{1}{2187}$ …

Order of operations

B – Brackets **O** – pOwers **DM** – Division and Multiplication **AS** – Addition and Subtraction	**B** – Brackets **I** – Indices **DM** – Division and Multiplication **AS** – Addition and Subtraction

BODMAS and BIDMAS are ways of remembering the order in which mathematical operations are carried out.

Example 12.5 ▷

Evaluate:

a $2 \times 3^2 + 6 \div 2$ **b** $(2 + 3)^2 \times 8 - 6$

Show each step of the calculation.

a Firstly, work out the power or index number, which gives $2 \times 9 + 6 \div 2$
 Secondly, the division, which gives $2 \times 9 + 3$
 Thirdly, the multiplication, which gives $18 + 3$
 Finally, the addition to give 21

b Firstly, work out the bracket, which gives $5^2 \times 8 - 6$
 Secondly, the power or index number, which gives $25 \times 8 - 6$
 Thirdly, the multiplication, which gives $200 - 6$
 Finally, the subtraction to give 194

Note: If we have a calculation that is a string of additions and subtractions, or a string of multiplications and divisions, then we do the calculation from left to right.

Example 12.6 ▷

Calculate:

a $\dfrac{(2 + 6)^2}{2 \times 4^2}$ **b** $3.1 + [4.2 - (1.7 + 1.5) \div 1.6]$

a $\dfrac{(2 + 6)^2}{2 \times 4^2} = \dfrac{8^2}{2 \times 16} = \dfrac{64}{32} = 2$

b $3.1 + [4.2 - (1.7 + 1.5) \div 1.6] = 3.1 + (4.2 - 3.2 \div 1.6)$
 $= 3.1 + (4.2 - 2)$
 $= 3.1 + 2.2$
 $= 5.3$

Note: If there are 'nested brackets', then the inside ones are calculated first.

Exercise 12C

1. Write the operation that you do first in each of these calculations, and then work out each one.

   a $5 + 4 \times 7$ b $18 - 6 \div 3$

   c $7 \times 7 + 2$ d $16 \div 4 - 2$

   e $(5 + 4) \times 7$ f $(18 - 6) \div 3$

   g $7 \times (7 + 2)$ h $16 \div (4 - 2)$

   i $5 + 9 - 7 - 2$ j $2 \times 6 \div 3 \times 4$

   k $12 - 15 + 7$ l $12 \div 3 \times 6 \div 2$

2. Work out the following, showing each step of the calculation.

   a $3 + 4 + 4^2$ b $3 + (4 + 4)^2$ c $3 \times 4 + 4^2$ d $3 \times (4 + 4)^2$

   e $5 + 3^2 - 7$ f $(5 + 3)^2 - 7$ g $2 \times 6^2 + 2$ h $2 \times (6^2 + 2)$

   i $\dfrac{200}{4 \times 5}$ j $\dfrac{80 + 20}{4 \times 5}$ k $\sqrt{(4^2 + 3^2)}$ l $\dfrac{(2 + 3)^2}{6 - 1}$

   m $3.2 - (5.4 + 6.1) + (5.7 - 2.1)$ n $8 \times (12 \div 4) \div (2 \times 2)$

3. Write out each of the following and insert brackets to make the calculation true.

   a $3 \times 7 + 1 = 24$ b $3 + 7 \times 2 = 20$

   c $2 \times 3 + 1 \times 4 = 32$ d $2 + 3^2 = 25$

   e $5 \times 5 + 5 \div 5 = 26$ f $5 \times 5 + 5 \div 5 = 10$

   g $5 \times 5 + 5 \div 5 = 30$ h $5 \times 5 + 5 \div 5 = 6$

   i $15 - 3^2 = 144$

4. Work out the following (calculate the inside bracket first).

   a $120 \div [25 - (3 - 2)]$ b $120 \div (25 - 3 - 2)$

   c $5 + [8 \times (6 - 3)]$ d $5 + (8 \times 6 - 3)$

   e $[120 \div (60 - 20)] + 20$ f $(120 \div 60 - 20) + 20$

   g $[120 \div (20 \div 4)] + 3$ h $(120 \div 20 \div 4) + 3$

   i $[(3 + 4)^2 - 5] \times 2$

Extension Work

By putting brackets in different places, one calculation can be made to give many different answers. For example, without brackets:

$4 \times 6 + 4 - 3 \times 8 + 1 = 24 + 4 - 24 + 1 = 5$

With brackets, this could be:

$4 \times (6 + 4) - 3 \times (8 + 1) = 4 \times 10 - 3 \times 9 = 40 - 27 = 13$

1. By putting brackets into the appropriate places in the same calculation, obtain answers of:

   a 33 b 17 c 252

2. Similarly, put brackets into $12 \div 6 - 2 \times 1 + 5 \times 3$ to make:

   a 54 b 15 c 0

Multiplying decimals

This section will give you more practice on multiplying integers and decimals.

Example 12.7

Find:

a　0.03×0.05　　**b**　900×0.004　　**c**　$50 \times 0.04 \times 0.008$

a　$3 \times 5 = 15$. There are four decimal places in the multiplication, so there are four in the answer. Therefore $0.03 \times 0.05 = 0.0015$

b　Rewrite as equivalent products, i.e. $900 \times 0.004 = 90 \times 0.04 = 9 \times 0.4 = 3.6$

c　Do this in two parts. Firstly, $50 \times 0.04 = 5 \times 0.4 = 2$. Then rewrite 2×0.008 as $2 \times 8 = 16$ but with three decimal places in the answer.
So $50 \times 0.04 \times 0.008 = 0.016$

Example 12.8

Without a calculator, work out 13.4×0.63.

There are many ways to do this. Three are shown. In all cases you should first estimate the answer:

$$13.4 \times 0.63 \approx 13 \times 0.6 = 1.3 \times 6 = 7.8$$

Remember also that there are three decimal places in the product (13.4×0.63), so there will be three in the answer.

In two methods the decimal points are ignored and put back into the answer.

Column method

```
    134
 ×   63
    402
   8040
   8442
```

Box method 1

	100	30	4	Total
60	6000	1800	240	8040
3	300	90	12	402
			Total	8442

Box method 2

	10	3	0.4	Total
0.6	6	1.8	0.24	8.04
0.03	0.3	0.09	0.012	0.402
			Total	8.442

By all three methods the answer is $13.4 \times 0.63 = 8.442$

1　Without using a calculator, work out the following.

a	400×0.5	**b**	0.07×200
c	0.3×400	**d**	0.06×500
e	0.07×400	**f**	0.008×200
g	0.005×700	**h**	0.003×4000
i	0.004×7000	**j**	300×0.009
k	900×0.01	**l**	900×0.04
m	600×0.1	**n**	700×0.01
o	800×0.001	**p**	900×0.0001

2 Without using a calculator, work out the following.

    a $0.002 \times 500 \times 300$

    b $0.03 \times 0.04 \times 60\,000$

    c $0.4 \times 0.02 \times 800$

    d $400 \times 600 \times 0.05$

    e $40 \times 0.006 \times 20$

    f $0.3 \times 0.08 \times 4000$

3 Without using a calculator, work out the answers to the following. Use any method you are happy with.

    a 73×9.4

    b 5.82×4.5

    c 12.3×2.7

    d 1.24×10.3

    e 2.78×0.51

    f 12.6×0.15

    g 2.63×6.5

    h 0.68×0.42

4 A rectangle is 2.46 m by 0.67 m. What is the area of the rectangle?

Extension   **Work**

1 Work out:

    a 1.2^2 **b** 1.7^2 **c** $1.7^2 - 1.2^2$ **d** 0.5×2.9

2 Work out:

    a 1.5^2 **b** 2.1^2 **c** $2.1^2 - 1.5^2$ **d** 0.6×3.6

3 Look for a connection between the calculations in parts **c** and **d** of **1** and **2**. Then write down the answer to $3.1^2 - 2.1^2$. Check your answer with a calculator.

Dividing decimals

This section will give you more practice on dividing integers and decimals.

Example 12.9   Work out:

    a $0.12 \div 0.03$ **b** $600 \div 0.15$

    a   Simplify the division by rewriting as equivalent divisions. In this case, multiply both numbers by 10 until the divisor (0.03) becomes a simple whole number (3). This is equivalent to shifting the decimal point to the right by the same amount in both numbers. So:

$$0.12 \div 0.03 = 1.2 \div 0.3 = 12 \div 3 = 4$$

    b   Rewriting as equivalent divisions:

$$600 \div 0.15 = 6000 \div 1.5 = 60\,000 \div 15 = 4000$$

Example 12.10 ▷

Work out:

a   32.8 ÷ 40   **b**   7.6 ÷ 800

a   Simplify the division by rewriting as equivalent divisions. In this case, divide both numbers by 10 until the divisor (40) becomes a simple whole number (4). This is equivalent to shifting the decimal point to the left by the same amount in both numbers. So:

$$32.8 ÷ 40 = 3.28 ÷ 4 = 0.82$$

It may be easier to set this out as a short division problem:

$$\frac{0.82}{4\overline{)3.28}}$$

b   Rewriting as equivalent divisions:

$$7.6 ÷ 800 = 0.76 ÷ 80 = 0.076 ÷ 8 = 0.0095$$

As a short division problem:

$$\frac{0.0095}{8\overline{)0.076\,^40}}$$

Example 12.11 ▷

Work out: 4.32 ÷ 1.2

First estimate the answer: 4.32 ÷ 1.2 ≈ 4 ÷ 1 = 4

Write without the decimal points, i.e. 432 ÷ 12, and use repeated subtraction (chunking):

$$
\begin{array}{r}
432 \\
-\ \ 360 \quad (30 \times 12) \\
\hline
72 \\
-\ \ \ 72 \quad\ (6 \times 12) \\
\hline
0 \quad (36 \times 12)
\end{array}
$$

The answer is 4.32 ÷ 1.2 = 3.6

Exercise 12E

1 Without using a calculator, work out the following.

    a 0.36 ÷ 0.02   **b** 0.48 ÷ 0.5

    c 0.45 ÷ 0.02   **d** 0.18 ÷ 0.03

    e 0.24 ÷ 0.02   **f** 0.48 ÷ 0.3

    g 0.39 ÷ 0.3   **h** 0.24 ÷ 0.05

2 Without using a calculator, work out the following.

    a 600 ÷ 0.4   **b** 500 ÷ 0.25

    c 300 ÷ 0.08   **d** 300 ÷ 0.02

    e 60 ÷ 0.015   **f** 60 ÷ 0.25

    g 500 ÷ 0.02   **h** 40 ÷ 0.25

6

3 Without using a calculator, work out the following.

a $3.2 \div 40$ b $2.8 \div 400$

c $24 \div 400$ d $36 \div 90$

e $4.8 \div 80$ f $4.8 \div 200$

g $3.5 \div 700$ h $0.16 \div 400$

4 Without using a calculator, work out the following. Use any method you are happy with.

a $3.36 \div 1.4$ b $1.56 \div 2.4$

c $5.688 \div 3.6$ d $20.28 \div 5.2$

e $22.23 \div 6.5$ f $2.89 \div 3.4$

g $5.75 \div 23$ h $2.304 \div 0.24$

5 A rectangle has an area of 3.915 cm². The length is 2.7 cm. Calculate the width.

Extension Work

1 Given that $46 \times 34 = 1564$, work out:

a 4.6×17 b 2.3×1.7

c $1564 \div 0.34$ d $15.64 \div 0.23$

2 Given that $39 \times 32 = 1248$, work out:

a 3.9×16 b 0.13×32

c 3900×0.08 d 0.0039×32

3 Given that $2.8 \times 0.55 = 1.540$, work out:

a 14×55 b $154 \div 11$

c $15.4 \div 0.28$ d 0.014×5500

LEVEL BOOSTER

5
I can simplify fractions by cancelling common factors.
I can add and subtract simple fractions.
I know the correct order of operations, including using brackets.
I can multiply simple decimals without using a calculator.

6
I can add and subtract fractions by writing them with a common denominator.
I can multiply and divide decimals.

7
I know the effect of multiplying and dividing by numbers between 0 and 1.
I can solve problems involving multiplication and division of numbers of any size.

1 *2005 Paper 2*

Use your calculator to work out the answers.

$(48 + 57) \times (61 - 19) =$

$\dfrac{48 + 57}{61 - 19} =$

2 *2005 Paper 1*

How many eighths are there in one quarter?

Now work out $\frac{3}{4} + \frac{1}{8}$

3 *2007 Paper 1*

Copy these fraction sums and write in the missing numbers.

$$\frac{1}{4} + \frac{\boxed{}}{8} = 1 \qquad\qquad \frac{1}{3} + \frac{8}{\boxed{}} = 1$$

4 *2004 Paper 2*

Some numbers are smaller than their squares.

For example: $7 < 7^2$

Which numbers are **equal** to their squares?

FM Shopping for bargains

The more you buy, the more you save

Collect 15 points for every litre

When you have 5000 points you receive a £5 voucher to spend in store

Petrol £1.20 per litre
Diesel £1.30 per litre

1
a How many litres would you need to buy to collect a voucher?

b Petrol is £1.20 a litre.

How much would you spend on petrol before you receive a voucher?

c Estimate the number of weeks it would take to receive a voucher if you use an average of 30 litres of petrol each week.

d The saving is equivalent to 1.5p per litre.

Work out the percentage saving per litre.

2 Nina uses an average of 40 litres of diesel each week. Diesel is £1.30 per litre.

a How much does she spend on diesel each week?

b Her car uses 1 litre of diesel for every 14 miles travelled. If Nina drives 140 fewer miles each week, how much will she save each week?

c If the price of diesel goes up by 10p a litre, how much more would she spend on diesel in a year (52 weeks)?

d Work out the percentage increase.

3 Here is some information about three business people and their company cars.

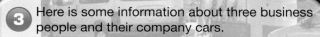

	Car fuel	Annual distance travelled (km)	CO_2 emissions (grams per km)
Managing director	Diesel	14 000	140
Secretary	Petrol	8 000	200
Delivery driver	Diesel	22 000	110

The company wants to encourage each person to reduce the CO_2 emissions.

a Work out the annual amount of CO_2 emissions for each car.
Give your answer in kilograms.

b The company wants each person to reduce the CO_2 emissions by reducing each person's travelling by 15%.
Work out the reduction in CO_2 emissions for each car.
Give your answer in kilograms.

Chocolate
Only £1 Was £1.19

Mint sauce
3 for £2 Normally 85p each

Almost Butter
Buy one get one free £1.38

Milk
2 for £2 or £1.25 each

Cheese
Save £1 was £3.25

Scotch eggs
Were £1.15 Save 20% Now 92p

Grillsteaks
520g Half price
Was £2.99 Now £1.49

Baby shampoo
Save $\frac{1}{3}$ Was £2.47 Now £1.64

Luxury Crisps
2 for £2.50 £1.49 each

Yoghurts
48p each Buy 3 get 3 free

Bread 95p

Coffee £3.90

Baked beans 45p

Orange juice £1.30

4 You have £20 to spend but you have to buy, bread, coffee, baked beans and orange juice.

a How much do these four items cost altogether?

b How much does this leave you to spend on other items?

c Using the offers, make **two** different shopping lists of items you could now afford to buy. Try to spend as close to £20 altogether as possible. (*Hint:* You can buy single items but then you would not get the offer price.)

5 You decide to take up all the offers shown.

a How much will you save on each offer compared with the full price?

b How much will you save altogether?

6 The shopping can be ordered on the Internet and delivered to your home.

The delivery charge is £4.50.

The journey to the supermarket and back is 8 miles altogether.

It costs 60p per mile to run your car.

Explain the advantages and disadvantages of having the shopping delivered.

This chapter is going to show you

- How to expand and then simplify expressions
- How to solve a range of linear equations
- How to solve equations by trial and improvement
- How to construct equations and solve them
- How to work with negative gradients
- How to change the subject of a formula

What you should already know

- How to solve simple equations
- How to use the arithmetic of negative numbers
- How to find the gradient of a line

Expand and simplify

In algebra we often have to rearrange **expressions** and **equations**. You have met two methods for doing this before: expansion and simplification.

Expansion means removing the brackets from an expression by multiplying each term inside the brackets by the term outside the brackets. When a negative term multiplies a bracket, it changes all the signs in the bracket.

Simplification means collecting **like terms** so as to write an expression as simply as possible. Sometimes you need to expand brackets first, then simplify.

Example 13.1

Expand:

a $2(x + 3y)$ **b** $m(5p - 2)$

a $2(x + 3y) = 2x + 6y$

b $m(5p - 2) = 5mp - 2m$

Example 13.2

Expand:

a $4 - (a + b)$ **b** $10 - (2x - 3y)$ **c** $T - 3(2m + 4n)$

a $4 - (a + b) = 4 - a - b$

b $10 - (2x - 3y) = 10 - 2x + 3y$

c $T - 3(2m + 4n) = T - 6m - 12n$

Example 13.3

Simplify:

a $5a + b + 2a + 5b$ **b** $4c + 3d - c - 2d$ **c** $4x - 2y + 2x - 3y$

a $5a + b + 2a + 5b = 7a + 6b$

b $4c + 3d - c - 2d = 3c + d$

c $4x - 2y + 2x - 3y = 6x - 5y$

Example 13.4

Expand and simplify:

a $3a + c + 2(a + 3c)$ **b** $10t - 3(2t - 4m)$

a $3a + c + 2(a + 3c) = 3a + c + 2a + 6c = 5a + 7c$

b $10t - 3(2t - 4m) = 10t - 6t + 12m = 4t + 12m$

Exercise 13A

1 Simplify the following.

a $3m + 2k + m$ **b** $2p + 3q + 5p$ **c** $4t + 3d - t$ **d** $5k + g - 2k$

e $5p + 2p + 3m$ **f** $2w + 5w + k$ **g** $m + 3m - 2k$ **h** $3x + 5x - 4t$

i $3k + 4m + 2m$ **j** $2t + 3w + w$ **k** $5x + 6m - 2m$ **l** $4y - 2p + 5p$

2 Expand the following.

a $3(2a + 3b)$ **b** $2(4t - 3k)$ **c** $5(n + 3p)$ **d** $4(2q - p)$

e $a(3 + t)$ **f** $b(4 + 3m)$ **g** $x(5y - t)$ **h** $y(3x - 2n)$

i $a(m + n)$ **j** $a(3p - t)$ **k** $x(6 + 3y)$ **l** $t(2k - p)$

3 Expand and simplify the following.

a $3x + 2(4x + 5)$ **b** $8a - 3(2a + 5)$ **c** $12t - 2(3t - 4)$

d $4x + 2(3x - 4)$ **e** $5t - 4(2t - 3)$ **f** $12m - 2(4m - 5)$

g $6(2k + 3) - 5k$ **h** $5(3n - 2) - 4n$ **i** $2(6x + 5) - 7x$

4 Expand and simplify the following.

a $2(3k + 4) + 3(4k + 2)$ **b** $5(2x + 1) + 2(3x + 5)$ **c** $3(5m + 2) + 4(3m + 1)$

d $5(2k + 3) - 2(k + 3)$ **e** $4(3t + 4) - 3(5t + 4)$ **f** $2(6k + 7) - 3(2k + 3)$

g $4(3 + 2m) - 2(5 + m)$ **h** $5(4 + 3d) - 3(4 + 2d)$ **i** $3(5 + 4k) - 2(3 + 5k)$

5 Solve the following equations.

a $3(x + 1) + 2(x - 1) = 21$ **b** $4(x + 3) + 3(x - 2) = 41$

c $4(2x + 1) + 5(3x + 2) = 83$ **d** $5(2x + 3) - 2(3x + 1) = 29$

e $4(6x + 5) - 2(4x + 3) = 54$ **f** $3(4x + 5) - 5(2x - 3) = 37$

6 Solve the following equations.

a $\dfrac{6x + 7}{4x - 1} = 2$ **b** $\dfrac{4x + 5}{x + 6} - 2 = 0$ **c** $\dfrac{11 - 2x}{1 - 4x} = 1.2$

Extension Work

In a magic square, each row and each column add up to the same amount.

Show that the square opposite is a magic square.

$x + m$	$x + y - m$	$x - y$
$x - y - m$	x	$x + y + m$
$x + y$	$x - y + m$	$x - m$

Solving equations by trial and improvement

So far, the equations you have met have been **linear**. This means that they do not contain **powers** of the variable. They are solved by adding, subtracting, multiplying or dividing both sides of the equation by the same terms.

Equations that do contain powers are called **non-linear**. Sometimes they are solved by **trial and improvement**. The aim is to find a close approximation to the solution.

Example 13.5 ▷

Solve the equation $x^2 + x = 34$ to one decimal place.

Try an integer to start with.
- Try $x = 5$: the left-hand side (LHS) of the equation is $5^2 + 5 = 30$, which is too small.

Try a bigger integer.
- Try $x = 6$: the LHS is $6^2 + 6 = 42$, which is too big.

So the solution lies between 5 and 6. Try the middle of this range.
- Try $x = 5.5$: the LHS is $5.5^2 + 5.5 = 35.75$, which is too big (the next guess should be smaller).
- Try $x = 5.3$: the LHS is $5.3^2 + 5.3 = 33.39$, which is too small.
- Try $x = 5.4$: the LHS is $5.4^2 + 5.4 = 34.56$, which is too big.

So the solution lies between 5.3 and 5.4. One of these is the answer correct to 1 dp. Try the middle of this range.
- Try $x = 5.35$: the LHS is $5.35^2 + 5.35 = 33.9725$ which is too small.

So the solution is bigger than 5.35 but smaller than 5.4. All of the numbers in this range round up to 5.4. So the solution is $x = 5.4$ correct to 1 dp.

The table summarises the calculations. You should make a table for each equation you solve.

x	$x^2 + x$	Comment
5	$5^2 + 5 = 30$	too small
6	$6^2 + 6 = 42$	too big (so x lies between 5 and 6)
5.5	$5.5^2 + 5.5 = 35.75$	too big
5.3	$5.3^2 + 5.3 = 33.39$	too small
5.4	$5.4^2 + 5.4 = 34.56$	too big (so x lies between 5.3 and 5.4)
5.35	$5.35^2 + 5.35 = 33.9725$	too small (so x rounds up to 5.4)

Example 13.6 ▶ Find a positive solution to the equation $x^3 + x = 52$ to one decimal place.

The solution can be followed in the table.

x	$x^3 + x$	Comment
4	$4^3 + 4 = 68$	too big
3	$3^3 + 3 = 30$	too small (so x lies between 3 and 4)
3.5	$3.5^3 + 3.5 = 46.375$	too small
3.7	$3.7^3 + 3.7 = 54.353$	too big
3.6	$3.6^3 + 3.6 = 50.256$	too small (so x lies between 3.6 and 3.7)
3.65	$3.65^3 + 3.65 = 52.277$	too big (so x rounds down to 3.6)

The solution is $x = 3.6$ to 1 dp.

Exercise 13B

(1) The solutions of each of the following equations lie between two consecutive integers. In each case, make a table and find the integers.

a $x^2 + x = 60$ **b** $x^2 - x = 40$ **c** $x^2 + x = 120$

d $x^3 + x = 25$ **e** $x^3 - x = 75$ **f** $x^3 + x = 150$

(2) The solutions of each of the following equations lie between two consecutive numbers with one decimal place. In each case, make a table and find the numbers.

a $x^2 + x = 75$ **b** $x^2 - x = 17$ **c** $x^2 + x = 115$

d $x^3 + x = 53$ **e** $x^3 - x = 76$ **f** $x^3 + x = 140$

(3) Jess and Paul both solved the equation $x^3 + x = 74$ by trial and improvement. However, they used different methods, as shown in the tables.

Jess				Paul		
x	$x^3 + x$	Comment		x	$x^3 + x$	Comment
4	68.00	too small		4	68.00	too small
4.1	73.02	too small		5	130.00	too big
4.2	78.29	too big		4.5	95.63	too big
4.11	73.54	too small		4.2	78.29	too big
4.12	74.05	too big		4.1	73.02	too small
4.111	73.59	too small		4.15	75.62	too big
4.112	73.64	too small		4.12	74.05	too big
4.113	73.69	too small		4.11	73.54	too small
4.114	73.74	too small		4.115	73.80	too small
4.115	73.80	too small		4.118	73.95	too small
4.116	73.85	too small		4.119	74.00	it's there
4.117	73.90	too small				
4.118	73.95	too small				
4.119	74.00	spot on				

The answer is $x = 4.119$.   The solution is $x = 4.119$.

Explain which of the two methods is more efficient for:

a   finding the solution to one decimal place.

b   finding the solution to two decimal places.

c   finding the solution to three decimal places.

Extension Work

Use a spreadsheet to find the solutions to the equation $x^3 - 10x^2 + 26x = 19$ to one decimal place. There are three positive solutions between 0 and 10.

Constructing equations

The first step in solving a problem with algebra is to write or **construct** an **equation**.

You need to choose a letter to stand for each variable in the problem. This might be x or the first letter of a suitable word. For example, t is often used to stand for time.

Example 13.7

I think of a number, add 7 to it, multiply it by 5, and get the answer 60. What is the number I first thought of?

Let my number be x:

'Add 7 to it' gives $x + 7$

'Multiply it by 5' gives $5(x + 7)$

'I get the answer 60' allows us to construct the equation $5(x + 7) = 60$

We can solve this now:
$$5(x + 7) = 60$$
Divide both sides by 5: $x + 7 = 12$
Subtract 7 from both sides: $x = 5$

Exercise 13C

1   Write an expression for each of the following.

a   Two numbers add up to 100. If one of the numbers is x, write an expression for the other.

b   The difference between two numbers is 8. If the smaller of the two numbers is y, write an expression for the larger number.

c   Jim and Ann have 18 marbles between them. If Jim has p marbles, how many marbles has Ann?

d   Lenny rides a bike at an average speed of 8 km/h. Write an expression for the distance he travels in t hours.

e   If n is an even number, find an expression for the next consecutive even number.

2   Solve each of the following problems by constructing an equation and then solving it.

a   A mother is four times as old as her son now. The mother's age is 48 years. Find the son's age. Let the son's age be x years.

b   If n is an odd number:

   i   Write an expression for the sum of the next *three* consecutive odd numbers.

   ii   If the sum of these *four* numbers is 32, find n.

c The sum of two consecutive even numbers is 54. Find the numbers. Let the smaller number be n.

d If the sum of two consecutive odd numbers is 208, what are the numbers? Let the smaller number be n.

e John weighs 3 kg more than his brother. The total weight is 185 kg. How much does John weigh? Let John's weight be w kg.

f Joy's Auntie Mary is four times as old as Joy. If the sum of their ages is 70, find their ages. Let Joy be x years old.

g A teacher bought 20 books in a sale. Some cost £8 each and the others cost £3 each. She spent £110 in all. How many of the £8 books did she buy? Let x be the number of £8 books she bought.

h The sum of six consecutive even numbers is 174. What is the smallest of the numbers? Let the smallest number be n.

i The sum of seven consecutive odd numbers is 133. What is the largest of the numbers? Let the largest number be n.

3 a The sum of two numbers is 56, and their difference is 14. What is their product?

b The sum of two numbers is 43, and their product is 450. What is their difference?

c The difference of two numbers is 12, and their product is 448. What is their sum?

d The sum of two numbers is 11, and twice the first plus half the second is 10. What is their product?

Extension Work

Carlos wanted to create a cuboid with a volume as close to 180 cm³ as possible.

The length had to be twice the width. The height had to be 3 cm less than the width. Find the width, length and height that Carlos will have to use to make his cuboid. Give your answer to two decimal places.

You may find a spreadsheet useful for this.

Problems with graphs

In Chapter 7 it was found that the graph of any linear equation is a straight line. The equation written in the form $y = mx + c$ gives the **gradient** m of the line and the **intercept** c on the y-axis.

The gradient m of a straight line was defined as the increase in the y coordinate for an increase of 1 in the x coordinate. It is found by dividing the **vertical rise** of the line by its corresponding **horizontal run**.

The gradient is positive if it runs from the bottom left of the graph to the top right, and negative if it runs from top left to bottom right.

The intercept c is the value of y when $x = 0$.

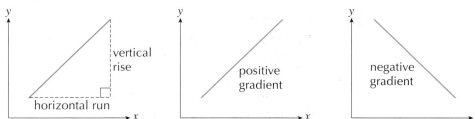

Exercise 13D

1 Each diagram shows the horizontal run and the vertical rise of a straight line. Find the gradient of each line below.

a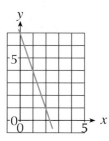

b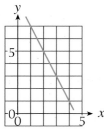

c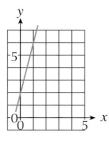

d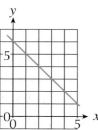

e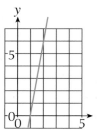

f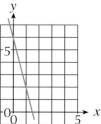

2 Find the gradient and the *y*-axis intercept of each of the following equations.

a $y = 4x + 1$ **b** $y = 3x - 1$ **c** $y = 5x$ **d** $y = -2x + 3$

3 Write the equation of the line in the form $y = mx + c$, where:

a $m = 3$ and $c = 2$ **b** $m = 4$ and $c = -3$

c $m = -2$ and $c = 5$ **d** $m = -4$ and $c = -1$

e $m = 4$ and $c = 0$ **f** $m = 0$ and $c = 8$

4 Find the gradient, the *y*-axis intercept and the equation of each linear graph shown below.

a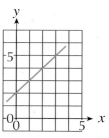

b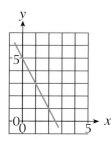

c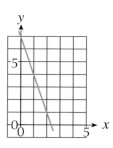

d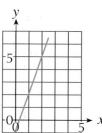

e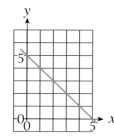

f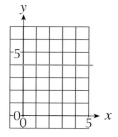

5 Look at the following equations.

    i $y = 2x + 5$ **ii** $y = 3x + 2$ **iii** $y = 2x - 3$

    iv $y = 2 - x$ **v** $y + 5 = 3x$ **vi** $y = x$

Which of the graphs described by these equations satisfy the following conditions?

a   Passes through the origin

b   Has a gradient of 2

c   Passes through the point (0, 2)

d   Has a gradient of 1

e   Are parallel to each other

Extension Work

1   Draw the following points on a coordinate grid.

    i   Find the gradient of the line joining the points.

    ii   Extend the line through the points to cross the y-axis if necessary.

    iii   Write down the equation of the line that passes through the points.

        a   (0, 3) and (2, 9)   **b**   (2, 5) and (6, 17)   **c**   (2, 10) and (3, 4)

        d   (3, 9) and (5, 3)   **e**   (−1, 2) and (1, 8)   **f**   (−3, 8) and (−1, −2)

2   For the equations below:

    i   plot the point where the graph crosses the y-axis.

    ii   draw a line from that point with the appropriate gradient.

    iii   label the graph you have drawn.

        a $y = 2x + 3$ **b** $y = 3x - 2$ **c** $y = -2x + 6$

Real-life graphs

Graphs with **axes** are used to show a **relationship** between two **variables**. The variable that controls the relationship usually goes on the horizontal axis. The variable that depends on that control goes on the vertical axis.

Example 13.8 ▷

Draw a sketch graph to illustrate that a hot cup of tea will take about 20 minutes to go cold.

The graph is as shown. The two axes needed are temperature and time. Time goes on the horizontal axis.

The temperature starts hot at 0 minutes, and is at cold after 20 minutes.

The graph needs a negative gradient.

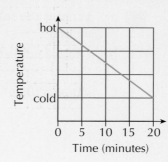

Exercise 13E

1 Sketch graphs to illustrate the following descriptions, clearly labelling each axis.

   a The more sunshine we have, the hotter it becomes.

   b The longer the distance, the longer it takes to travel.

   c In 2 hours all the water in a saucer had evaporated.

   d My petrol tank starts a journey full, with 40 litres of petrol. When my journey has finished, 300 km later, my tank has just 5 litres of petrol left in it.

   e The more petrol I buy, the more I have to pay.

2 The graph shows a car park's charges.

   a How much are the car park charges for the following durations.

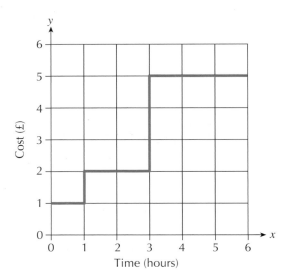

   i 30 minutes

   ii less than 1 hour

   iii 2 hours

   iv 2 hours 59 minutes

   v 3 hours 30 minutes

   vi 6 hours

   b How long can I park for:

   i £1?

   ii £2?

   iii £5?

   c This type of graph is called a step graph. Explain why it is called this.

 3 A taxi's meter reads £2 at the start of every journey. Once 2 miles have been travelled, an extra £3 is added to the fare. The reading then increases in steps of £3 for each whole mile covered up to 5 miles. For journeys over 5 miles, £1 is added per extra mile.

   a Draw a step graph to show the charges for journeys up to 10 miles.

   b How much is charged for the following journeys?

   i half a mile

   ii 1 mile

   iii 3 miles

   iv 5 miles

   v 6 miles

   vi 10 miles

4 **a** What is the relationship between the radius r and the circumference C of a circle?

   b Draw a graph to show this relationship. Put r on the horizontal axis and C on the vertical axis.

   c What is the gradient of this line?

5 Match the four graphs to the following situations.

  a The amount John gets paid against the number of hours he works

  b The temperature of an oven against the time it is switched on

  c The amount of tea in a cup as it is drunk

  d The cost of posting a letter compared to the weight

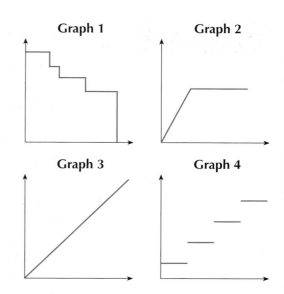

Graph 1   **Graph 2**

Graph 3   **Graph 4**

Extension Work

1 Harry decides to take a bath.

The graph shows the depth of water in the bath.

Match each section of the graph to the events below.

  a The bath gets topped up with hot water.

  b Harry lays back for a soak.

  c Harry gets in the bath.

  d The hot and cold tap are turned on.

  e The cold tap is turned off and only the hot tap is left on.

  f Harry washes himself.

  g The plug is pulled and the bath empties.

  h Harry gets out of the bath.

  i The hot tap is turned off and Harry gets ready to get in.

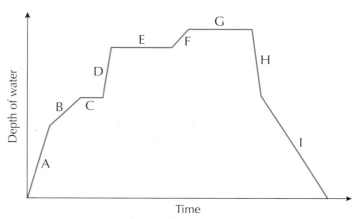

2 Draw graphs to show these other bath stories.

  a Jade turns the taps on, then starts talking to her friend on the phone. The bath overflows. Jade rushed back in and pulls the plug.

  b Jane decides to wash her dog. She fills the bath with a few inches of water then puts the dog in. The dog jumps around and whilst being washed splashes most of the water out of the bath. The plug is then pulled and the small amount of water left empties out.

  c Jake fills the bath then gets in. Then the phone rings and Jake gets out dripping a lot of water on the floor. He gets back in the bath, finishes his bath, gets out and pulls the plug.

Change of subject

Look at the following formula:

$$P = 4a + 2$$

The formula states the value of the variable P in terms of a.

We say P is the **subject** of the formula. Often we need to rearrange a formula to make another variable into the subject.

This is done in a very similar way to how we solve equations. We add, subtract, multiply or divide both sides of the equation by the same amount until we obtain the new subject.

Example 13.9 ▷

Change the formula $E = 5t + 3$ to make t the subject.

The formula needs altering so that t is on its own on the left-hand side of the formula.

Subtract 3 from both sides: $E - 3 = 5t$

Divide both sides by 5: $\dfrac{E - 3}{5} = t$

Turn it round so that t is on the left-hand side: $t = \dfrac{E - 3}{5}$

Example 13.10 ▷

Rewrite the formula $N = \dfrac{m}{2} - 1$ to express m in terms of N.

Add 1 to both sides of the equation: $N + 1 = \dfrac{m}{2}$

Multiply both sides by 2: $2(N + 1) = m$

Turn it round so that m is on the left-hand side: $m = 2(N + 1)$

Exercise 13F

1 Rewrite each of the following formulae as indicated.

   a $A = 2k$; express k in terms of A

   b $A = \dfrac{h}{2}$; express h in terms of A

   c $C = 2\pi r$; express r in terms of C

   d $A = 3x + 2$; express x in terms of A

2 Rewrite each of the following formulae as indicated.

   a $C = \pi D$; make D the subject of the formula

   b $P = 2(a + b)$; make a the subject of the formula

   c $S = 3r(h + 1)$; make h the subject of the formula

   d $V = \pi r^2 h$; make h the subject of the formula

   e $S = 5t + 4$; make t the subject of the formula

7

3 Given $E = 5n + 8$:

    a   Find E when $n = 15$

    b   Make n the subject of the formula

    c   Find n when $E = 23$

4 Given $S = a + 3$:

    a   Find S when $a = 7$

    b   Make a the subject of the formula

    c   Find a when $S = 24$

5 Given $y = 5x - 2$:

    a   Find y when $x = 2$

    b   Make x the subject of the formula

    c   Find x when $y = 5$

6 Given $T = \dfrac{R}{2}$:

    a   Find T when $R = 20$

    b   Make R the subject of the formula

    c   Find R when $T = 16$

7 Given $V = 12r$:

    a   Find V when $r = 5$

    b   Make r the subject of the formula

    c   Find r when $V = 36$

8 Use the formula $S = 7m + 8$ to find the value of m when $S = 36$.

9 Use the formula $I = \dfrac{PTR}{100}$ to find the value of T when $P = 4$, $I = 10$ and $R = 20$.

10 Use the formula $A = \dfrac{h(a + b)}{2}$ to find the value of b when $h = 8$, $a = 3$ and $A = 60$.

Extension **Work**

1   The area of a circle is given by $A = \pi r^2$. Make r the subject of the formula.

2   The volume of a cone is given by $V = \frac{1}{3}\pi r^2 h$. Make r the subject of the formula.

3   The surface area of a sphere is given by the formula $A = 4\pi r^2$. Make r the subject of the formula.

5 I can use algebra to represent a practical situation.

6 I can expand and simplify expressions with brackets.

I can solve linear equations with brackets where the solution may be fractional or negative.

I can solve equations with the unknown value on both sides where the solution may be fractional or negative.

I can use algebra to set up an equation to represent a practical situation.

I can calculate the gradient of a straight line drawn on a coordinate grid and can distinguish between a positive and a negative gradient.

I can plot a straight-line graph using the gradient–intercept method.

I can draw and interpret graphs that describe real-life situations.

7 I can solve equations involving algebraic fractions.

I can find the equation of a line using the gradient–intercept method.

I can change the subject of a formula with at most two variables.

National Test questions

1 *2006 Paper 2*

Multiply out this expression.

Write your answer as simply as possible.

$$5(x + 2) + 3(7 + x)$$

2 *2007 Paper 2*

Jenny wants to multiply out the brackets in the expression $3(2a + 1)$.

She writes:

$$3(2a + 1) = 6a + 1$$

Show why Jenny is **wrong**.

3 *2004 Paper 1*

a Rearrange the equations.

$$b + 4 = a \qquad b = \ldots$$

$$4d = c \qquad d = \ldots$$

$$m - 3 = 4k \qquad m = \ldots$$

b Rearrange the equation to make t the subject.

$$5(2 + t) = w$$

4 *2003 Paper 1*

For each part of the question, write down the statement that is true.

a   When x is even,   When x is even,
      $(x - 2)^2$ is even. $(x - 2)^2$ is odd.

      Show how you know it is true for **all** even values of x

b   When x is even,   When x is even,
      $(x - 1)(x + 1)$ is even. $(x - 1)(x + 1)$ is odd.

      Show how you know it is true for **all** even values of x.

FM Train timetable

Use the timetable to answer the questions.

Sheffield - Barnsley - Huddersfield/Leeds

Mondays to Fridays

									G													
Sheffield	0516	0536	0550	0614	0636	0649	0704	0725	0736	0751	0808	0836	0851	0908	0936	0951	1008	1036	1051	1108	1136	1151
Meadowhall	0522	0542	0556	0620	0642	0655	0710	0731	0742	0757	0814	0842	0857	0914	0942	0957	1014	1042	1057	1114	1142	1157
Chapeltown	0528	0548	—	0626	0648	—	0716	—	0748	—	0820	0848	—	0920	0948	—	1020	1048	—	1120	1148	—
Elsecar	0533	—	—	0631	—	—	0721	—	—	—	0825	—	—	0925	—	—	1025	—	—	1125	—	—
Wombwell	0537	0555	—	0635	0655	—	0725	—	0755	—	0829	0855	—	0929	0955	—	1029	1055	—	1129	1155	—
Barnsley	0542	0601	0611	0641	0701	0710	0731	0748	0801	0812	0835	0901	0912k	0935	1001	1012	1035	1101	1112	1135	1201	1212
Dodworth	—	0607	—	—	0707	—	—	—	0807	—	—	0907	—	—	1007	—	—	1107	—	—	1207	—
Silkstone Common	—	0611	—	—	0711	—	—	—	0811	—	—	0911	—	—	1011	—	—	1111	—	—	1211	—
Penistone	—	0618	—	—	0718	—	—	—	0825n	—	—	0918	—	—	1018	—	—	1118	—	—	1218	—
Denby Dale	—	0625	—	—	0724	—	—	—	0831	—	—	0924	—	—	1024	—	—	1124	—	—	1224	—
Shepley	—	0630	—	—	0729	—	—	—	0836	—	—	0929	—	—	1029	—	—	1129	—	—	1229	—
Stocksmoor	—	0632	—	—	0732	—	—	—	0839	—	—	0932	—	—	1032	—	—	1132	—	—	1232	—
Brockholes	—	06360	—	—	0736	—	—	—	0843	—	—	0936	—	—	1036	—	—	1136	—	—	1236	—
Honley	—	639	—	—	0738	—	—	—	0845	—	—	0938	—	—	1038	—	—	1138	—	—	1238	—
Berry Brow	—	0642	—	—	0741	—	—	—	0848	—	—	0941	—	—	1041	—	—	1141	—	—	1241	—
Lockwood	—	0644	—	—	0744	—	—	—	0851	—	—	0944	—	—	1044	—	—	1144	—	—	1244	—
Huddersfield	—	0650	—	—	0749	—	—	—	0856	—	—	0949	—	—	1049	—	—	1149	—	—	1249	—
Darton	—	—	—	0646	—	—	0736	—	—	—	0840	—	—	0940	—	—	1040	—	—	1140	—	—
Wakefield Kirkgate	—	—	0629	0658	—	0729	0747	—	—	0829	0852	—	0929	0952	—	1029	1052	—	1129	1152	—	1229
Normanton	—	—	0633	0702	—	0733	0752	—	—	—	0856	—	—	0956	—	—	1056	—	—	1156	—	—
Castleford	—	—	—	0710	—	—	0800	—	—	—	0904	—	—	1004	—	—	1104	—	—	1204	—	—
Woodlesford	—	—	—	0719	—	—	0809	—	—	—	0913	—	—	1013	—	—	1113	—	—	1213	—	—
Leeds	—	—	0650	0733	—	0750	0823	—	—	0851	0927	—	0950	1027	—	1050	1127	—	1150	1227	—	1250

Notes: G Through train from Retford   k Arrives 7 minutes earlier   n Arrives 1818

1 How long does the 0536 from Sheffield take to get to Huddersfield?

2 How long does the 1008 from Sheffield take to get to Leeds?

3 How long does the 0635 from Wombwell take to get to Normanton?

4 What is the last station before Huddersfield?

5 If you arrive at Sheffield station at 0730, how long will you have to wait for the next train to Leeds?

6 Only two trains a day from Sheffield in the morning do not go any further than Barnsley. What times do these trains leave Sheffield?

7 **a** The first 'fast' train to Leeds leaves Sheffield at 0550. How many stations, except Sheffield and Leeds, does it stop at?

   b How long does the this train take to get from Sheffield to Wakefield Kirkgate?

   c How many stations does a 'slow' train from Sheffield to Leeds stop at, except at Sheffield and Leeds?

8 Ken lives in Penistone. He wants to catch the 0718 to Huddersfield. It takes him 15 minutes to walk to the station. On the way he buys a paper which can take up to 2 minutes. He likes to be at the station at least 5 minutes early. What time should he leave home?

9 What is special about the 0751 fast train to Leeds from Sheffield?

10 If you arrive at Sheffield station at half past eight in the morning, how long do you have to wait before you can catch a train to Elsecar?

11 Frank, who lives in Barnsley, has an interview in Leeds at 11 am. The hotel where the interview is being held is 5 minutes' walk from the station. What is the time of the latest train that Frank can catch from Barnsley?

12 Mary, who lives in Wombwell, is meeting her friend for coffee in Huddersfield at 10 am. The café is 10 minutes from the station. What time train should Mary catch to get to Huddersfield in time?

13 Ahmed lives in Elsecar and has to get to Huddersfield to catch a train that leaves Huddersfield at 0757. Which train should he catch from Elsecar?

14 What time does the 0851 from Sheffield **arrive** at Barnsley station?

15 How long does the 0736 from Sheffield take to get to Penistone?

This chapter is going to show you

- How to investigate problems involving numbers and measures
- How to identify important information in a question
- How to interpret information from graphs
- How to use examples to prove a statement is true or false
- How to divide a quantity using proportion or ratio
- How to solve problems involving ratios and proportions
- How to compare two ratios

What you should already know

- When to use symbols, words or algebra to describe a problem
- When to use tables, diagrams and graphs
- How to break down a calculation into simpler steps
- How to solve simple problems using ratio and proportion

Number and measures

A newspaper has 48 pages. The pages have stories, adverts or both on them. 50% of the pages have both. Twice as many pages have adverts only as have stories only. How many pages have stories only?

Example 14.1 ▶ Use the digits 1, 2, 3 and 4 once only to make the largest possible product.

To make large numbers, the larger digits need to have the greatest value. So try a few examples:

$41 \times 32 = 1312$
$42 \times 31 = 1302$
$43 \times 21 = 903$
$431 \times 2 = 862$

There are other possibilities, but these all give smaller answers.

So the biggest product is $41 \times 32 = 1312$.

Exercise 14A

1 a Three consecutive numbers add up to 171. What are the numbers?

b Three consecutive numbers add up to 255. What are the numbers?

c Three consecutive numbers add up to 375. What are the numbers?

d Show that it is likely that all three consecutive numbers add up to a multiple of 3.

2 a Find two consecutive odd numbers with a product of 143.

b Find two consecutive odd numbers with a product of 575.

c Find two consecutive odd numbers with a product of 783.

d Do you think the product of two consecutive odd numbers will always be odd?

3 a Find two consecutive even numbers with a product of 288.

b Find two consecutive even numbers with a product of 728.

c Find two consecutive even numbers with a product of 1224.

d Do you think the product of two consecutive even numbers will always be even?

4 a Copy and complete the table.

Power of 3	Answer	Units digit
3^1	3	3
3^2	9	9
3^3	27	7
3^4	81	1
3^5	243	
3^6		
3^7		
3^8		

b What is the units digit of the answer to 3^{44}?

5 A dog and a cat run around a circular track of length 48 m. They both set off in the same direction from the starting line at the same time. The dog runs at 6 m per second and the cat runs at 4 m per second. How long is it before the dog and the cat are together again?

6 Amy is 6 years older than Bill. Two years ago Amy was three times as old as Bill. How old will Amy be in 4 years' time?

7 A map has a scale of 1 cm to $2\frac{1}{2}$ km. The road between two towns is 5 cm on the map, to the nearest centimetre.

a Calculate the shortest possible actual distance between the two towns.

b Calculate the difference between the shortest and longest possible distances between the two towns.

8 Which is the greater mass, 3 kg or 7 pounds (lb)? Explain your answer.

9 Which is the greater length, 10 miles or 15 kilometres? Explain your answer.

10 Which is the greater area, 1 square mile or 1 square kilometre? Explain your answer.

Extension Work

Write down a three-digit number using three different digits. Reverse the digits and write down this new number. You should now have two different three-digit numbers. Subtract the smaller number from the bigger number.

Your answer will have either two or three digits. If it has two digits (for example 99), rewrite it with three (099).

Now reverse the digits of your answer and write down that number. Add this number to your previous answer. Your final answer should be a four-digit number.

Either repeat using different numbers, or compare your answer with someone else's. Write down what you notice.

What happens if you do not use different digits at the start?

Using algebra, graphs and diagrams to solve problems

Of three chickens (A, B and C), A and B have a total mass of 4.1 kg, A and C have a total mass of 5.8 kg, and B and C have a total mass of 6.5 kg. What is the mass of each chicken?

Example 14.2 ▷ A gardener has a fixed charge of £5 and an hourly rate of £3 per hour. Write down an equation for the total charge £C when the gardener is hired for n hours. State the cost of hiring the gardener for 6 hours.

The formula is:

$C = 5$ (for the fixed charge) plus $3 \times n$ (for the hours worked)

$C = 5 + 3n$

If $n = 6$ then $C = 5 + (3 \times 6) = 23$

So the charge is £23.

Example 14.3 ▷ I think of a number, add 3 and then double it. The answer is 16. What is the number?

| ? | → | + 3 | → | × 2 | → | 16 |

Working this flowchart backwards:

| 5 | ← | − 3 | ← | ÷ 2 | ← | 16 |

The answer is 5.

1 A man and his suitcase weigh 84.1 kg, to the nearest tenth of a kilogram. The suitcase weighs 12 kg to the nearest kilogram. What is the heaviest that the man could weigh?

2 The sum of two numbers is 325 and the difference is 17. What is the product of the two numbers?

FM **3** **a** A tool-hire company has a fixed charge of £12 plus £5 per day to hire a tool. Write the total hire charge £C as a formula in terms of the number of days n.

b Work out the cost for 10 days.

c A different company represents its charges on the graph shown.

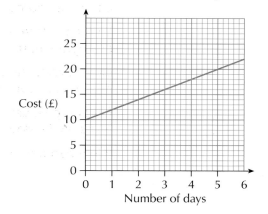

Use the graph to work out the fixed charge and the daily rate.

4 **a** Draw the next pattern in the sequence.

b How many squares will the fifth pattern have?

c Write down a rule to work out the number of squares in the next pattern.

5 I think of a number, double it and add 1. The answer is 33.

a Write down an equation to represent this information.

b What is the number?

6 I think of a number, square it and subtract 5. The answer is 31.

a Write down an equation to represent this information.

b What is the number?

7 I think of a number, double it and add 5. The answer is the same as the number plus 12.

a Write down an equation to represent this information.

b What is the number?

FM **8** Each year a man invests £50 more than the year before. In the first year he invested £100.

a How much does he invest in the 10th year?

b Write down a formula for the amount he invests in the nth year.

9 A grid has 100 squares. If the squares are labelled 1p, 2p, 4p, 8p, 16p, … , what is the label on the 100th square? Write your answer as a power of 2.

10 There are 32 teams in a knockout tournament. In the first round there will be 16 matches. How many matches will there be altogether?

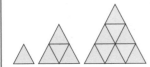

Extension Work

Equilateral triangles are pieced together to make a pattern of triangles as shown. The first diagram has only one small triangle.

1   How many small triangles are in the next two patterns?

2   Extend the patterns to see if you can work out a formula for the number of small triangles in the *n*th pattern.

3   What is the special name given to this pattern?

Logic and proof

Look at the recipe, which is for four people. How much of each ingredient is needed to make a chocolate cake for six people?

Chocolate cake
500 g flour
100 g sugar
35 g cocoa powder
60 g butter

Example 14.4 ▷

Take any three consecutive numbers. Multiply the first by the third. Square the second. Work out the difference between the two answers.

For example, take 7, 8, 9:

$7 \times 9 \quad = 63$

$8^2 = 8 \times 8 = 64$

difference $= 1$

Whichever numbers you choose, you will always get an answer of 1.

Example 14.5 ▷

Prove that the sum of three odd integers is always odd. (Remember: An integer is a positive whole number.)

Call any integer *m*.

Then $2m$ is an even integer, because any multiple of 2 is even.

Therefore $2m + 1$ is an odd integer, because any even integer plus 1 is odd.

In just the same way, we can call any other two integers *n* and *p*, and make two odd integers $2n + 1$ and $2p + 1$.

We now have three odd integers: $2m + 1$, $2n + 1$, $2p + 1$. The proof requires us to add (sum) them:

$$\begin{aligned} \text{Sum} \quad &= (2m + 1) + (2n + 1) + (2p + 1) \\ &= 2m + 2n + 2p + 2 + 1 \quad \text{(rearrange)} \\ &= 2(m + n + p + 1) + 1 \quad \text{(take factor 2)} \\ &= \text{even} + 1 \quad \text{(multiple of 2 is even)} \\ &= \text{odd} \quad \text{(any even plus 1 is odd)} \end{aligned}$$

So we have proved that the sum of three odd integers is always odd.

Exercise 14C

1 Copy and complete the following number problems. Each box represents one digit.

a
$$\begin{array}{r} \square\,5\,\square \\ +\ \ \square\,7 \\ \hline 5\ 4\ 9 \end{array}$$

b
$$\begin{array}{r} \square\,1\,6 \\ -\ \ 5\,\square \\ \hline 7\,\square\,9 \end{array}$$

c
$$\begin{array}{r} \square\,3 \\ \times\ \ 1\,\square \\ \hline 5\ 1\ 6 \end{array}$$

d $1\,\square\,\square\,^2 = \square\,2\,3\,2\,\square$

e $4\,\square\,^2 = 1\,\square\,\square\,1$

f $\sqrt{1\,\square\,\square\,2\,\square} = \square\,\square\,3$

2 Give an example to show that the sum of three odd numbers is always odd.

3 Prove that the sum of two consecutive numbers is always odd.

4 Show by example that the product of three consecutive numbers is divisible by 6.

5 Explain why the only even prime number is 2.

6 Show that the product of two consecutive numbers is always even.

7 a Find the three numbers below 30 that have exactly three factors.
   b What do you notice about these numbers?

8 Find the numbers less than 30 that all have exactly six factors.

9 What is special about all numbers with exactly three factors?

FM **10** Which bottle in the diagram is the best value for money?

FM **11** Which is the better value for money?

a 6 litres for £7.50 or 3 litres for £3.80
b 4.5 kg for £1.80 or 8 kg for £4.00
c 200 g for £1.60 or 300 g for £2.10
d Six chocolate bars for £1.50 or four chocolate bars for 90p

FM **12** A recipe uses 750 g of meat and makes a meal for five people. How many grams of meat would be needed if the meal was for eight people?

Extension Work

1 Write down a prime number that is not 2 or 3. Now write down the nearest multiple of 6 to your prime number. Work out the difference between your prime number and the nearest multiple of 6. Choose another prime number and repeat the process. What do you notice?

2 Can you prove that your result will work every time?

Proportion

Look at the picture.
Can you work out how many pints are in 3 litres?

A litre of water is a pint and three-quarters

Example 14.6

A café sells 200 cups of tea, 150 cups of coffee and 250 other drinks in a day.

What proportion of the drinks sold are:

a cups of tea? **b** cups of coffee?

a There are 200 cups of tea out of 600 cups altogether, so the proportion of cups of tea is $\frac{200}{600} = \frac{1}{3}$.

b There are 150 cups of coffee out of 600 cups altogether, so the proportion of cups of coffee is $\frac{150}{600} = \frac{1}{4}$.

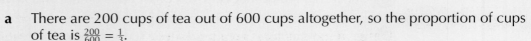

Exercise 14D

1 An orange drink is made using one part juice to four parts water. What proportion of the drink is juice? Give your answer as a fraction, decimal or percentage.

2 A woman spends £75 on food and £25 on clothing. What proportion of her spending is on food?

3 A supermarket uses $\frac{3}{4}$ of its space for food and the rest for non-food items. What is the ratio of food to non-food items?

4 A green paint is made by mixing blue and yellow paint in the ratio 3 : 7. How many litres of blue and yellow paint are needed to make:

a 20 litres of green paint? **b** 5 litres of green paint?

5 A café generally sells tea and coffee in the ratio of 3 : 5.

a How many of each drink will have been sold if 136 drinks were sold altogether?

b One day 39 cups of tea were sold, how many drinks were sold that day altogether?

c One weekend 115 cups of coffee were sold, how many cups of tea were sold?

6 A supermarket tries to divide its stores between food and other goods in the ratio of 7 : 3.

    a One store has 540 m² floor space. How much is allocated to each?

    b Another store has 123 m² allocated to non-food goods. How much is allocated to food?

7 Grannie's recipe for Lemon Punch is to use lemon juice and cola in the ratio of 3 : 17.

    a Grannie wanted to make 5 litres of punch. How much of each ingredient does she need?

    b One evening, Grannie found that she only had 300 ml of lemon juice. What is the most Lemon Punch she could make with that?

    c Joy, Grannie's granddaughter, brought round four 2-litre bottles of cola. What is the most punch Grannie could make with that?

8 In 30 minutes, 40 litres of water run through a pipe. How much water will run through the pipe in 12 minutes?

9 A recipe for fish pie for four people uses: 550 g of cod; 150 ml of milk; 1 kg of potatoes; 200 g of cheese.

    a Jonathan makes a fish pie for 10 people. How many millilitres of milk does he use?

    b Edna uses 350 g of cheese. How many people could she make fish pie for?

Extension Work

Design a spreadsheet that a shopkeeper could use to increase the price of items by 20%.

Ratio

John and Mary are sharing out some sweets. John wants twice as many sweets as Mary, and there are 21 sweets altogether. Can you work out how many sweets they each get?

Example 14.7 ▷ Alice and Michael have 128 CDs altogether. Alice has three times as many as Michael. How many CDs do they each have?

If Alice has three times as many as Michael, then the ratio is 3 : 1. This means that altogether there are four (3 + 1) parts to share out.

Four parts is all 128 CDs, so one part is 128 ÷ 4 = 32 CDs.

So Michael has 32 CDs and Alice has 32 × 3 = 96 CDs.

You can check your answer: 32 + 96 = 128.

Example 14.8 ▷ James and Briony are two goalkeepers. James has let in twice as many goals as Briony. Altogether they have let in 27 goals. How many goals has James let in?

James has let in twice as many goals as Briony. So if Briony has let in x goals, then James has let in $2x$ goals.

Altogether, this means that $3x = 27$. So $x = 9$ and $2x = 18$.

So James has let in 18 goals.

Example 14.9 ▷ The ratio of shots taken to goals scored by two football teams are:

Team A   7 : 2
Team B   11 : 3

a   Change each ratio into the form n : 1.

b   State which team is more accurate.

a   Team A   7 : 2 = 3.5 : 1
Team B   11 : 3 = 3.67 : 1

b   Team A is more accurate as they take fewer shots for each goal scored.

Exercise 14E

(1) Harriet and Richard go shopping and buy 66 items altogether. Harriet buys twice as many items as Richard. How many items does Harriet buy?

(2) At a concert the numbers of males to females are in the ratio 3 : 2. There are 350 people altogether. How many females are at the concert?

(3) 180 people see a film at the cinema. The numbers of children to adults are in the ratio 5 : 4. How many children see the film?

(4) In a fishing contest the number of trout caught to the number of carp caught is in the ratio 1 : 2. The total number of trout and carp is 72. How many carp were caught?

(5) A bakery makes 1400 loaves. The ratio of white to brown is 4 : 3. How many brown loaves did the bakery make?

(6) A do-it-yourself shop sells paints. The ratio of gloss paint to emulsion paint sold on one day is 2 : 3. If they sell 85 litres of paint, how much gloss paint do they sell?

(7) The table shows some information about pupils in a school. There are 1224 pupils in the school.

	Left-handed	Right-handed
Girls	96	540
Boys	84	504

a What percentage of the pupils are girls?

b What is the ratio of left-handed pupils to right-handed pupils?
Write your ratio in the form of 1 : n.

c One pupils was chosen at random from the whole school.
What was the probability that the pupil chosen is a right-handed boy?

8 Alison and Murray have a collection of 132 books, but Alison put into the collection twice as many as Murray. How many books did each put into the collection?

9 Some cricketers are more likely to take wickets than others. Consider the following statistics, showing some players' ratio of wickets to overs taken.

Sidebottam   4 : 11
Trueman   2 : 3
Old   3 : 13

a Change each ratio into 1 : n.

b State which cricketer took more wickets per over.

10 A cake mixture uses currants and raisins in the ratio 3 : 2. A different cake mixture uses currants and raisins in the ratio 5 : 4.

a Change each ratio into the form n : 1.

b Which cake mixture has the greater proportion of currants to raisins?

11 Purple paint is made using two parts of blue paint to three parts of red paint. A girl has 100 ml of each colour. What is the maximum amount of purple paint that she can make?

Extension Work

Draw a cube of side 1 cm and write down the volume. Double the length of the sides and write down the volume of the new cube. Work out the ratio of the new volume to the previous volume. Double the side length several more times, working out the new : previous volume ratio each time.

Repeat this exercise, but triple or quadruple the side length each time instead.

Can you find a connection between the new : previous volume ratio and the new : previous side ratio?

LEVEL BOOSTER

6
I am able to interpret information presented in a variety of forms.
I can justify answers by testing for particular cases.
I can calculate using ratios in appropriate situations.

7
I can solve problems using proportional change.
I can justify my solutions to problems.

1   *2005 Paper 1*

   a   Look at this information:

> Two numbers **multiply** to make zero.

One of the statements below is true.

Write it down.

> Both numbers must be zero.
> At least one number must be zero.
> Exactly one number must be zero.
> Neither number can be zero.

   b   Now look at this information:

> Two numbers **add** to make zero.

If **one** number is **zero**, what is the other number?

If **neither** number is **zero**, give an example of what the numbers could be.

2   *2006 Paper 1*

   a   Give an example to show the statement below is **not** correct:

> When you multiply a number by 2, the answer is always greater than 2.

   b   Now give an example to show the statement below is **not** correct:

> When you subtract a number from 2, the answer is always less than 2.

3   *2005 Paper 2*

In one week Jamal watched television for **26 hours.**

In that week:

> He watched television for the **same** length of time on Monday, Tuesday, Wednesday and Thursday.
>
> On each of Friday, Saturday and Sunday, he watched television for **twice as long** as on Monday.

How long did he spend watching television on **Saturday**?

Write your answer in hours and minutes.

4 To take the whole of a school on a trip requires a lot of transport.

a A school of 1800, including pupils and staff, created a table showing bus capacity and how many buses would be needed.

Complete the table.

Bus capacity	24	30	40	50	60		
Number of buses			45		30	25	24

b Write an equation using symbols to connect P, the number of people in the school, B, the capacity of a bus, and N, the number of buses.

c One bus company estimated that on a school trip they will travel at an average speed of 36 miles per hour. The headmaster is thinking about a trip that would be 45 miles away.

How long, in hours and minutes, is the estimate for the time of this journey. Show your working.

d Another school had a quote for their trip needing 60 buses. If they were to have used buses with an increased capacity of 100%, how many buses would have been needed?

e How many buses would have been needed if the capacity of buses had been increased by 50%?

f The petrol tank on a small bus, measures x by y by z and it takes 1 minute 30 seconds to fill.

How long will it take to fill a large bus petrol tank measuring $2x$ by $2y$ by $2z$ at the same rate?

This chapter is going to show you

- How to draw plans, elevations and scale drawings
- How to solve problems using coordinates
- How to use map scales
- How to find a locus
- How to use bearings
- How to solve problems with cuboids

What you should already know

- How to draw nets of 3-D shapes
- How to plot coordinates in all four quadrants
- How to measure and draw angles
- How to calculate the surface area and volume of cuboids

Plans and elevations

A **plan** is the **view** of a 3-D shape when it is looked at from above. An **elevation** is the view of a 3-D shape when it is looked at from the front or from the side.

Example **15.1**

The 3-D shape shown is drawn on centimetre isometric dotted paper. Notice that the paper must be used the correct way round, so always check that the dots form vertical columns.

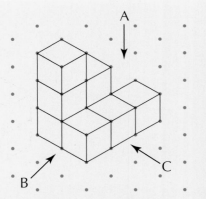

The plan, front elevation and side elevation can be drawn on centimetre-squared paper:

Plan from A

Front elevation from B

Side elevation from C

Exercise 15A

1 Draw each of the following cuboids accurately on an isometric grid.

a

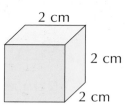
2 cm
2 cm
2 cm

b

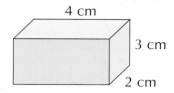
4 cm
3 cm
2 cm

c

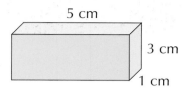
5 cm
3 cm
1 cm

2 Draw each of the following 3-D shapes accurately on an isometric grid.

a

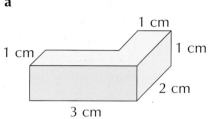
1 cm
1 cm
1 cm
2 cm
3 cm

b

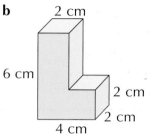
2 cm
6 cm
2 cm
2 cm
4 cm

c

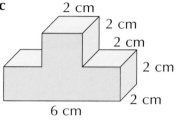
2 cm
2 cm
2 cm
2 cm
2 cm
6 cm

3 Copy each of the following 3-D shapes onto an isometric grid.

a

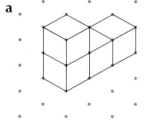

b

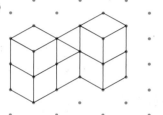

c

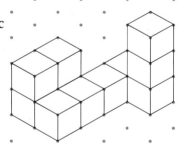

d

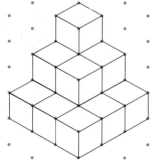

For each one, draw on centimetre-squared paper:

i the plan.   **ii** the front elevation.   **iii** the side elevation.

4 The plan, front elevation and side elevation of a 3-D solid are made up of cubes as shown. Draw the solid on an isometric grid.

Plan

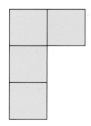

Front elevation

Side elevation

5 The diagrams below are the views of various 3-D shapes from directly above.

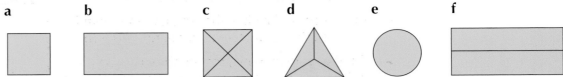

a   b   c   d   e   f

For each one, write down the name of a 3-D shape that could have this plan.

6 Make a 3-D solid from multi-link cubes. On centimetre-squared paper draw its plan, front elevation and side elevation. Show these to a partner, and ask them to construct the solid using multi-link cubes. Compare the two solids made.

Extension Work

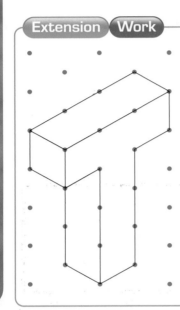

1 The letter T is drawn on an isometric grid, as shown on the left.

   a Draw other capital letters that can be drawn on an isometric grid.

   b Explain why only certain capital letters can be drawn easily on the grid.

   c Design a poster, using any of these letters, to make a logo for a person who has these letters as their initials.

2 The diagram on the right is another way of representing a cube in 2-D.

This representation is known as a Schlegel diagram, named after a famous German mathematician. Investigate Schlegel diagrams, using reference books or the Internet.

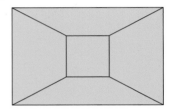

Scale drawings

A **scale drawing** is a smaller drawing of an actual object. A **scale** must always be clearly given by the side of the scale drawing.

Scale: 1 cm to 3 m

Example 15.2 ▶

Shown is a scale drawing of Rebecca's room.

- On the scale drawing, the length of the room is 5 cm, so the actual length of the room is 5 m.

- On the scale drawing, the width of the room is 3.5 cm, so the actual width of the room is 3.5 m.

- On the scale drawing, the width of the window is 2 cm, so the actual width of the window is 2 m.

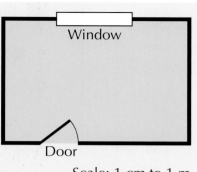

Scale: 1 cm to 1 m

Exercise 15B

1 The lines shown are drawn using a scale of 1 cm to 10 m. Write down the length each line represents.

a ▬▬▬▬▬

b ▬▬▬▬▬▬▬▬▬▬

c ▬▬▬▬▬▬▬

d ▬▬▬▬▬▬▬▬▬▬▬

e ▬▬▬▬▬▬▬▬

FM 2 The diagram shows a scale drawing for a school hall.

(a) Find the actual length of the hall.

(b) Find the actual width of the hall.

(c) Find the actual distance between the opposite corners of the hall.

Scale: 1 cm to 5 m

FM 3 The diagram shown is Ryan's scale drawing for his mathematics classroom. Nathan notices that Ryan has not put a scale on the drawing, but he knows that the length of the classroom is 8 m.

(a) What scale has Ryan used?

(b) What is the actual width of the classroom?

(c) What is the actual area of the classroom?

4 Copy and complete the table below for a scale drawing in which the scale is 4 cm to 1 m.

	Actual length	Length on scale drawing
a	4 m	
b	1.5 m	
c	50 cm	
d		12 cm
e		10 cm
f		4.8 cm

5 The plan shown is for a bungalow.

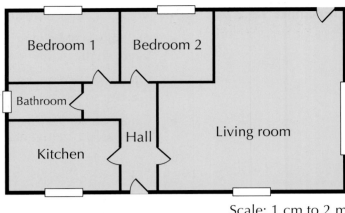

a Find the actual dimensions of each of the following rooms.
  i The kitchen
  ii The bathroom
  iii Bedroom 1
  iv Bedroom 2

b Calculate the actual area of the living room.

Scale: 1 cm to 2 m

6 The diagram shows the plan of a football pitch. It is not drawn accurately. Use the measurements on the diagram to make a scale drawing of the pitch (choose your own scale).

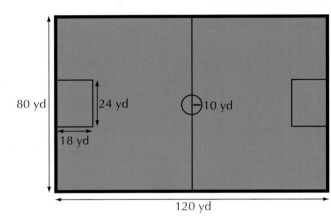

80 yd   24 yd   10 yd

18 yd

120 yd

Extension Work

1 On centimetre-squared paper, design a layout for a bedroom. Make cut-outs for any furniture you wish to have in the room. Use a scale of 2 cm to 1 m.

2 You will need a metre rule or a tape measure for this activity. Draw a plan of your classroom, including the desks and any other furniture in the room. Choose your own scale.

Finding the mid-point of a line segment

The next example will remind you how to plot points in all four quadrants using *x* and *y* **coordinates**.

It will also show you how to find the **mid-point** of a **line segment** that joins two points.

Example 15.3

The coordinates of the points A, B, C and D on the grid are A(4, 4), B(−2, 4), C(2, 1) and D(2, −3).

The mid-point of the line segment that joins A and B is X (X is usually referred to as the mid-point of AB). From the diagram, the coordinates of X are (1, 4). Notice that the *y* coordinate is the same for the three points on the line.

The mid-point of CD is Y. From the diagram, the coordinates of Y are (2, −1). Notice that the *x* coordinate is the same for the three points on the line.

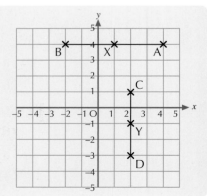

Exercise 15C

1 Copy the grid on the right and plot the points A, B, C, D, E and F.

    a Write down the coordinates of the points A, B, C, D, E and F.

    b Using the grid to help, write down the coordinates of the mid-point of each of the following line segments.

       i AB

      ii CD

     iii BE

      iv EF

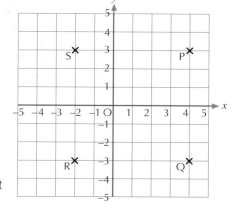

2 Copy the grid on the right and plot the points P, Q, R and S.

    a Write down the coordinates of the points P, Q, R and S.

    b Join the points to form the rectangle PQRS. Using the grid to help, write down the coordinates of the mid-point of each of the following lines.

       i PQ   **ii** QR

     iii PS   **iv** SR

    c Write down the coordinates of the mid-point of the diagonal PR.

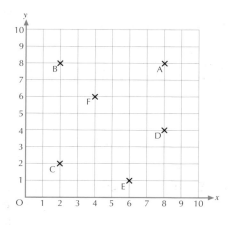

3 a Copy and complete the table, using the points on the grid shown. The first row of the table has been completed for you.

	Coordinates of the first point on the line segment	Coordinates of the second point on the line segment	Coordinates of the mid-point of the line segment
AB	A(8, 8)	B(2, 8)	(5, 8)
AD			
BC			
BF			
AF			
CE			

b Can you spot a connection between the coordinates of the first and second points and the coordinates of the mid-point? Write down a rule in your own words.

4 By using the rule you found in Question 3 or by plotting the points on a coordinate grid, find the mid-points of the line that joins each of the following pairs of coordinate points.

    a A(3, 2) and B(3, 6)   **b** C(4, 6) and D(6, 10)   **c** E(3, 2) and F(5, 4)

    d G(8, 6) and H(2, 3)   **e** I(5, 6) and J(−3 , −2)

The aim is to find a formula for the mid-point of a line segment AB.

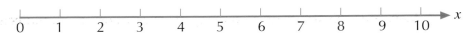

On the x-axis above, what number lies halfway between 4 and 8? Can you see a way of getting the answer without using the number line? The answer is the mean of 4 and 8 or $\frac{4 + 8}{2} = 6$.

Test this rule by trying other numbers.

x_1 and x_2 lie on the x-axis, as shown below. What number lies halfway between x_1 and x_2? The answer is the mean of x_1 and x_2, which is $\frac{x_1 + x_2}{2}$.

The same rule will work for numbers on the y-axis.

On the y-axis shown, what number lies halfway between y_1 and y_2? The answer is the mean of y_1 and y_2, which is $\frac{y_1 + y_2}{2}$.

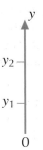

This rule can now be applied to find the coordinates of the mid-point of the line AB on the diagram shown.

Point A has coordinates (x_1, y_1) and point B has coordinates (x_2, y_2). Using the above rule for both axes, we find that the coordinates of the mid-point of AB are given by the formula:

$$\left(\frac{x_1 + x_2}{2}, \frac{y_1 + y_2}{2} \right)$$

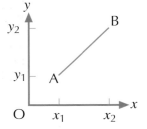

Points A, B, C, D and E are plotted on the grid shown. Use the formula above to find the mid-point for each of the following line segments.

a   AB
b   BC
c   CD
d   DE
e   AE

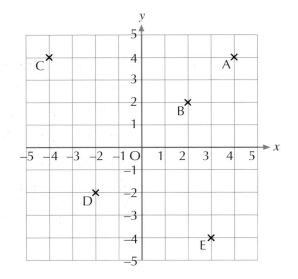

Map scales

Maps are **scale drawings** used to represent areas of land in subjects such as geography.

Distance on a map can be shown in two different ways, as in the examples below.

The first way is to give a **map scale**. This gives a distance on the map and an equivalent distance on the ground. This is shown in Example 15.4.

The second way is to give a map ratio. A map ratio has no units and will look something like 1 : 10 000. Example 15.5 explains how to use a map ratio.

A direct distance is 'as the crow flies'. String can be used to estimate map distance along paths and roads.

Example 15.4 ▷

The map shows part of south-east England. Find the actual direct distance between Maidstone and Dover.

The direct distance between Maidstone and Dover on the map is 5.5 cm. The scale is 1 cm to 10 km. So 5.5 cm represents 5.5 × 10 km = 55 km.

The actual distance between Maidstone and Dover is 55 km.

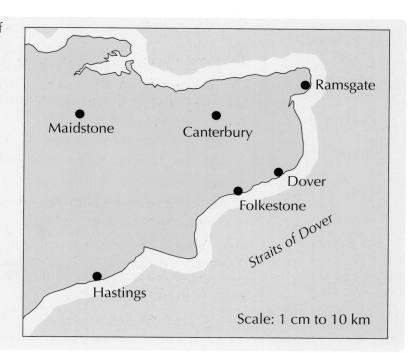

Scale: 1 cm to 10 km

Example 15.5 ▷

The scale of the map in Example 15.4 is 1 cm to 10 km.

There are 100 cm in a metre, and 1000 metres in a kilometre.

So 10 km = 10 × 100 × 1000 = 1 000 000 cm.

Therefore 1 cm to 10 km can also be written as 1 cm to 1 000 000 cm.

So the map ratio will be given as 1 : 1 000 000.

When the ratio is used to find actual distances, each centimetre on the map will represent 1 000 000 cm or 10 km on the ground. Similarly, each inch on the map will represent 1 000 000 inches or 15.78 miles on the ground.

Exercise 15D

1. Write each of the following map scales as a map ratio.

   a 1 cm to 1 m
   b 1 cm to 4 m
   c 4 cm to 1 m
   d 1 cm to 1 km
   e 2 cm to 1 km

2. Using the map in Example 15.4, find the actual direct distance between:

   a Maidstone and Hastings
   b Canterbury and Ramsgate
   c Folkestone and Dover

3. The map ratio on a map is 1 : 50 000. The direct distance between two towns on the map is 4 cm. What is the actual direct distance between the two towns?

4. The map ratio on a map is 1 : 100 000. Peter has just been for a walk. Using a piece of string, he measures the map distance of his walk and finds it to be 12.5 cm. How far did he walk?

5. The map ratio on a map of Europe is 1 : 20 000 000. The actual direct distance between Paris and Rome is 1100 kilometres. What is the direct distance on the map?

FM 6. The map shows York city centre. Find the actual direct distance between each of the following.

   a The station and the football ground
   b The National Railway Museum and the Castle Museum
   c York Minster and the Barbican Centre
   d The station and the law courts

FM **7** The map shows the path taken by a group of fell walkers in the Lake District. They start at the car park in Glenridding and walk on the path to Helvellyn.

Use a piece of string to find the actual distance of the walk between Glenridding and Helvellyn.

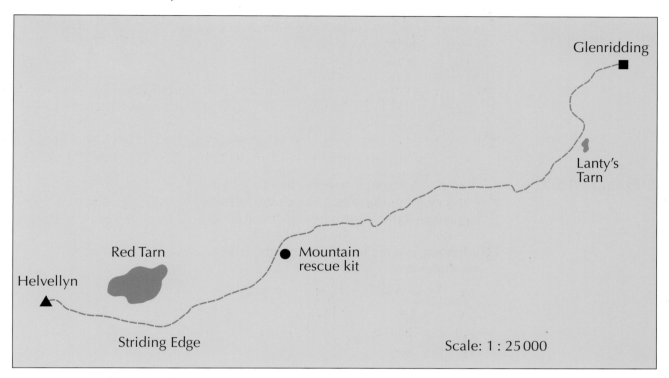

Glenridding

Lanty's Tarn

Red Tarn

Mountain rescue kit

Helvellyn

Striding Edge

Scale: 1 : 25 000

---

1 Write each of the following imperial map scales as a map ratio.
   a 1 inch to 1 mile
   b 1 inch to 1 yard
   c 3 inches to $\frac{1}{2}$ mile
   d 1 inch to 50 yards

2 Ask your teacher for a map of Great Britain. Using the scale given on the map, find the direct distances between various towns and cities.

3 Use the Internet to look for maps of the area where you live and find the scale that is used. Print out copies of the maps and find the distances between local landmarks.

Loci

The trail from the jet aircraft has traced out a path. The path of the jet is known as a **locus** (the plural is **loci**). A locus is a set of points that satisfies a given set of conditions or a rule.

It is useful to think of a locus as a path traced out by a single moving point.

Example 15.6 ▷

Mr Yeates is walking along a straight track that is equidistant from two trees (equidistant means 'the same distance'). The sketch shows his locus. The locus can be described as the perpendicular bisector of the imaginary line joining the two trees.

In some cases, the locus can be drawn accurately if measurements are given.

• Tree

Locus _____

• Tree

Example 15.7 ▷

Mr McGinty's goat is tethered to a post by a rope 2 m long. The sketch shows the locus of the goat as it moves around the post with the rope remaining taut. The locus can be described as a circle with centre at the post and radius 2 m.

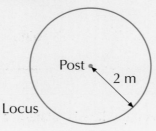

Post •

2 m

Locus

Exercise 15E

1 Draw a sketch and describe the locus for each of the following situations.

   a A cricket ball being hit for a six by a batsman

   b The Earth as it orbits the Sun

   c A bullet from a rifle

   d The tip of Big Ben's minute hand as it moves from 3 o'clock to half past three

   e A parachutist after jumping from a plane

   f The pendulum of a grandfather clock

2 Barn A and barn B are 500 m apart. A farmer drives his tractor between the barns so that he is equidistant from each one. On a sketch of the diagram, draw the locus of the farmer.

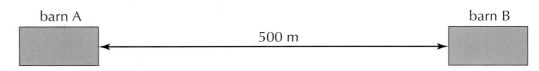

barn A   500 m   barn B

3 The two fences on the diagram border a park.
Kathryn enters the park at an entrance at X. She
then walks through the park so that she is
equidistant from each fence.

    a On a sketch of the diagram, draw
Kathryn's locus.

    b Describe the locus.

4 A toy car is moving so that it is always a fixed distance from a point X at the edge of
the room, as shown on the diagram.

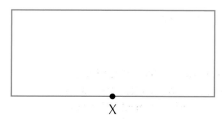

    a On a sketch of the diagram, draw the locus of the car.

    b Describe the locus.

5 The line AB is 20 cm long and C is its mid-point.

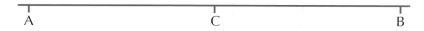

    a Describe the locus of A if the line is rotated about C.

    b Describe the locus of A if the line is rotated about B.

6 The line AB is 6 cm long.

A ——————————————— B

Draw the line AB. Then draw an accurate diagram to show all the points that are
3 cm or less from AB.

7 The diagram is a plan of a yard with part of a building in it. The building is shown in
grey. A guard dog is tethered to the base of the wall of the building, at the point
marked ✕. The guard dog's chain is 3 m long.

Draw a scale diagram to
show the area of the yard
where the dog can patrol.
Use a scale of 1 cm to 1 m.

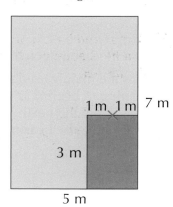

1   The diagram on the right shows the dimensions of a building. A path is to be laid around the building so that the edge of the path is always 1 m away from the building. Make a scale drawing to show the edge of the path around the building. Use a scale of 1 cm to 1 m.

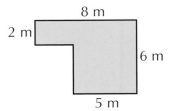

2   The diagram shows the position of two ticket meters in a large car park in a city centre. When Mrs Kitson buys her parking ticket, she always walks to the nearer meter. On a sketch of the car park, using a ruler and compasses, divide the car park into two areas in which parking is nearer to one or other of the two meters.

3   Use reference material or the Internet to find out about contours, isotherms and isobars. How are these related to a locus?

4   If you have access to ICT facilities, find out how to generate shapes and paths, using programs such as Logo. For example, find out how to draw regular polygons, star shapes and spiral shapes.

Bearings

There are four main directions on a compass – north (N), south (S), east (E) and west (W). These directions are examples of **compass bearings**. A **bearing** is a specified direction in relation to due **north**. The symbol for due north is:

N
↑

You have probably seen this symbol on maps in geography.

Bearings are mainly used for navigation purposes at sea, in the air and in sports such as orienteering. A bearing is measured in degrees (°). The angle is always measured *clockwise* from the **north** line. A bearing is always given using three digits and is referred to as a **three-figure bearing**. For example, the bearing for the direction east is 090°.

Example 15.8 ▶ On the diagram, the three-figure bearing of B from A is 035° and the three-figure bearing of A from B is 215°.

Remember: Imagine yourself at one point. Face north. Then turn clockwise through the bearing angle until you face the other point.

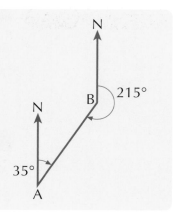

Example 15.9 ▶ The diagram shows the positions of Manchester and Leeds on a map.

The bearing of Leeds from Manchester is 050°.

To find the bearing of Manchester from Leeds, use the dotted line to find the alternate angle of 50° and then add 180°. The bearing is 230°.

Notice that the two bearings have a difference of 180°. Such bearings are often referred to as 'back bearings'.

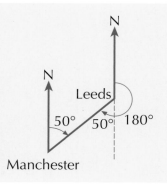

Exercise 15F

1 Write down each of the following compass bearings as three-figure bearings.

   a South   **b** West   **c** North-east   **d** South-west

2 Write down the three-figure bearing of B from A for each of the following.

   a 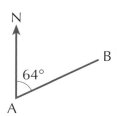   **b**    **c** 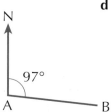   **d**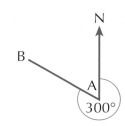

3 Find the three-figure bearing of X from Y for each of the following.

   a 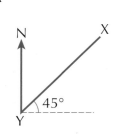   **b**    **c** 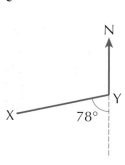   **d**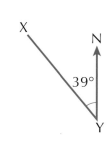

4 Draw a rough sketch to show each of the following bearings (mark the angle on each sketch).

    a From a ship A, the bearing of a light-house B is 030°

    b From a town C, the bearing of town D is 138°

    c From a gate E, the bearing of a trigonometric point F is 220°

    d From a control tower G, the bearing of an aircraft H is 333°

5 The two diagrams show the positions of towns and cities in England.

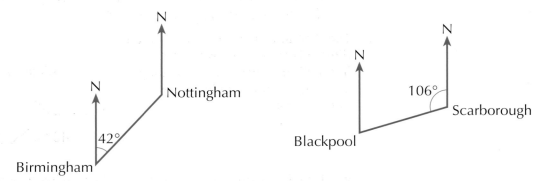

Find the bearing of each of the following.

    a Nottingham from Birmingham   **b** Birmingham from Nottingham

    c Scarborough from Blackpool   **d** Blackpool from Scarborough

6 Terri and Josh are planning a walk on Ilkley Moor in Yorkshire. The scale drawing below shows the route they will take, starting from Black Pots.

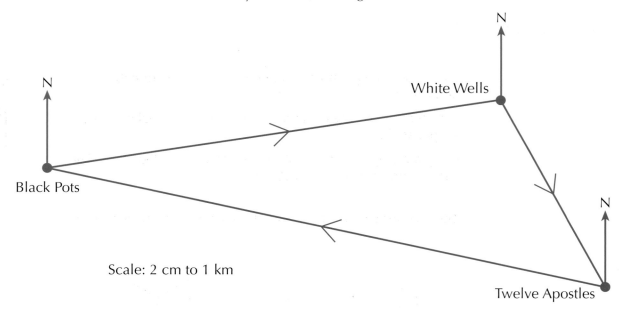

Scale: 2 cm to 1 km

    a What is the total distance of their walk if they keep to a direct route between the landmarks?

    b They have to take three-figure bearings between each landmark because of poor visibility. Use a protractor to find the bearings of the following.

        i White Wells from Black Pots   **ii** Twelve Apostles from White Wells

        iii Black Pots from Twelve Apostles

1 A liner travels from a port X on a bearing of 140° for 120 nautical miles to a port Y. It then travels from port Y on a bearing of 250° for a further 160 nautical miles to a port Z.

   a Make a scale drawing to show the journey of the liner. Use a scale of 1 cm to 20 nautical miles.

   b Use your scale drawing to find:
      i the direct distance the liner travels from port Z to return to port X.
      ii the bearing of port X from port Z

2 The diagram shows the approximate direct distances between three international airports. The bearing of Stansted airport from Heathrow airport is 040°.

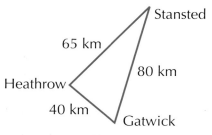

   a Use this information to make a scale drawing to show the positions of the airports. Use a scale of 1 cm to 10 km.

   b Use your scale drawing to find:
      i the bearing of Gatwick airport from Heathrow airport.
      ii the bearing of Gatwick airport from Stansted airport.

A cube investigation

For this **investigation** you will need a collection of **cubes** and centimetre isometric dotted paper.

Two cubes can only be arranged in one way to make a solid shape, as shown.

Copy the diagram onto centimetre isometric dotted paper. The surface area of the solid is 10 cm².

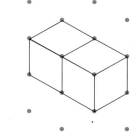

Three cubes can be arranged in two different ways, as shown.

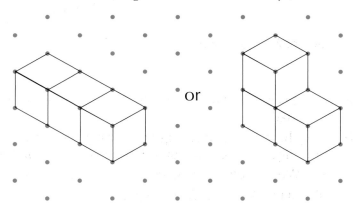

or

Copy the diagrams onto centimetre isometric dotted paper. The **surface area** of both solids is 14 cm².

Here is an arrangement of four cubes.

The surface area of the solid is 18 cm².

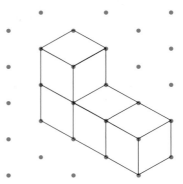

Exercise 15G

1 How many different arrangements can you make using four cubes? Draw all the different arrangements on centimetre isometric dotted paper.

2 Make a table to show the surface areas of the different solids that you have made using four cubes. What are the least and greatest surface areas for the different solids?

Write down anything else you notice, for example, about the touching faces of the cubes.

3 Look at the surface areas of the solids made from two, three and four cubes.

What do you think are the least and greatest surface areas of a solid made from five cubes?

LEVEL BOOSTER

5
I can use scales and make scale drawings.
I can find coordinates of the mid-point of a line segment.
I can convert a map scale to a map ratio.
I can give three-figure bearings.

6
I can draw plans and elevations.
I can use map scales.
I can use three-figure bearings when solving problems.
I can find the surface area of a cuboid.

7
I can find the locus of a moving point.

National Test questions

1 *1999 Paper 2*

The diagram shows a model made with nine cubes. Five of the cubes are grey. The other four cubes are white.

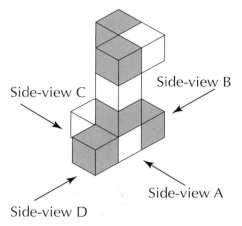

Side-view C

Side-view B

Side-view A

Side-view D

a The drawings below show the four side-views of the model. Which side-view does each drawing show?

i   **ii**   **iii**   **iv**

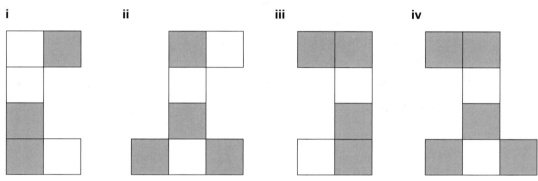

b Copy and complete the top-view of the model by shading the squares that are grey.

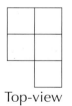

Top-view

c Imagine you turn the model upside down. What will the new top-view of the model look like? Copy and complete the new top-view of the model by shading the squares that are grey.

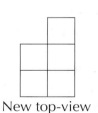

New top-view

2 *2006 Paper 2*

Each shape below is made from **five cubes** that are joined together.

Copy and complete the missing diagrams below.

Shape drawn on an isometric grid	**View from above** of the shape drawn on a square grid

3 *2000 Paper 1*

The plan shows the position of three towns, each marked with an X.

The scale of the plan is 1 cm to 10 km.

The towns need a new radio mast. The new radio mast must be:

nearer to Ashby than Ceewater

less than 45 km from Beaton.

Copy or trace the plan. Show on the copy the region where the new radio mast can be placed. Leave in your construction lines.

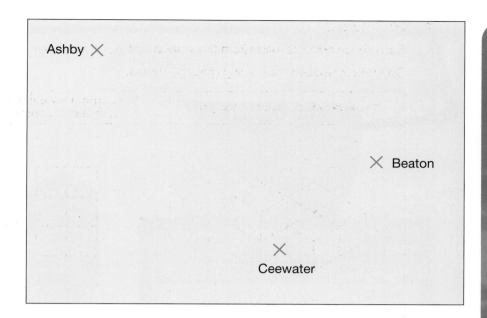

Ashby ✕

✕ Beaton

✕
Ceewater

4 *2001 Paper 2*

A gardener wants to plant a tree.

She wants it to be more than 8 m away from the vegetable plot.

She wants it to be more than 18 m away from the greenhouse.

The plan below shows part of the garden. The scale is 1 cm to 4 m.

Copy or trace the plan. Show *accurately* on the copy the region of the garden where she can plant the tree. Label this region R.

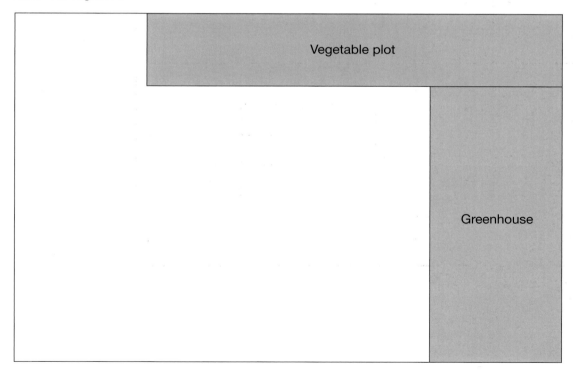

Vegetable plot

Greenhouse

Photographs

FastPrint advertises the cost of photograph prints in their shop.

Print size	Price each	
3" × 2" (4)	£0.99	
	Quantity	**Price**
13 cm × 9 cm	1–99	£0.10 each
	100–249	£0.09 each
	250+	£0.08 each
	Quantity	**Price**
6" × 4"	1–49	£0.15 each
	50–99	£0.12 each
	100–249	£0.09 each
	250–499	£0.08 each
	500–750	£0.06 each
	751+	£0.05 each
7" × 5"	£0.29	
8" × 6"	£0.45	
10" × 8"	£1.20	
12" × 8"	£1.20	
45 cm × 30 cm	£6.99	

1 A school decides to use FastPrint to buy prints of a year group photograph. Pupils can choose the size of the prints they want. They can also choose to buy more than one size.

The school's order is as follows:

128	13 cm × 9 cm prints
87	6" × 4" prints
75	10" × 8" prints
and 60	12" × 8" prints

What is the total cost of buying these prints?

2 The print sizes are given in both imperial units (" means inches) and metric units.

a Use the conversion factor 1 cm = 0.394 inches to change the 13 cm × 9 cm and the 45 cm × 30 cm print sizes into imperial sizes. Give your answers to one decimal place.

b Which pairs of prints are twice the size in area?

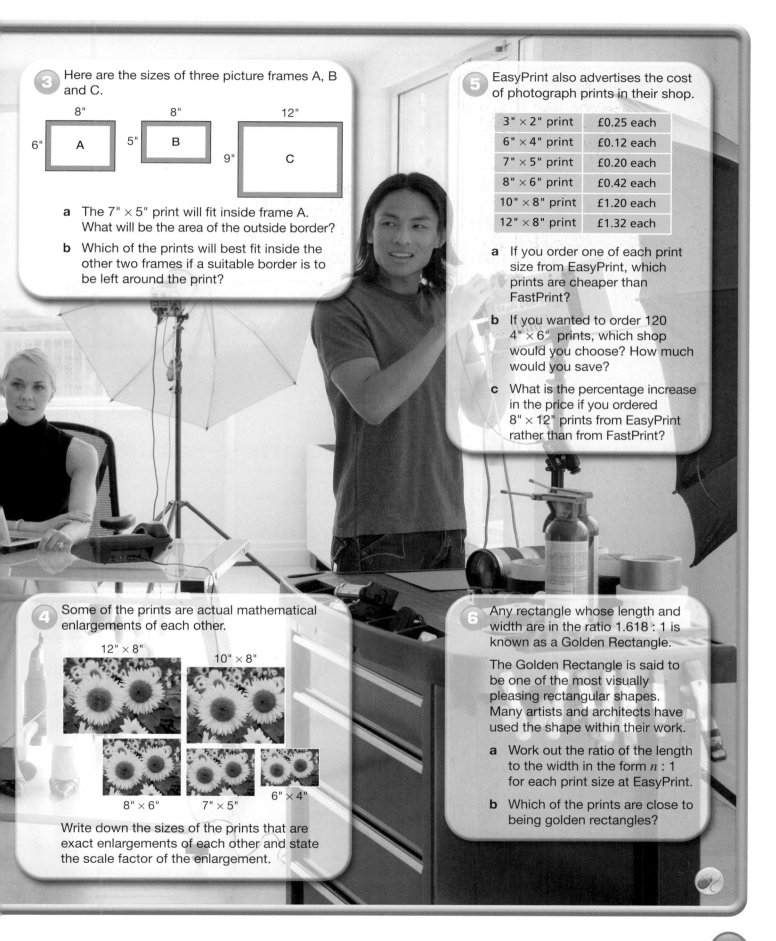

3 Here are the sizes of three picture frames A, B and C.

8"
6" | A |

8"
5" | B |

12"
9" | C |

a The 7" × 5" print will fit inside frame A. What will be the area of the outside border?

b Which of the prints will best fit inside the other two frames if a suitable border is to be left around the print?

5 EasyPrint also advertises the cost of photograph prints in their shop.

3" × 2" print	£0.25 each
6" × 4" print	£0.12 each
7" × 5" print	£0.20 each
8" × 6" print	£0.42 each
10" × 8" print	£1.20 each
12" × 8" print	£1.32 each

a If you order one of each print size from EasyPrint, which prints are cheaper than FastPrint?

b If you wanted to order 120 4" × 6" prints, which shop would you choose? How much would you save?

c What is the percentage increase in the price if you ordered 8" × 12" prints from EasyPrint rather than from FastPrint?

4 Some of the prints are actual mathematical enlargements of each other.

12" × 8"

10" × 8"

8" × 6"   7" × 5"   6" × 4"

Write down the sizes of the prints that are exact enlargements of each other and state the scale factor of the enlargement.

6 Any rectangle whose length and width are in the ratio 1.618 : 1 is known as a Golden Rectangle.

The Golden Rectangle is said to be one of the most visually pleasing rectangular shapes. Many artists and architects have used the shape within their work.

a Work out the ratio of the length to the width in the form $n : 1$ for each print size at EasyPrint.

b Which of the prints are close to being golden rectangles?

This chapter is going to show you

- How to plan tasks and collect data
- How to calculate a mean using an assumed mean
- How to construct frequency diagrams for continuous data
- How to construct simple line graphs for time series
- How to compare two distributions by using an average and the range
- How to compare theoretical probabilities with experimental probabilities

What you should already know

- How to construct frequency tables for discrete data
- How to find the mode, median, range and modal class for grouped data
- How to calculate the mean from a simple frequency table
- How to construct graphs and diagrams to represent data
- How to write a short report from a statistical survey

Collecting data for frequency tables

When collecting **data** you will need to ask yourself questions such as the following:

- Does my **data collection** sheet record all the relevant facts?
- Is it detailed (accurate) enough?
- Is my experiment reliable? Does it need repeating several times?
- Have I tested my questions on a small sample first?

Example 16.1 ▷ The journey times, in minutes, for a group of 16 railway travellers are shown below:

25, 47, 12, 32, 28, 17, 20, 43, 15, 34, 45, 22, 19, 36, 44, 17

Construct a frequency table to represent the data.

The data should be collected into a small number of equal classes. The range of journey times is $47 - 12 = 35$ minutes. So a suitable class size is 10 minutes.

The class intervals are written in the form $10 < T \leq 20$. This means 10 minutes to 20 minutes, including 20 minutes but excluding 10 minutes.

There are six times in the group $10 < T \leq 20$: 12, 17, 20, 15, 19 and 17.
There are three times in the group $20 < T \leq 30$: 25, 28, and 22.
There are three times in the group $30 < T \leq 40$: 32, 34 and 36.
There are four times in the group $40 < T \leq 50$: 47, 43, 45 and 44.

Putting all this information into a table gives:

Time T (minutes)	Frequency
$10 < T \leq 20$	6
$20 < T \leq 30$	3
$30 < T \leq 40$	3
$40 < T \leq 50$	4

Example 16.2 ▷ Look at the different methods of collecting data shown, and then decide which is the most suitable method for each of the two tasks **a** and **b**. Briefly outline a plan for each task.

Methods of collecting data
Construct a questionnaire
Do research on the Internet
Carry out an experiment
Use a software database (e.g. an encyclopaedia CD)
Visit a library for books and other print sources

a Compare the reaction times of two groups of pupils.

b Compare the age distribution of the populations of different countries.

a This task would require an experiment.

The plan would consider:
- the detailed design of the reaction time experiment.
- what results to expect (a hypothesis).
- the number of pupils in each group.
- how the pupils would be selected to ensure that there was no bias.
- how to record the data.
- how to analyse the results and report the findings.

b This task would use data obtained from the Internet, a software database or a library.

The plan would consider:
- which countries and what data to look at.
- what results to expect (a hypothesis).
- the most efficient way of obtaining the data.
- how many years of data to compare.
- how to record the data.
- how to analyse the results and report the findings.

Exercise 16A

1 The heights (in metres) of 20 people are as follows:

1.65, 1.53, 1.71, 1.62, 1.48, 1.74, 1.56, 1.55, 1.80, 1.85, 1.58, 1.61, 1.82, 1.67, 1.47, 1.76, 1.79, 1.66, 1.68, 1.73

Copy and complete the frequency table.

Height h (metres)	Frequency
$1.40 < h \leq 1.50$	
$1.50 < h \leq 1.60$	
$1.60 < h \leq 1.70$	
$1.70 < h \leq 1.80$	
$1.80 < h \leq 1.90$	

2 The masses (in kilograms) of fish caught one day by a fisherman are as follows:

0.3, 5.6, 3.2, 0.4, 0.6, 1.1, 2.4, 4.8, 0.5, 1.6, 5.1, 4.3, 3.7, 3.5

Copy and complete the frequency table.

Mass M (kilograms)	Frequency
$0 < M \leq 1$	
$1 < M \leq 2$	
...	
...	
...	
...	

3 Look at the different methods of collecting data in Example 16.2. Decide which is the most suitable method for each of the following tasks. Briefly outline a plan for each task including the points mentioned in Example 16.2.

a Comparing how easy two newspapers are to read

b Testing someone's memory in a game

c Finding out people's opinions on smoking

4 Criticise each of the following methods of collecting data.

a Recording long jump data for a whole school in one set of data

b Collecting data about the age of the population of a country and putting it into groups of five years, i.e. 0–5, 6–10 etc.

c Giving a questionnaire about fitness to a small sample of members of a sports club

d Testing boys' reaction times in the morning and girls' reaction times in the afternoon using a different test

Extension **Work**

Write out a plan for collecting, analysing and reporting on data about the different types of housing or shops around your school. In your plan, make sure that you consider the scope of the task, a hypothesis, how to collect the data, how to record the data, and how to analyse the results and present a report. Remember to state any difficulties that you may have.

Assumed mean and working with statistics

The father's age is double the combined age of his children. Two years ago the children had an average age of 7 years. The difference in the children's ages is 2 years. How old is the father?

Example 16.3 ▷

Find the mean of the four numbers 26.8, 27.2, 34.1, 36.4. Use 30 as the assumed mean.

Subtracting 30 from each number gives: −3.2, −2.8, 4.1, 6.4

Adding these numbers up gives: −3.2 + −2.8 + 4.1 + 6.4 = 4.5

So the mean of these numbers is: 4.5 ÷ 4 = 1.125

Adding the 30 back on gives a mean for the original numbers of:
   30 + 1.125 = 31.125

Example 16.4 ▷

A set of numbers has a mean of 6 and a range of 7.

What happens to   **i** the mean and   **ii** range when the numbers are:

a   multiplied by 2?   **b**   increased by 5?

a   **i**   As each number has doubled, the mean will also double. For example, if the numbers were 3, 5 and 10, then the new numbers would be 6, 10 and 20.

The old mean is $\frac{3 + 5 + 10}{3} = 6$ and the new mean is $\frac{6 + 10 + 20}{3} = 12$.

   ii   The old range is 10 − 3 = 7 and the new range is 20 − 6 = 14. So the range also doubles.

b   **i**   As each number has increased by 5, the mean will also increase by 5. For example, if the numbers were 3, 5 and 10, then the new numbers would be 8, 10 and 15.

The old mean is $\frac{3 + 5 + 10}{3} = 6$ and the new mean is $\frac{8 + 10 + 15}{3} = 11$.

   ii   The old range is 10 − 3 = 7 and the new range is 15 − 8 = 7, which is still the same.

Exercise 16B

1 Find the mean of 34, 35, 37, 39, 42. Use 37 as the assumed mean.

2 Find the mean of 18, 19, 20, 21, 27. Use 20 as the assumed mean.

3 The heights, in centimetres, of five brothers are 110, 112, 115, 119 and 124. Find their mean height using an assumed mean of 110 cm.

4 Four pupils each use a trundle wheel to measure the length of their school field in metres. Their results are 161.0, 164.5, 162.5 and 165.0. Find the mean of their results using an assumed mean of 160 m.

5 A box of matches has 'Average contents 600' written on it. Sunil counts the matches in 10 boxes and obtains the following results: 588, 592, 600, 601, 603, 603, 604, 605, 605, 607. Calculate the mean number of matches using an assumed mean of 600. Comment on your answer.

6 The mean of five numbers 5, 9, 10, 20 and x is 10. Find the value of x.

7 Write down three numbers with a mean of 7 and a range of 4.

8 Write down three numbers with a median of 6 and a range of 3.

9 The mean of five numbers is 7, the mode is 10 and the range is 7. What are five possible numbers?

10 The mean of a set of numbers is 5 and the range is 6. The numbers are now doubled.
  a What is the new mean?
  b What is the new range?

11 The mean of a set of numbers is 11 and the range is 8. The numbers are now increased by 5.
  a What is the new mean?
  b What is the new range?

12 The mode of a set of numbers is 15 and the range is 6. The numbers are now halved.
  a What is the new mode?
  b What is the new range?

Extension **Work**

Draw two straight lines of different lengths. Ask other pupils to estimate the lengths of the lines and record the results. Calculate the mean and range of the estimates for each line. Compare the accuracy of the estimates for the two lines. You could then extend this by repeating for two curved lines and compare the accuracy of the estimates for straight and curved lines.

Drawing frequency diagrams

Look at the picture. How could the organisers record the finishing times to find out when most of the runners finish?

Example 16.5 ▶ Construct a frequency diagram for the data about journey times shown.

Journey times t (minutes)	Frequency
$0 < t \leq 15$	4
$15 < t \leq 30$	5
$30 < t \leq 45$	10
$45 < t \leq 60$	6

It is important that the diagram has a title and labels as shown.

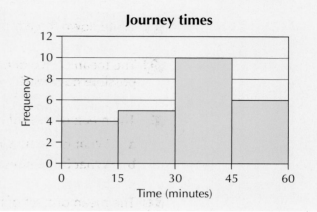

Example 16.6 ▶ Look at the graph for ice-cream sales. In which month were sales at their highest? Give a reason why you think this happened.

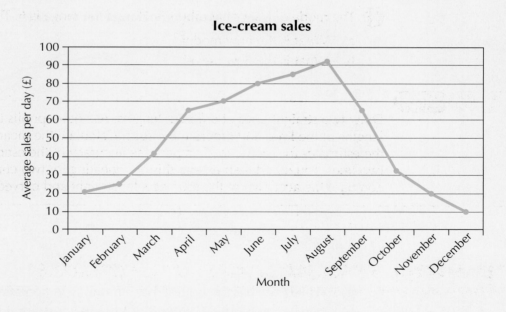

The highest sales were in August (£92 per day). This was probably because the weather was warmer, as people tend to buy ice-creams in warm weather.

Exercise 16C

1 For each frequency table, construct a frequency diagram.

a Aircraft flight times:

Time T (h)	Frequency
0 < T ≤ 1	3
1 < T ≤ 2	6
2 < T ≤ 3	8
3 < T ≤ 4	7
4 < T ≤ 5	4

b Temperatures of capital cities:

Temperature T (°C)	Frequency
0 < T ≤ 5	2
5 < T ≤ 10	6
10 < T ≤ 15	11
15 < T ≤ 20	12
20 < T ≤ 25	7

c Length of metal rods:

Length l (cm)	Frequency
0 < l ≤ 10	9
10 < l ≤ 20	12
20 < l ≤ 30	6
30 < l ≤ 40	3

d Mass of animals on a farm:

Mass M (kg)	Frequency
0 < M ≤ 20	15
20 < M ≤ 40	23
40 < M ≤ 60	32
60 < M ≤ 80	12
80 < M ≤ 100	6

FM 2 The graph below shows the mean monthly temperature for two cities.

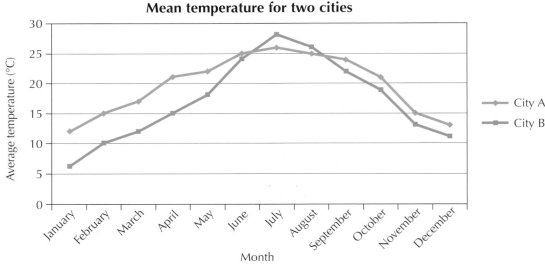

Mean temperature for two cities

a Which city has the hottest mean monthly temperature?
b Which city has the coldest mean monthly temperature?
c How many months of the year is the temperature higher in city A than city B?
d What is the difference in average temperature between the two cities in February?
e Which city has the greater range of temperature over the year? Explain your answer.

Extension Work

Use a travel brochure to compare the temperatures of two European destinations.
Make a poster to advertise one destination as being better than the other.

Comparing data

79 m   153 m

Look at the picture. What is the range of the golfer's shots?

Example 16.7 ▷ The table shows the mean and range of basketball scores for two teams:

	Team A	Team B
Mean	75	84
Range	20	10

Compare the mean and range and explain what they tell you.

The means tell you that the average score for team B is higher than that for team A, so they have higher scores generally.

The range compares the difference in their lowest and highest scores. Team A have the greater range, so there is more variation in their scores. You could say that they are less consistent.

Exercise 16D

1 A factory worker records the start and finish times of a series of the same job.

Job number	1	2	3	4	5
Start time	9.00 am	9.20 am	9.50 am	10.10 am	10.20 am
Finish time	9.15 am	9.45 am	10.06 am	10.18 am	10.37 am

Work out the range of the time taken for this job.

2 The minimum and maximum temperatures are recorded for four counties in England in April.

County	Northumberland	Leicestershire	Oxfordshire	Surrey
Minimum	2 °C	4 °C	4 °C	4.5 °C
Maximum	12 °C	15 °C	16.5 °C	17.5 °C

a   Find the range of the temperatures for each county.
b   Comment on any differences you notice.

3 The table shows the mean and range of a set of test scores for Jon and Matt.

	Jon	Matt
Mean	64	71
Range	35	23

Compare the mean and range and explain what they tell you.

4 Fiona recorded how long, to the nearest hour, Everlast, Powercell and Electro batteries lasted in her CD player. She did five trials of each make of battery. Her results are as follows.

Everlast	Powercell	Electro
6	4	9
5	6	8
6	3	9
6	3	9
7	4	9

a Find the mean and range of the lifetime for each make of battery.

b Everlast batteries cost £1.00 each, Powercell 50p each, and Electro £1.50 each. Which type of battery would you buy, and why?

5 A teacher has two routes to school. One week he uses a motorway, and another week he uses country lanes. He records how long it takes him to get to school each day for the two weeks. The results are shown in the table.

	Time taken using motorway (minutes)	Time taken using country lanes (minutes)
Monday	35	22
Tuesday	20	25
Wednesday	15	24
Thursday	14	27
Friday	16	22

a Find the mean and range for each type of journey.

b Which route to school should he use, and why?

Extension Work

7

Use an atlas or another data source (the Internet or a software program) to compare the populations of the four largest cities in China and the United States of America, using the mean and the range.

Comparing sets of data

Two cars A and B each cost £20 000 when they were new.

The graphs show how the values of the cars fell over eight years.

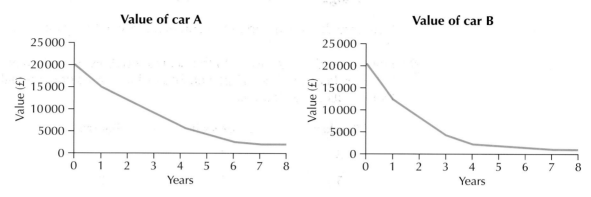

Value of car A

Value of car B

Which car fell in value more? How can you tell?

Example 16.8 ▷

A teacher is comparing the reasons for absence of pupils who have time off school. The charts show the reasons for absence of two different year groups.

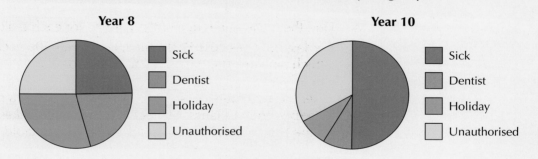

Year 8

Year 10

- Sick
- Dentist
- Holiday
- Unauthorised

One hundred pupils in Year 8 had time off school, and 40 pupils in Year 10.

The teacher says, 'The charts show that more pupils were off sick in Year 10.' Explain why the charts do not show this.

In Year 8 the number of pupils off sick was a quarter of 100, which is 25.

In Year 10 the number of pupils off sick was a half of 40, which is 20. So fewer pupils were off sick in Year 10.

Exercise 16E

1 The graph shows the attendance at two concerts, a classical concert and a rock concert.

Comment on the proportion of children attending each concert.

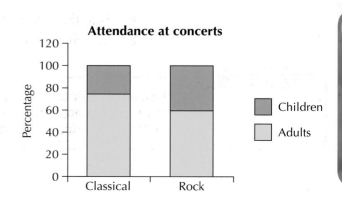

Attendance at concerts

- Children
- Adults

2 One hundred pupils took two tests, a science test and a maths test. The results are shown on the graph.

Which test did the pupils find more difficult? Explain your answer.

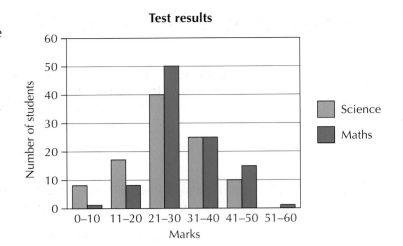

Test results

3 The chart shows the percentage of trains that were on time and late during one day.

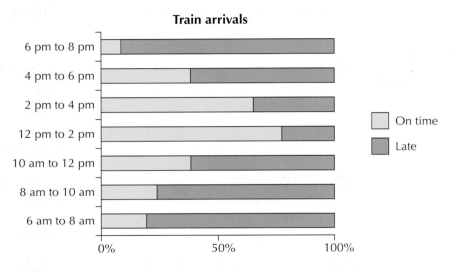

Train arrivals

a Compare the times late for different parts of the day.

b Comment on what you would expect to happen between 8 pm and 10 pm.

Extension Work

Here are two sets of data for the weights of a sample of two different makes of 400 gram chocolate bars.

1 Calculate the mean and range of the data for each sample.

2 Draw charts to compare the two makes of chocolate.

3 Comment on which one you would buy.

Chucky Bar (grams)	Choctastic (grams)
401	391
407	410
405	407
404	402
403	413
404	395

Experimental and theoretical probability

Look at the picture. Would you say the chance of the jigsaw pieces coming out of the box face up is evens, or do more pieces come out face down every time?

Example 16.9 ▷

Design and carry out an experiment to test whether drawing pins usually land with the pin pointing up or the pin pointing down.

Count out 50 drawing pins, then drop them onto a table.

Record the number with the pin pointing up and the number with the pin pointing down.

Suppose that 30 point up and 20 point down.

We could then say that the experimental probability of a pin pointing up is: $\frac{30}{50} = \frac{3}{5}$.

Exercise 16F

1 Darren says that if someone is asked to think of a number from 1 to 10, they will pick 3 or 7 more often than any other number.

   a What is the theoretical probability that a person will choose 3 or 7?

   b Design and carry out an experiment to test Darren's prediction.

   c Compare the experimental and theoretical probabilities.

2 a What is the theoretical probability that an ordinary fair dice lands on the number 6?

   b What is the theoretical probability that an ordinary fair dice lands on an odd number?

   c Design and carry out an experiment to test these theoretical probabilities.

3 Five cards, numbered 1, 2, 3, 4 and 5, are placed face down in a row as shown. Cards are picked at random.

   a What is the theoretical probability that a person chooses the card with the number 2 on it?

   b A gambler predicts that when people pick a card they will rarely pick the end ones. Design and carry out an experiment to test his prediction.

4 a What is the theoretical probability that a coin lands on heads?

   b Design and carry out an experiment to test this theoretical probability.

5 Two fair dice are thrown.

   a Copy and complete the sample space diagram for the total scores.

   b What is the theoretical probability of a total score of 7?

   c Design and carry out an experiment to test whether you think two dice are fair.

First dice

	1	2	3	4	5	6
1						
2						
3						
4						
5						
6						

Second dice

Extension Work

Use computer software to simulate an experiment, for example tossing a coin or rolling a dice. Work out the experimental probabilities after 10, 20, 30 results, and compare with the theoretical probability. Write down any pattern that you notice. Repeat the experiment to see whether any pattern is repeated.

LEVEL BOOSTER

6
I can collect and record continuous data, choosing appropriate class intervals over a sensible range to create frequency tables.

I can construct and interpret frequency diagrams.

I can identify all the outcomes when dealing with a combination of two experiments, using diagrams or tables.

7
I can find the average and range from frequency diagrams.

I can compare distributions and comment on what I find.

National Test questions

1 *2005 Paper 2*

Here is some information about all the pupils in class 9A:
A teacher is going to choose a pupil from 9A at random.

	Number of boys	Number of girls
Right-handed	13	14
Left-handed	1	2

a What is the probability that the pupil chosen will be a **girl**?

b What is the probability that the pupil chosen will be **left-handed**?

c The teacher chooses the pupil at random.
She tells the class that the pupil is **left-handed**.

What is the probability that this left-handed pupil is a **boy**?

2 *2002 Paper 2*

a From 5th May 2000 to 5th May 2001 a swimming club had the same members.

Copy and complete the table to show information about the ages of these members.

Ages of members	
Mean (5th May 2000)	24 years 3 months
Range (5th May 2000)	4 years 8 months
Mean (5th May 2001)	
Range (5th May 2001)	

b The table shows information about members of a
different club.

Ages of members	
Mean	17 years 5 months
Range	2 years 0 months

A new member, aged 18 years 5 months, is going to join the club.

What will happen to the mean age of the members? Choose the correct statement from the following:

It will increase by more than 1 year.

It will increase by exactly 1 year.

It will increase by less than 1 year.

It will stay the same.

It is not possible to tell.

What will happen to the range of ages of the members? Choose the correct statement from the
following:

It will increase by more than 1 year.

It will increase by exactly 1 year.

It will increase by less than 1 year.

It will stay the same.

It is not possible to tell.

3 *2002 Paper 2*

The percentage charts show information about the wing length of adult blackbirds, measured to the
nearest millimetre.

Use the data to decide whether
these statements are true or false,
or whether there is not enough
information to tell. Explain your
answer.

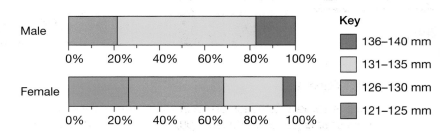

a The smallest male's wing
length is larger than the
smallest female's wing length.

b The biggest male's wing length is larger than the biggest female's wing length.

Questionnaire

Cris created a questionnaire for her Year 8 classmates. She went round asking 40 boys and 40 girls the following questions.

a   What is your favourite band or artist?   **b**   How many CDs do you possess?

c   Which is your favourite Wii sporting game?

This is a summary of her results.

Boy/Girl	Music	CDs	Wii Game	Boy/Girl	Music	CDs	Wii Game
Boy	Fall out Boy	12	Bowling	Girl	Kate Nash	17	Bowling
Girl	Arctic Monkeys	17	Bowling	Boy	Foo Fighters	32	Golf
Boy	Panic! at Disco	27	Boxing	Girl	Arctic Monkeys	43	Bowling
Girl	Kate Nash	34	Bowling	Girl	Spice Girls	26	Golf
Girl	Fall out Boy	32	Bowling	Boy	Kate Nash	32	Boxing
Boy	Foo Fighters	29	Boxing	Boy	Foo Fighters	44	Boxing
Boy	Arctic Monkeys	43	Golf	Boy	Arctic Monkeys	53	Boxing
Boy	Foo Fighters	41	Boxing	Girl	Kate Nash	45	Bowling
Girl	Arctic Monkeys	23	Bowling	Girl	Foo Fighters	36	Bowling
Girl	Arctic Monkeys	16	Golf	Boy	Fall out Boy	28	Boxing
Boy	Foo Fighters	26	Boxing	Boy	Arctic Monkeys	16	Tennis
Girl	Fall out Boy	37	Bowling	Girl	Foo Fighters	19	Tennis
Girl	Foo Fighters	24	Bowling	Boy	Panic! at Disco	20	Golf
Boy	Arctic Monkeys	16	Golf	Girl	Fall out Boy	31	Bowling
Boy	Fall out Boy	33	Boxing	Girl	Fall out Boy	40	Bowling
Girl	Kate Nash	45	Bowling	Boy	Arctic Monkeys	43	Bowling
Boy	Foo Fighters	52	Tennis	Girl	Panic! at Disco	55	Golf
Girl	Foo Fighters	37	Tennis	Girl	Foo Fighters	23	Bowling
Girl	Kate Nash	13	Bowling	Boy	Kate Nash	27	Baseball
Girl	Panic! at Disco	31	Bowling	Boy	Arctic Monkeys	35	Boxing
Boy	Kate Nash	50	Golf	Girl	Kate Nash	31	Golf
Boy	Arctic Monkeys	43	Bowling	Boy	Foo Fighters	28	Bowling
Boy	Foo Fighters	25	Boxing	Boy	Panic! at Disco	46	Boxing
Girl	Arctic Monkeys	30	Bowling	Boy	Fall out Boy	34	Boxing
Boy	Fall out Boy	17	Bowling	Girl	Arctic Monkeys	26	Bowling
Girl	Kate Nash	29	Tennis	Boy	Fall out Boy	18	Bowling
Girl	Spice Girls	31	Golf	Girl	Foo Fighters	22	Tennis
Girl	Arctic Monkeys	48	Bowling	Girl	Foo Fighters	40	Boxing
Boy	Foo Fighters	38	Boxing	Boy	Arctic Monkeys	51	Golf
Boy	Panic! at Disco	21	Bowling	Boy	Arctic Monkeys	42	Golf
Boy	Fall out Boy	20	Tennis	Girl	Kate Nash	46	Tennis
Girl	Kate Nash	37	Golf	Girl	Kate Nash	34	Boxing
Boy	Foo Fighters	48	Boxing	Boy	Foo Fighters	50	Boxing
Boy	Foo Fighters	23	Golf	Girl	Arctic Monkeys	43	Bowling
Boy	Arctic Monkeys	19	Bowling	Boy	Foo Fighters	54	Baseball
Girl	Kate Nash	24	Bowling	Girl	Panic! at Disco	23	Bowling
Girl	Arctic Monkeys	52	Bowling	Boy	Foo Fighters	33	Boxing
Boy	Kate Nash	49	Tennis	Boy	Fall out Boy	41	Boxing
Boy	Foo Fighters	38	Golf	Girl	Fall out Boy	37	Bowling
Girl	Panic! at Disco	25	Bowling	Girl	Kate Nash	46	Tennis

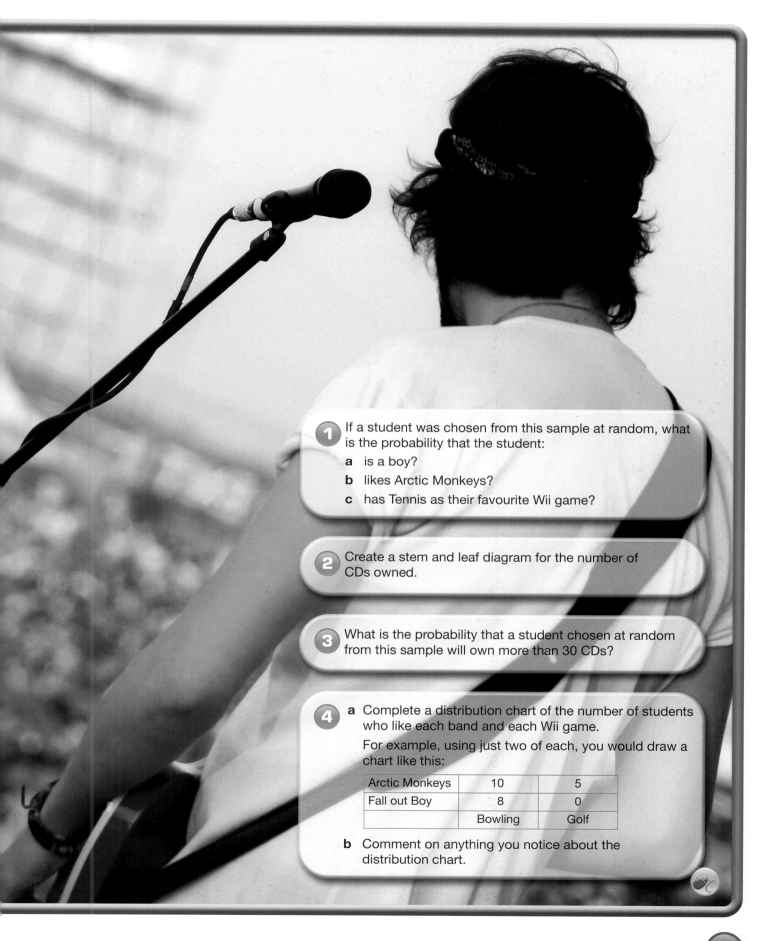

1 If a student was chosen from this sample at random, what is the probability that the student:
   a is a boy?
   b likes Arctic Monkeys?
   c has Tennis as their favourite Wii game?

2 Create a stem and leaf diagram for the number of CDs owned.

3 What is the probability that a student chosen at random from this sample will own more than 30 CDs?

4 a Complete a distribution chart of the number of students who like each band and each Wii game.
   For example, using just two of each, you would draw a chart like this:

Arctic Monkeys	10	5
Fall out Boy	8	0
	Bowling	Golf

   b Comment on anything you notice about the distribution chart.

Index

251